Workshop on Open Infrastructures and Analysis Frameworks for HLT 2014

Held at COLING 2014

Dublin, Ireland
23 August 2014

ISBN: 978-1-63439-220-4

Printed from e-media with permission by:

Curran Associates, Inc.
57 Morehouse Lane
Red Hook, NY 12571

Some format issues inherent in the e-media version may also appear in this print version.

Printed by Curran Associates, Inc. (2014)

For permission requests, please contact the Association for Computational Linguistics at the address below.

Association for Computational Linguistics
209 N. Eighth Street
Stroudsburg, Pennsylvania 18360

Phone: 1-570-476-8006
Fax: 1-570-476-0860

acl@aclweb.org

Additional copies of this publication are available from:

Curran Associates, Inc.
57 Morehouse Lane
Red Hook, NY 12571 USA
Phone: 845-758-0400
Fax: 845-758-2634
Email: curran@proceedings.com
Web: www.proceedings.com

Preface

The Workshop on Open Infrastructures and Analysis Frameworks for Human Language Technology (HLT) provides a forum for discussion of requirements for an envisaged open “global laboratory" for HLT research and development. Recent advances in digital storage and networking, coupled with the extension of HLT into ever broader areas and the persistence of difficulties in software portability, have led to an increased focus on development and deployment of web-based infrastructures that allow users to access tools and other resources and combine them to create novel solutions that can be efficiently composed, tuned, evaluated, disseminated and consumed. This in turn engenders collaborative development and deployment among individuals and teams across the globe. It also increases the need for robust, widely available evaluation methods and tools, means to achieve interoperability of software and data from diverse sources, means to handle licensing for limited access resources distributed over the web, and, perhaps crucially, the need to develop strategies for multi-site collaborative work.

For many decades, NLP has suffered from low software engineering standards, resulting in a limited degree of re-usability of code and interoperability of different modules within larger NLP systems. While this did not really hamper success in limited task areas, it caused serious problems for building complex integrated software systems, e.g., for information extraction or machine translation. This lack of integration has led to duplicated software development, work-arounds for programs written in different (versions of) programming languages, and ad-hoc tweaking of interfaces between modules developed at different sites.

In recent years, several efforts have been devoted to the development of frameworks to to allow the easy integration of varied tools through common type systems and standardized communication methods for components analyzing unstructured textual information. These include two frameworks, UIMA and GATE, which have been widely adopted within the HLT community to facilitate the creation of reusable HLT components that can be assembled to address different HLT tasks depending on their order, combination and configuration. At the same time, major projects in the US, EU, and Asia have recently undertaken the development of web service platforms for HLT, in order to exploit the growing number of web-based tools and services available for HLT-related tasks including corpus annotation, configuration and execution of tool pipelines, and evaluation of results and automatic parameter tuning. These platforms may also integrate modules and pipelines from existing frameworks such as UIMA and GATE, in order to achieve interoperability with a wide variety of modules from different sources.

Many of the issues and challenges surrounding these developments have been addressed individually in particular projects and workshops, but there are ramifications that cut across all of them. This workshop brings together participants representing the range of interests that comprise the comprehensive picture for community-driven, distributed, collaborative, web-based development and use for language processing software and resources, including developers of HLT infrastructures as well as those who will use these services and infrastructures, especially for multi-site collaborative work. The program includes presentations describing approaches to the range of challenges posed by such development, including legal issues concerning licensing of components and tools; the technical aspects of packaging and distribution of components; means to assemble complex processing pipelines and manage large bodies of data; means to visualize, explore, and further deploy analysis results; and issues surrounding the preservation of analysis results, provenance documentation, and evaluation and reproducibility. The overall goal is to work toward eliminating the fragmentation and duplication of effort that currently characterizes the field by establishing the basis of a community effort to develop and support the global laboratory for HLT development and research.

Workshop Committee

Program Co-Chairs

Jens Grivolla, Universitat Pompeu Fabra (Spain)

Nancy Ide, Vassar College (USA)

General Organizers

Kalina Bontcheva, University of Sheffield (UK)

Christopher Cieri, Linguistic Data Consortium (USA)

Eric Nyberg, Carnegie Mellon University (USA)

James Pustejovsky, Brandeis University (USA)

Jonathan Wright, Linguistic Data Consortium (USA)

Program Committee:

Al Asswad, Mohammad, Cornell University
Nuria Bel, Universitat Pompeu Fabra
Steven Bethard, University of Alabama at Birmingham
Philipp Cimiano, Universität Bielefeld
Joan Codina, Universitat Pompeu Fabra
Kevin Cohen, University of Colorado School of Medicine
Azad Dehghan, University of Manchester
Leon Derczynski, University of Sheffield
Richard Eckart de Castilho, TU Darmstadt
Nicolai Erbs, TU Darmstadt
Thilo Götz, IBM Deutschland
Mark A. Greenwood, University of Sheffield
Nicolas Hernandez, University of Nantes
Yoshinobu Kano, Japan Science and Technology Agency
Peter Klügl, University of Würzburg
Marie-Jean Meurs, Concordia University
Yohei Murakama, Kyoto University
Kamel Nebhi, University of Geneva
Renaud Richardet, École Polytechnique Fédérale De Lausanne
Carlos Rodríguez-Penagos, Barcelona Media
Horacio Saggion, Universitat Pompeu Fabra
Bahar Sateli, Concordia University
Chunqi Shi, Brandeis University
Keith Suderman, Vassar College
Michael Tanenblatt, Thomas J. Watson Research Center
Martin Toepfer, Universität Würzburg
Katrin Tomanek, VigLink Inc.
Marc Verhagen, Brandeis University
Karin Verspoor, University of Melbourne
Graham Wilcock, University of Helsinki
René Witte, Concordia University
Torsten Zesch, University of Duisburg-Essen

Table of Contents

Conference Program

Saturday, August 23, 2014

8:45–9:00	Opening Remarks
9:00–9:30	*A broad-coverage collection of portable NLP components for building shareable analysis pipelines* Richard Eckart de Castilho and Iryna Gurevych
9:30–10:00	*Integrating UIMA with Alveo, a human communication science virtual laboratory* Dominique Estival, Steve Cassidy, Karin Verspoor, Andrew MacKinlay and Denis Burnham
10:00–10:30	*Towards Model Driven Architectures for Human Language Technologies* Alessandro di Bari, Guido Vetere and Kateryna Tymoshenko
10:30–11:00	Coffee break
11:00–11:30	*The Language Application Grid Web Service Exchange Vocabulary* Nancy Ide, James Pustejovsky, Keith Suderman and Marc Verhagen
11:30–12:00	*Significance of Bridging Real-world Documents and NLP Technologies* Tadayoshi Hara, Goran Topic, Yusuke Miyao and Akiko Aizawa
12:00–12:30	*A Conceptual Framework of Online Natural Language Processing Pipeline Application* Chunqi Shi, James Pustejovsky and Marc Verhagen
12:30–14:00	Lunch
14:00–14:30	*Command-line utilities for managing and exploring annotated corpora* Joel Nothman, Tim Dawborn and James R. Curran
14:30–15:00	*SSF: A Common Representation Scheme for Language Analysis for Language Technology Infrastructure Development* Akshar Bharati, Rajeev Sangal, Dipti Misra Sharma and Anil Kumar Singh
15:00–15:30	Coffee break
15:30–16:00	*Quo Vadis UIMA?* Thilo Götz, Jörn Kottmann and Alexander Lang

Saturday, August 23, 2014 (continued)

16:00–16:30 *Integrated Tools for Query-driven Development of Light-weight Ontologies and Information Extraction Components*
Martin Toepfer, Georg Fette, Philip-Daniel Beck, Peter Kluegl and Frank Puppe

16:30–17:00 *Intellectual Property Rights Management with Web Service Grids*
Christopher Cieri and Denise DiPersio

17:00–17:30 *EUMSSI: a Platform for Multimodal Analysis and Recommendation using UIMA*
Jens Grivolla, Maite Melero, Toni Badia, Cosmin Cabulea, Yannick Estève, Eelco Herder, Jean-Marc Odobez, Susanne Preuß and Raúl Marín

17:30–18:00 Discussion : How to build a global community

A broad-coverage collection of portable NLP components for building shareable analysis pipelines

Richard Eckart de Castilho[1] **Iryna Gurevych**[1,2]
(1) Ubiquitous Knowledge Processing Lab (UKP-TUDA)
Dept. of Computer Science, Technische Universität Darmstadt
(2) Ubiquitous Knowledge Processing Lab (UKP-DIPF)
German Institute for Educational Research and Educational Information
`http://www.ukp.tu-darmstadt.de`

Abstract

Due to the diversity of natural language processing (NLP) tools and resources, combining them into processing pipelines is an important issue, and sharing these pipelines with others remains a problem. We present DKPro Core, a broad-coverage component collection integrating a wide range of third-party NLP tools and making them interoperable. Contrary to other recent endeavors that rely heavily on web services, our collection consists only of portable components distributed via a repository, making it particularly interesting with respect to sharing pipelines with other researchers, embedding NLP pipelines in applications, and the use on high-performance computing clusters. Our collection is augmented by a novel concept for automatically selecting and acquiring resources required by the components at runtime from a repository. Based on these contributions, we demonstrate a way to describe a pipeline such that all required software and resources can be automatically obtained, making it easy to share it with others, e.g. in order to reproduce results or as examples in teaching, documentation, or publications.

1 Introduction

Sharing is a central concept to scientific work and to software development. In science, information about experimental setups and results is shared with fellow researchers, not only to disseminate new insights, but also to allow others to validate results or to improve on them. In software development, libraries and component-based architectures are a central mechanism to promote the reuse of software. Portable software must operate in the same way across system platforms. In the context of scientific research, this is an important factor related to the reproducibility of results created from software-based experiments.

The NLP software landscape provides a wealth of reusable software in the form of NLP tools addressing language analysis at different levels from tokenization to sentiment analysis. These tools are combined into NLP pipelines that form essential parts of experiments in natural language research and beyond, e.g. in the emerging digital humanities. Therefore, it is essential that such pipelines can easily be shared between researchers, to reproduce results, to evolve experiments, and to allow for a better understanding of the exact details of an experiment (cf. Fokkens et al. (2013)).

Analyzing the current state of the art, we find that despite considerable effort that has been going into processing frameworks enabling interoperability, workbenches to build and run pipelines, and all kinds of online services, it is still not possible to create a readily shareable description of an NLP pipeline. A pipeline description is basically a configuration file referencing the components and resources used by the pipeline. Currently, these references are ambiguous, e.g. because they do not incorporate version information. This causes a reproducibility problem, e.g. when a pipeline is part of an experiment, because the use of a different version can easily lead to different results. A sharable description must be self-contained in the sense that it uniquely identifies all involved components and resources, permitting the execution environment for the pipeline to be set up reproducibly, in the best case automatically. Currently, the task of setting up the environment is largely left to the user and requires time and diligence.

Proceedings of the Workshop on Open Infrastructures and Analysis Frameworks for HLT, pages 1–11,
Dublin, Ireland, August 23rd 2014.

In this paper, we present a novel concept for self-contained NLP pipeline descriptions supported by a broad-coverage collection of interoperable NLP components. Our approach is enabled by the combination of distributing portable NLP components and resources through a repository and by an auto-configuration mechanism allowing components to select suitable resources at runtime and to obtain them automatically from the repository. Our contributions facilitate the sharing of pipelines, e.g. as part of publications or examples in documentation, and allow users to maintain control by providing the ability to create backups of components and resources for a later reproduction of results.

Section 2 reflects on the state of the art and identifies the need for a broad-coverage component collection of portable components, as well as the need for self-contained pipeline descriptions. Section 3.1 describes a novel concept for the automatic selection and acquisition of resources. Section 3.2 presents a broad-coverage collection of portable components integrating this concept. Section 3.3 demonstrates a shareable workflow based on these contributions. Section 4 gives further examples of how our contributions could be applied. Finally, Section 5 summarizes the paper and suggests future research directions.

2 State of the art

In this section, we examine the current state of the art related to describing NLP pipelines, kinds of component collections, publishing of components and resources, and the selection of resources to use with a component. We start by defining the terminology used throughout the rest of this paper.

Definition of terminology We make a distinction between a *tool* and a *component*. Most NLP tools are standalone tools addressing one particular task, e.g. dependency parsing, relying on separate tokenizers, part-of-speech (POS) taggers, etc. These tools cannot be easily combined into pipelines, because their input/output formats are often not compatible and because they lack a uniform programming interface.

We speak of a *component* when a tool has been integrated into a *processing framework*, usually by implementing an adapter between the tool and the framework. The framework defines a uniform programming interface, data model, and processing model enabling interoperability between the components.

Through integration with the framework, components become easily composeable into *pipelines*. A *pipeline* consists of *components* processing input documents one after the other and passing the output on to the next component. Each component adds *annotations* to the document, e.g. sentence and token boundaries, POS tags, syntactic constituents, or dependency relations, etc. These steps build upon each other, e.g. a component for dependency parsing requires at least sentences, tokens, and POS tags.

Many components are generic engines that require some *resource* (e.g. a *probabilistic model* or *knowledge base*) that configures them for a specific language, tagset, domain, etc. We use the term *resource selection* for the task of choosing a resource and configuring a component to use it. The task of obtaining the resource we call *resource acquisition*.

As Thompson et al. (2011) point out, achieving a consensus on the exact representation of different linguistic theories as annotations and thereby attaining full conceptual interoperability between components from different vendors is currently not considered feasible. Thus, frameworks leave the type system (kinds of annotations) unspecified. Therefore, the technical integration with a framework alone does not make the tools interoperable on the conceptual level (cf. Chiarcos et al. (2008)). As a consequence, multiple *component collections* exist, each providing interoperable components centered around a particular combination of processing framework and type system (e.g. Buyko and Hahn (2008), Kano et al. (2011), Wu et al. (2013)). Each of these defines its own concepts of tokens, sentence, syntactic structures, discourse structures, etc. Yet, even these type systems leave certain aspects underspecified, e.g. the various tagsets used to categorize parts-of-speech, syntactic constituents, etc.

2.1 Sharing pipelines

Processing frameworks offer a way to construct pipeline descriptions that instruct the framework to configure and execute a pipeline of NLP components.

GATE (Cunningham et al., 2002) and Apache UIMA (Ferrucci and Lally, 2004) are currently the most prominent processing frameworks. Both describe pipelines by means of XML documents. These refer to individual components by name and expect that the user has taken precautions that these components are accessible by the framework. Neither framework includes provisions to automatically obtain the components or resources they require, e.g. from a repository (Section 2.2). In fact, the pipeline descriptions do not contain sufficient information to uniquely identify components. Components are referred to only by name, but not by version. The same is true for resources which are often referred to only by filename.

Thus, both of the major processing frameworks to not offer self-contained descriptions for pipelines. When such pipeline descriptions are shared with another person, the recipient requires additional information about which exact versions of tools and resources are needed to run the pipeline.

2.2 Publishing components and resources

In this section, we examine different approaches to publishing NLP components and resources so that they can be more easily found, accessed, or obtained in order to execute a particular pipeline.

Directories META-SHARE (Thompson et al., 2011) and the CLARIN Virtual Language Observatory (VLO) (Uytvanck et al., 2010) are two directories of language resources, including NLP tools and resources. These directories currently target primarily human users and offer rich metadata and a user interface to browse it or to find specific kinds of entries. However, these directories to not contain sufficient information to programmatically download the software or resources, or to access them as services.

Repositories Repositories are online services from which components and resources can be obtained.

The Central Repository (2014) is a repository within the Java-ecosystem used to distribute Java libraries and resources they require, so-called *artifacts*. It relies on concepts that have evolved around the Maven project (Sonatype Company, 2008). Meanwhile, these are supported by many build tools, development environments, and even by some programming languages (cf. Section 3.3). Several NLP tools (e.g. ClearNLP (2014), Stanford CoreNLP (Manning et al., 2014), MaltParser (Nivre et al., 2007), ClearTK (Ogren et al., 2009)) are already distributed via this medium, some including their resources.

There are many Maven repositories on the internet. They are organized as a loosely federated network. The Central Repository merely serves as the default point of contact built into clients. Repositories have the ability to access each other and to cache those artifacts required by their immediate users. This provides resilience against network failures or remote data loss. Artifacts can be addressed across the federation by a set of coordinates (*groupId*, *artifactId*, and *version*).

Another kind of repositories are plug-in repositories, such as those used by GATE (Cunningham et al., 2002). From these, the user can conveniently download and install components within the GATE workbench. These plug-in repositories are specific to GATE, whereas the Maven repositories are a generic infrastructure widely used by the Java community and that is supported by many tools and applications.

Online Workbenches While many NLP tools are offered as *portable software* for offline use, we observe a trend in recent years towards offering NLP tools as *web-services* for online use, sometimes as the only way to access them. Hinrichs et al. (2010) cite incompatibilities between the software and the user's machine and insufficiently powerful workstations as reasons for this approach. Another reason may be the ability to set up a *walled garden* in which the service provider is able to control the use of services, e.g. to academic researchers or to paying commercial customers.

Argo (Rak et al., 2013) is a web-based workbench. It offers access to a collection of UIMA-based NLP-services that can be executed in different environments. Rak et al. mention in particular a cluster environment but also plan support for a number of cloud platforms. For this reason, we assume that most of the components are integrated into Argo as portable software that can be deployed to these platforms on-demand. Yet, it appears that the components are only accessible through Argo and that they are not distributed separately for use in other UIMA-based environments.

U-Compare (Kano et al., 2011) is a Java application for building and running UIMA-based pipelines and comparing their results. While some components accessible through the workbench run locally, many components are only stubs calling out to web-services running at different remote locations.

WebLicht (Hinrichs et al., 2010) is a distributed infrastructure of NLP services hosted at different locations. They exchange data in an XML format called TCF (*Text Corpus Format*). Pipelines can be built and run using the web-based WebLicht workbench. Within this walled garden platform, authenticated academic users have access to resources that are free for academic research, but not otherwise.

Online Marketplaces AnnoMarket (Tablan et al., 2013) is another distributed infrastructure of NLP services based on GATE. It does not seem to offer a workbench to compose custom pipelines. Instead, it offers a set of pre-configured components and exposes them as web-services to be programmatically accessed. It is the only commercial offering in this overview that the user has to pay for.

Note on service-based approaches Service-based approaches have also been taken in other scientific domains to facilitate the creation of shareable and repeatable experiments, e.g. on platforms such as myExperiment (Goble et al., 2010). However, Gómez-Pérez et al. (2013) found service-based workflows to be subject to decay as services are updated and change their input/output formats, their results, or as they become temporarily unavailable due to network problems. We also expect they can become permanently unavailable, e.g. due to a lack of funding unless supported by a sound business model.

Furthermore, to our knowledge none of the offerings above allow the user to export their pipelines including all necessary software and resources, e.g. to make a backup or to deploy it on a private computing infrastructure, e.g. a private cloud or cluster system.

2.3 Component collections

We define a component collection as a set of interoperable components. The interoperability between the components is enabled by conventions that are typically rendered as a common annotation type system, a common API, or both.

Standalone NLP tools Most NLP tools are not comprehensive suites that cover all tasks from tokenization to e.g. coreference resolution, but are rather standalone tools addressing only a particular task, e.g. dependency parsing, relying on separate tokenizers, POS-taggers, etc. Examples of such standalone tools are MaltParser (Nivre et al., 2007) and HunPos (Halácsy et al., 2007). The major part of the analysis logic is implemented within the tool, such that they tend not to rely significantly on third-party libraries. However, many third-party resources can be found on the internet for popular standalone tools.

NLP tool suites Some vendors offer tool suites that cover multiple analysis tasks, e.g. ClearNLP, CoreNLP, and OpenNLP. They consist of a set of interoperable tools. Some even go so far as to include a proprietary processing framework and pipeline mechanism. For example, CoreNLP allows the user to implement custom analysis components and to register them with their framework. OpenNLP, on the other hand, provides UIMA-wrappers for their tools. These wrappers are configurable for different UIMA type systems, but unfortunately the configuration mechanism is not powerful enough to accommodate for the design of various major type systems.

We also refer to such tool suites as *single vendor collections*. As for standalone tools, the major part of the analysis logic is a part of the suite and tends not to rely significantly on third-party libraries. Also, again many third-parties offer resources for popular tool suites.

Special purpose collections Special purpose collections combine NLP tools into a comprehensive modular pipeline for a specific purpose.

The Apache cTAKES project (Savova et al., 2010) offers a UIMA-based pipeline for the analysis of medical records which includes components from ClearNLP, OpenNLP, and more for the basic language analysis. These third-party components are used in conjunction with resources created specifically for the domain of medical records. Higher-level tasks use original components from the project, e.g. to identify drugs or relations specific to the medical domain.

Broad-coverage collections Broad-coverage collections cover multiple analysis tasks, but they do not focus on a specific purpose. Instead, they provide the user with a choice for each analysis task by integrating tools from different vendors capable of doing the same task. Because the languages supported by each tool differ, this allows the collection to cover more languages than individual tools or even tool suites alone. Additionally, broad-coverage collections allow comparing different tools against each other.

The U-Compare workbench (Kano et al., 2011) focusses specifically on the ability to compare tools against each other. It offers a GUI for building analysis pipelines and comparing their results. U-Compare also offers a collection of UIMA-based components centered around the U-Compare type system. It started integrating analysis tools primarily from the biomedical domain, but many more tools were integrated as part of the META-NET project (Thompson et al., 2011). This makes the collection accessible through U-Compare one of the largest collections of interoperable NLP components available.

ClearTK (Ogren et al., 2009) is actually a machine-learning framework based on Apache UIMA. However, it also integrates various NLP tools from different vendors and for this reason we list it under the broad-coverage collections. The tools are integrated to provide features for the machine-learning algorithms. The main reason for ClearTK not to use components from other existing UIMA component collections may have been the lack of a comprehensive UIMA component collection for NLP at the time ClearTK was in its early stages.

Note on cross-collection interoperability An alternative to broad-coverage collections that integrate many tools and make them interoperable would be to achieve cross-collection interoperability. That means, many vendors would provide small collections or even individual components and the end users would combine them into pipelines as desired. However, even within a framework like UIMA or GATE, a) some conventions, like a common type system, would need to be respected, b) extensive mapping between the individual components would be required, or c) the components would need to be adaptable to arbitrary type systems through configuration. Until at least one of these points has been resolved in a user-friendly way, we consider broad-coverage collections to be the most convenient solution for the user. The insights gained in building the broad-coverage collections may eventually contribute to finding solutions for these problems.

2.4 Resource selection and acquisition

Many NLP tools are generic, language-independent engines that are parametrized for a particular language with a resource, e.g. a probabilistic model, a set of rules, or another knowledge base. We call this *resource selection*. The selection can happen manually or automatically.

Manual selection is required, for example, in ClearTK or GATE. Components that require a resource offer a parameter pointing to the location from where this resource can be loaded, typically a location on the local file system. This entails that the resource is either bundled with the component or that the user must find and download the resource to the local machine. We call this step *resource acquisition*.

U-Compare (Kano et al., 2011), on the other hand, offers some components preconfigured with resources for certain languages. In particular, components that call out to remote web-services tend to support multiple languages. Based on the language they are invoked for, the service employs a particular resource. However, in this case the users cannot invoke the service with a custom resource from their local machine. Portable components that are bundled with U-Compare also allow for custom resources.

2.5 Need for shareable pipelines based on portable components

Current workflow descriptions are inconvenient to share with others because they are not self-contained. They do not uniquely identify components and resources. The responsibility to obtain, and install components and resources is largely left to the user. Web-based workbenches and marketplaces provide some remedy in this aspect as they remove the need for any local installation by the user. However, such online service-based approaches have been found to be a cause of workflow decay (Gómez-Pérez et al., 2013).

In consequence, we find that a shareable pipeline should rely on portable software and resources that can be automatically obtained from a repository. Once obtained, these remain within the control of the user, e.g. to create backups, or to run them on alternative environments, such as a private compute cluster. In the latter case, the use of remote services would likely cause a performance bottleneck. To make such an approach to shareable pipelines attractive, it must be supported by a broad-coverage collection from which pipelines can be assembled for various tasks.

3 Contributions

3.1 Automatic selection and acquisition of resources

We present a novel approach to the configuration of components with resources based on the data being processed. Resources are stored in a repository from where a component can obtain them on demand. The approach is based on a set of coordinates to address resources: *tool*, *language*, *variant*, and *version*.

In many cases, this removes the need for the user to explicitly configure the resource to be used. By overriding specific coordinates (mainly *variant*), the user can choose between different resources. Additionally, the user can disable resource-resolution via coordinates and instruct the component to use a model at a specific location, e.g. to use custom model from the local file system.

As an example, consider a part-of-speech-tagger component being used to process English text:

- *tool* – this coordinate is uniquely identified by the component being used, e.g. *opennlp-tagger*.
- *language* – this coordinate is obtained from the data being processed by the tagger, e.g. *en* or *de*.
- *variant* – as there can be multiple applicable resources per language, this coordinate is used to choose one of the resources. A default variant is provided by the component, possibly a different variant depending on the language, e.g. *fast* or *accurate*.
- *version* – resources are versioned, just as components are. New versions of a resource are created to fix bad data, to extend the data on which the resource is based, or to make it compatible with a new version of a tool. We note that generally, the versioning of tools and resources is independent of each other: a resource may be compatible with multiple versions of a tool and multiple versions of a resource may be compatible with one specific version of a tool. Furthermore, some vendors do not version resources properly or at all. For example, by comparing hash values, we observed that from version to version only some of the models packaged with CoreNLP change, while others remain identical. We also found the models (and even binaries) of TreeTagger (Schmid, 1994) to change from time to time without any apparent change in version. As a consequence, we decided to consequently use a time-based versioning scheme for resources. The independence between tool and resource versions also has another effect: users find it hard to manually select a resource version compatible with the tool version they use. Thus, we maintain a list of resources and default versions with each component and use it to fill in the *version* coordinate.

To operationalize this concept, we translate these coordinates into Maven coordinates and use these to resolve the resource against the Maven repository infrastructure. For example the coordinates *[tool: opennlp-tagger, language: en, variant: maxent, version: 20120616.1]* would be translated into *[groupId: de.tudarmstadt.ukp.dkpro.core, artifactId: de.tudarmstadt.ukp.dkpro.core.opennlp-model-tagger-en-maxent, version: 20120616.1]*.

Mind that some vendors already distribute resources for their tools via Maven repositories (cf. Section 2.2), but they do so at their own coordinates, e.g. at *[groupId: com.clearnlp, artifactId: clearnlp-general-en-dep, version: 1.2]* and these resources can become of a significant size.[1] To avoid republishing resources at coordinates matching our naming scheme, the artifact at the translated coordinates serves only as a proxy that does not contain the resource itself. Instead, it contains a redirection to the artifact containing the actual resource. This allows us to maintain a common coordinate scheme for all resources while being able to incorporate existing third-party resources. It also allows us to maintain additional metadata, e.g. about tagsets. When vendors do not distribute their resources via Maven, we package them and distribute them via our own public repository – if their license does not prohibit this.

3.2 The DKPro Core broad-coverage component collection or portable components

We present *DKPro Core*, a broad-coverage collection of NLP components based on the UIMA processing framework. Our collection relies only on portable software and resources and it is distributed via the Maven repository infrastructure. It also served as a use-case and test-bed for the development of our resource selection mechanism (Section 3.1). DKPro Core is provided as open-source software.[2]

[1] For example, the ClearNLP dependency parser model for general English (version 1.2) has about 721 MB.

[2] `https://code.google.com/p/dkpro-core-asl/`

Task	Components	Languages
Language identification	2	de, en, es, fr, +65
Tokenization and sentence boundary detection	5	de, en, es, fr, +25
Lemmatization	7	de, en
Stemming	1	de, en, es, fr, +11
Part-of-speech tagging	9	de, en, es, fr, +14
Morphological analysis	2	de, en, fr, it, +1
Named entity recognition	2	de, en, es, nl
Chunking	1	en
Constituency parsing	3	de, en, fr, zh, +1
Dependency parsing	5	de, en, es, fr, +7
Coreference analysis	1	en
Semantic role labelling	1	en
Spell checking and grammar checking	3	de, en, es, fr, +25

Figure 1: Analysis tasks covered by the DKPro Core component collection

The collection targets users with a strong interest in the ability to programmatically assemble pipelines, e.g. as part of dynamic scientific experiments or within NLP-enabled applications. For this reason, our collection employs the Apache uimaFIT library (Apache UIMA Community, 2013) to allow the implementation of pipelines with only a few lines of code (cf. Section 3.3).

Table 1 provides an overview over the analysis tasks currently covered by the collection.[3] Additionally, our collection provides diverse input/output modules that support different file formats ranging from simple text, over various corpus formats (CoNLL, TIGER-XML, BNC-XML, TCF, etc.), to tool-specific formats (IMS Open Corpus Workbench (Evert and Hardie, 2011), TGrep2 (Rohde, 2005), several UIMA-specific formats, etc.). These enable the processing of corpora from many sources and the further processing of results with specialized tools.

We primarily integrate third-party tools with the UIMA framework and include only few original components, mainly for reading and writing the different supported data formats. Our work focusses on the concerns related to interoperability and usability, such as the resource selection mechanism (Section 3.1).

It is our policy to integrate only third-party tools that are properly versioned and that are distributed via the Central Repository, generally including their full source code.[4] As a considerable portion of the tools we integrate do not initially meet this requirement, we regularly reach out to the respective communities and either help them publishing their tools the Central Repository or offer to do so on their behalf. The DKPro Core components themselves are also distributed via the Central Repository.

3.3 Self-contained executable pipeline example

We define a self-contained pipeline description as uniquely identifying all required components and resources. Assuming that the results of the pipeline are fully defined by these and by the input data, such a self-contained pipeline should allow for reproducible results. In particular, the results must not influenced by the platform the pipeline is run on.

We take a step further making self-contained pipelines also convenient for the users by removing the need to manually obtain and install the required components and resources. To do so, we rely on a generic bootstrapping mechanism which is capable of extracting the information about the required artifacts from the pipeline description and of obtaining them automatically from a repository.

We achieve this goal most illustratively through a combination of these ingredients: our auto-configuration mechanism (Section 3.1) which removes the need for explicit configuration and which identifies and fetches the required resources from the repository at runtime; our component collection (Section 3.2) that is published through a Maven repository; Groovy (2014) and its Grape[5] subsystem serving as a bootstrapping mechanism to fetch the components from the repository; uimaFIT providing a concise way of assembling a pipeline of UIMA components in Groovy and making it executable.

Listing 1 demonstrates such a self-contained and executable pipeline. The example consists of three

[3]Unfortunately, we cannot give a full account of the actually integrated third-party tools here, due to the lack of space.

[4]An exception to this rule are tools that need to be integrated as binaries because they are not implemented in Java.

[5]Groovy Adaptable Packaging Engine: `http://groovy.codehaus.org/Grape`

Listing 1: Executable pipeline implemented in Groovy

```
1 @Grab(group='de.tudarmstadt.ukp.dkpro.core',
2       module='de.tudarmstadt.ukp.dkpro.core.textcat-asl', version='1.6.1')
3 @Grab(group='de.tudarmstadt.ukp.dkpro.core',
4       module='de.tudarmstadt.ukp.dkpro.core.stanfordnlp-gpl', version='1.6.1')
5 @Grab(group='de.tudarmstadt.ukp.dkpro.core',
6       module='de.tudarmstadt.ukp.dkpro.core.maltparser-asl', version='1.6.1')
7 @Grab(group='de.tudarmstadt.ukp.dkpro.core',
8       module='de.tudarmstadt.ukp.dkpro.core.io.text-asl', version='1.6.1')
9 @Grab(group='de.tudarmstadt.ukp.dkpro.core',
10      module='de.tudarmstadt.ukp.dkpro.core.io.conll-asl', version='1.6.1')
11
12 import de.tudarmstadt.ukp.dkpro.core.textcat.*;
13 import de.tudarmstadt.ukp.dkpro.core.stanfordnlp.*;
14 import de.tudarmstadt.ukp.dkpro.core.maltparser.*;
15 import de.tudarmstadt.ukp.dkpro.core.io.text.*;
16 import de.tudarmstadt.ukp.dkpro.core.io.conll.*;
17 import static org.apache.uima.fit.factory.AnalysisEngineFactory.*;
18 import static org.apache.uima.fit.factory.CollectionReaderFactory.*;
19 import static org.apache.uima.fit.pipeline.SimplePipeline.*;
20
21 runPipeline(
22   createReaderDescription(TextReader,
23     TextReader.PARAM_SOURCE_LOCATION, args[0]),
24   createEngineDescription(LanguageIdentifier),
25   createEngineDescription(StanfordSegmenter),
26   createEngineDescription(StanfordPosTagger),
27   createEngineDescription(MaltParser),
28   createEngineDescription(Conll2006Writer,
29     Conll2006Writer.PARAM_TARGET_LOCATION, args[1]));
```

sections. Lines 1-10 identify the components used in the pipeline by name and version. Lines 12-19 are necessary boilerplate code making the components accessible within the Groovy script. Lines 21-29 employ uimaFIT to assemble and run a pipeline consisting of components from our collection.

When the Groovy script representing the pipeline is executed, it downloads all required artifacts. Afterwards, these artifacts remain on the user's system and they can be used again for a subsequent execution of the script. The user may also create backups of these artifacts or transfer them to a different system. Thus, in contrast to pipelines that rely on online services, our approach allows the user to maintain control over the involved software and resources.

The example pipeline given in Listing 1 can indeed be run on any computer that has Groovy installed. It is a life example of a self-contained NLP pipeline shared as part of a scientific publication. By means of this example, we demonstrate that we have reached our goal of providing a concept for shareable pipelines based on portable components and resources.

Due to its conciseness, we consider the Groovy script to provide the most illustrative example of the benefits provided by our contributions. However, there are alternative ways to operationalize our concepts. Alternatively we could use a Jython (2014) script and jip[6] to resolve the Maven dependencies, Java and Maven, or a variety of other JVM-based languages and build tools supporting Maven repositories.

4 Applications

The DKPro Core collection has already been successfully used for linguistic pre-processing in various tasks, including, but not limited to, temporal tagging (Strötgen and Gertz, 2010), text segmentation based on topic models (Riedl and Biemann, 2012), and textual entailment (Noh and Padó, 2013).

The portable components and resources from our collection can be integrated into online workbenches and can be run on cloud platforms by users that find this convenient. Combined with our concept for executable pipelines, users can be enabled to export self-contained pipelines from such workbenches and to archive them for later reproduction. Additionally, users can und run the pipelines on private hardware, possibly on sensitive data which users do not feel comfortable submitting to the cloud. We believe that service-based offerings should be based as much as possible on portable software, and we focussed in this paper on improving the availability and convenience of using such portable NLP software. Thus, we consider our approach not to be competing with service-based approaches but rather as complementing them.

[6]https://pypi.python.org/pypi/jip

Our concept of automatically selecting and acquiring resources can be immediately transferred to other component collections. Although our component collection is based on UIMA, this aspect has been implemented independent of the processing framework. Having experienced the convenience offered by this concept, we believe that integrating a pluggable resource resolving mechanism directly into processing frameworks such as GATE or UIMA would be beneficial. A pluggable mechanism would be important because we expect that the underlying repository infrastructures and coordinate systems are likely to evolve over time. For example, we could envisage an integrated resolving mechanism that allows combining the rich metadata offered by directories such as META-SHARE or the Virtual Language Observatory with the ability to automatically acquire software and resources offered by Maven or with the ability of invoking NLP tools as services such as via AnnoMarket.

Our concept of rendering self-contained pipelines as executable scripts facilitates the sharing of pipelines. This can be either only the script which then downloads its dependencies upon execution, or the dependencies can be resolved beforehand and included with the script. The concise pipeline description is also useful for examples in teaching, in documentation, or on community platforms like Stack Overflow.[7] We offer Groovy- and Jython-based quick-start examples for the DKPro Core collection to new users.

5 Summary and future work

In this paper, we have presented a novel concept for implementing shareable NLP pipelines supported by a broad-coverage collection of interoperable NLP components. Our approach is enabled by the combination of distributing portable NLP components and resources through a repository infrastructure and by an auto-configuration mechanism allowing components to select suitable resources at runtime and to obtain them automatically from the repository.

We have demonstrated that our contributions enable a concise and self-contained pipeline description, which can easily be shared, e.g. as examples in teaching, documentation, or publications. The reliance on portable artifacts allow the user to maintain control, e.g. by creating backups of the involved artifacts to reproduce results at a later time, even if the original repository may no longer be available.

In the future, we plan to investigate a mechanism to automatically detect misalignments between resources and components within a pipeline to provide the user with an indication when suboptimal results may occur and what may cause them. This is necessary because components in the collection are interoperable at the level of annotation types, whereas tagsets and tokenization are simply passed through. While this is a common approach, it leads to the situation that the results may be negatively affected due to diverging tokenizations used while generate the resources for the components. Also, the automatic resource selection mechanism may currently choose resources with incompatible tagsets, e.g. a POS-tagger model producing tagset X while a subsequent dependency parser would require tagset Y.

We also plan to extend the resource selection process to support additional metadata. Eventually, the *variant* coordinate should be replaced by a more fine-grained mechanism to select resources based e.g. on the domain, tagset, or other characteristics.

Acknowledgements

The project was partially funded by means of the German Federal Ministry of Education and Research (BMBF) under the promotional reference 01UG1110D, and partially by the Volkswagen Foundation as part of the Lichtenberg-Professorship Program under grant No. I/82806. The authors take the responsibility for the contents.

References

Apache UIMA Community. 2013. Apache uimaFIT guide and reference, version 2.0.0. Technical report, Apache UIMA.

[7] `http://stackoverflow.com` (Last accesses: 2014-02-14)

Ekaterina Buyko and Udo Hahn. 2008. Fully embedded type systems for the semantic annotation layer. In *ICGL 2008 - Proceedings of First International Conference on Global Interoperability for Language Resources*, pages 26–33, Hong Kong.

Central Repository. 2014. The Central Repository. URL `http://search.maven.org` (Last accessed: 2014-03-19), March. Sonatype Inc. (`http://www.sonatype.org/central`).

Christian Chiarcos, Stefanie Dipper, Michael Götze, Ulf Leser, Anke Lüdeling, Julia Ritz, and Manfred Stede. 2008. A flexible framework for integrating annotations from different tools and tagsets. *Traitement Automatique des Langues*, 49(2):271–293.

ClearNLP. 2014. Version 2.0.2 - fast and robust NLP components implemented in Java. URL `http://opennlp.apache.org` (Last accessed: 2014-03-19), January.

Hamish Cunningham, Diana Maynard, Kalina Bontcheva, and Valentin Tablan. 2002. GATE: an architecture for development of robust HLT applications. In *Proceedings of 40th Annual Meeting of the Association for Computational Linguistics*, pages 168–175, Philadelphia, Pennsylvania, USA, July. Association for Computational Linguistics.

Stefan Evert and Andrew Hardie. 2011. Twenty-first century corpus workbench: Updating a query architecture for the new millennium. In *Proceedings of the Corpus Linguistics 2011 conference*, Birmingham, UK, July. University of Birmingham.

David Ferrucci and Adam Lally. 2004. UIMA: an architectural approach to unstructured information processing in the corporate research environment. *Natural Language Engineering*, 10(3-4):327–348.

Antske Fokkens, Marieke van Erp, Marten Postma, Ted Pedersen, Piek Vossen, and Nuno Freire. 2013. Offspring from reproduction problems: What replication failure teaches us. In *Proceedings of the 51st Annual Meeting of the Association for Computational Linguistics (Volume 1: Long Papers)*, pages 1691–1701, Sofia, Bulgaria, August. Association for Computational Linguistics.

Carole A Goble, Jiten Bhagat, Sergejs Aleksejevs, Don Cruickshank, Danius Michaelides, David Newman, Mark Borkum, Sean Bechhofer, Marco Roos, Peter Li, et al. 2010. myExperiment: a repository and social network for the sharing of bioinformatics workflows. *Nucleic acids research*, 38(suppl 2):W677–W682.

José Manuel Gómez-Pérez, Esteban Garcıa-Cuesta, Jun Zhao, Aleix Garrido, José Enrique Ruiz, and Graham Klyne. 2013. How reliable is your workflow: Monitoring decay in scholarly publications. In *Proceedings of the 3rd Workshop on Semantic Publishing (SePublica 2013) at 10th Extended Semantic Web Conference*, page 75, Montpellier, France, May.

Groovy. 2014. Version 2.2.2 - A dynamic language for the Java platform. URL `http://groovy.codehaus.org` (Last accessed: 2014-03-19, February.

Péter Halácsy, András Kornai, and Csaba Oravecz. 2007. Hunpos – an open source trigram tagger. In *Proceedings of the 45th Annual Meeting of the Association for Computational Linguistics Companion Volume Proceedings of the Demo and Poster Sessions*, pages 209–212, Prague, Czech Republic, June. Association for Computational Linguistics.

Marie Hinrichs, Thomas Zastrow, and Erhard Hinrichs. 2010. WebLicht: Web-based LRT Services in a Distributed eScience Infrastructure. In Nicoletta Calzolari, Khalid Choukri, Bente Maegaard, Joseph Mariani, Jan Odijk, Stelios Piperidis, Mike Rosner, and Daniel Tapias, editors, *Proceedings of the Seventh International Conference on Language Resources and Evaluation (LREC'10)*, pages 489–493, Valletta, Malta, May. European Language Resources Association (ELRA).

Jython. 2014. Jython: Python for the Java Platform. URL `http://www.jython.org` (Last accessed: 2014-03-19.

Yoshinobu Kano, Makoto Miwa, Kevin Bretonnel Cohen, Lawrence E. Hunter, Sophia Ananiadou, and Jun'ichi Tsujii. 2011. U-Compare: A modular NLP workflow construction and evaluation system. *IBM Journal of Research and Development*, 55(3):11:1–11:10, May.

Christopher Manning, Mihai Surdeanu, John Bauer, Jenny Finkel, Steven Bethard, and David McClosky. 2014. The stanford corenlp natural language processing toolkit. In *Proceedings of 52nd Annual Meeting of the Association for Computational Linguistics: System Demonstrations*, pages 55–60, Baltimore, Maryland, June. Association for Computational Linguistics.

Joakim Nivre, Johan Hall, Jens Nilsson, Atanas Chanev, Gülsen Eryigit, Sandra Kübler, Svetoslav Marinov, and Erwin Marsi. 2007. Maltparser: A language-independent system for data-driven dependency parsing. *Natural Language Engineering*, 13(2):95–135.

Tae-Gil Noh and Sebastian Padó. 2013. Using UIMA to structure an open platform for textual entailment. In Peter Klügl, Richard Eckart de Castilho, and Katrin Tomanek, editors, *Proceedings of the 3rd Workshop on Unstructured Information Management Architecture (UIMA@GSCL 2013)*, pages 26–33, Darmstadt, Germany, Sep. CEUR-WS.org.

Philip V. Ogren, Philipp G. Wetzler, and Steven J. Bethard. 2009. ClearTK: a framework for statistical natural language processing. In Christian Chiarcos, Richard Eckart de Castilho, and Manfred Stede, editors, *Proceedings of the Biennial GSCL Conference 2009, 2nd UIMA@GSCL Workshop*, pages 241–248, Potsdam, Germany, September. Gunter Narr Verlag.

Rafal Rak, Andrew Rowley, Jacob Carter, and Sophia Ananiadou. 2013. Development and analysis of nlp pipelines in argo. In *Proceedings of the 51st Annual Meeting of the Association for Computational Linguistics: System Demonstrations*, pages 115–120, Sofia, Bulgaria, August. Association for Computational Linguistics.

Martin Riedl and Chris Biemann. 2012. Text segmentation with topic models. *JLCL*, 27(1):47–69.

Douglas LT Rohde. 2005. Tgrep2 user manual version 1.15. *Massachusetts Institute of Technology. http://tedlab.mit.edu/dr/Tgrep2*.

Guergana K. Savova, James J. Masanz, Philip V. Ogren, Jiaping Zheng, Sunghwan Sohn, Karin C. Kipper-Schuler, and Christopher G. Chute. 2010. Mayo clinical text analysis and knowledge extraction system (cTAKES): architecture, component evaluation and applications. *Journal of the American Medical Informatics Association*, 17(5):507–513.

Helmut Schmid. 1994. Probabilistic part-of-speech tagging using decision trees. In *Proceedings of International Conference on New Methods in Language Processing*, pages 44–49, Manchester, UK.

Sonatype Company. 2008. *Maven: The Definitive Guide*. O'Reilly Media, September. ISBN: 9780596517335.

Jannik Strötgen and Michael Gertz. 2010. HeidelTime: High Quality Rule-Based Extraction and Normalization of Temporal Expressions. In *Proceedings of the 5th International Workshop on Semantic Evaluation*, pages 321–324, Uppsala, Sweden, July. Association for Computational Linguistics.

Valentin Tablan, Kalina Bontcheva, Ian Roberts, Hamish Cunningham, and Marin Dimitrov. 2013. Annomarket: An open cloud platform for nlp. In *Proceedings of the 51st Annual Meeting of the Association for Computational Linguistics: System Demonstrations*, pages 19–24, Sofia, Bulgaria, August. Association for Computational Linguistics.

Paul Thompson, Yoshinobu Kano, John McNaught, Steve Pettifer, Teresa Attwood, John Keane, and Sophia Ananiadou. 2011. Promoting interoperability of resources in meta-share. In *Proceedings of the Workshop on Language Resources, Technology and Services in the Sharing Paradigm*, pages 50–58, Chiang Mai, Thailand, November. Asian Federation of Natural Language Processing.

Dieter Van Uytvanck, Claus Zinn, Daan Broeder, Peter Wittenburg, and Mariano Gardellini. 2010. Virtual Language Observatory: The portal to the language resources and technology universe. In Nicoletta Calzolari, Khalid Choukri, Bente Maegaard, Joseph Mariani, Jan Odijk, Stelios Piperidis, Mike Rosner, and Daniel Tapias, editors, *Proceedings of the Seventh International Conference on Language Resources and Evaluation (LREC'10)*, pages 900–903, Valletta, Malta, may. European Language Resources Association (ELRA).

Stephen Wu, Vinod Kaggal, Dmitriy Dligach, James Masanz, Pei Chen, Lee Becker, Wendy Chapman, Guergana Savova, Hongfang Liu, and Christopher Chute. 2013. A common type system for clinical natural language processing. *Journal of Biomedical Semantics*, 4(1):1.

Integrating UIMA with Alveo, a human communication science virtual laboratory

Dominique Estival
U. of Western Sydney
d.estival@uws.edu.au

Steve Cassidy
Macquarie University
steve.cassidy@mq.edu.au

Karin Verspoor
University of Melbourne
karin.verspoor@unimelb.edu.au

Andrew MacKinlay
RMIT
andrew.mackinlay@rmit.edu.au

Denis Burnham
U. of Western Sydney
d.burnham@uws.edu.au

Abstract

This paper describes two aspects of Alveo, a new virtual laboratory for human communication science (HCS). As a platform for HCS researchers, the integration of the Unstructured Information Management Architecture (UIMA) with Alveo was one of the aims during the development phase and we report on the choices that were made for the implementation. User acceptance testing (UAT) constituted an integral part of the development and evolution of Alveo and we present the distributed testing organisation, the test development process and the evolution of the tests. We conclude with some lessons learned regarding multi-site collaborative work on the development and deployment of HLT research infrastructure.

1 Introduction

The Alveo Virtual Laboratory provides a new platform for collaborative research in human communication science (HCS). [1] Funded by the Australian Government National eResearch Collaboration Tools and Resources (NeCTAR) program, it involves partners from 16 institutions in a range of disciplines: linguistics, natural language processing, speech science, psychology, as well as music and acoustic processing. The goal of the platform is to provide easy access to a variety of databases and a range of analysis tools, in order to foster inter-disciplinary research and facilitate the discovery of new methods for solving old problems or the application of known methods to new datasets (Estival, Cassidy, Sefton, & Burnham, 2013). The platform integrates a number of tools and enables non-technical users to process communication resources (including not only text and speech corpora but also music recordings and videos) using these tools in a straightforward manner. In this paper, we report on the recent integration of the Unstructured Information Management Architecture (UIMA) with Alveo. This integration is bi-directional, in that existing resources and annotations captured over those resources in Alveo can flow to a UIMA process, and new annotations produced by a UIMA process can be consumed and persisted by Alveo. We also introduce the general approach to user acceptance testing (UAT) of Alveo, focussing on the organisation and process acceptance adopted to meet the acceptance criteria required for the project and to ensure user uptake within the research community. Finally, we demonstrate the application of the testing process for acceptance of the UIMA integration.

Section 2 briefly describes Alveo and its components, in particular the tools and corpora already available on the platform and the workflow engine, then Section 3 describes the Alveo-UIMA integration. Section 4 describes the UAT requirement and the organisation of the testing among the Alveo project partners, outlines the actual testing process and gives examples of the tests, among them the UIMA tests, which were developed for the project. Section 5 discusses alternative strategies and we conclude with some lessons learned regarding multi-site collaborative work on the development and deployment of HLT research infrastructure.

Proceedings of the Workshop on Open Infrastructures and Analysis Frameworks for HLT, pages 12–22, Dublin, Ireland, August 23rd 2014.

2 The Alveo Virtual Laboratory

Alveo provides easy access to a range of databases relevant to human communication science disciplines, including speech, text, audio and video, some of which would previously have been difficult for researchers to access or even know about. The system implements a uniform and secure license management system for the diverse licensing and user agreement conditions required. Browsing, searching and dataset manipulation are also functionalities which are available in a consistent manner across the data collections through the web-based Discovery Interface. The first phase of the project (December 2012 – June 2014) saw the inclusion of the collections shown in Table 1.

1. PARADISEC (Pacific and Regional Archive for Digital Sources in Endangered Cultures): audio, video, text and image resources for Australian and Pacific Island languages (Thieberger, Barwick, Billington, & Vaughan, 2011)
2. AusTalk, audio-visual speech corpus of Australian English (Burnham et al., 2011)
3. The Australian National Corpus (S. Cassidy, Haugh, Peters, & Fallu, 2012) comprising: Australian Corpus of English (ACE); Australian Radio Talkback (ART); AustLit; Braided Channels; Corpus of Oz Early English (COOEE); Griffith Corpus of Spoken English (GCSAusE); International Corpus of English (ICE-AUS); Mitchell & Delbridge corpus; Monash Corpus of Spoken English (Musgrave & Haugh, 2009).
4. AVOZES, a visual speech corpus (Goecke & Millar, 2004)
5. UNSW Pixar Emotional Music Excerpts: Pixar movie theme music expressing different emotions
6. Sydney University Room Impulse Responses: environmental audio samples which, through convolution with speech or music, can create the effect of that speech or music in that acoustic environment
7. Macquarie University Battery of Emotional Prosody: sung sentences with different prosodic patterns
8. Colloquial Jakartan Indonesian corpus: audio and text, recorded in Jakarta in the early 1990's (ANU)
9. The ClueWeb dataset (http://lemurproject.org/clueweb12/).

Table 1: *Alveo* Data Collections

Through the web-based Discovery interface, the user can select items based on the results of faceted search across the collections and can organise selected data in Items Lists. Beyond browsing and searching, Alveo offers the possibility of analysing and processing the data with a range of tools. In the first phase of the project, the tools listed in Table 2 were integrated within Alveo.

1. EOPAS (PARADISEC tool) for text interlinear text and media analysis
2. NLTK (Natural Language Toolkit) for text analytics with linguistic data (Bird, Klein, & Loper, 2009)
3. EMU, for search, speech analysis and interactive labelling of spectrograms and waveforms (Steve Cassidy & Harrington, 2000)
4. AusNC Tools: KWIC, Concordance, Word Count, statistical summary and statistical analysis
5. Johnson-Charniak parser, to generate full parse trees for text sentences (Charniak & Johnson, 2005)
6. ParseEval, to evaluate the syllabic parse of consonant clusters (Shaw & Gafos, 2010)
7. HTK-modifications, a patch to HTK (Hidden Markov Model Toolkit, http://htk.eng.cam.ac.uk/) to enable missing data recognition
8. DeMoLib, for video analysis (http://staff.estem-uc.edu.au/roland/research/demolib-home/)
9. PsySound3, for physical and psycho-acoustical analysis of complex visual and auditory scenes (Cabrera, Ferguson, & Schubert, 2007)
10. ParGram, grammar for Indonesian (Arka, 2012)
11. INDRI, for information retrieval with large data sets (http://www.lemurproject.org/indri/)

Table 2: *Alveo* Tools

Most of these tools require significant expertise to set up and one of the Alveo project goals is to make this easier for non-technical researchers. The *Alveo* Workflow Engine is built around the Galaxy open source workflow management system (Goecks, Nekrutenko, Taylor, & Team, 2010), which was originally designed for use in the life sciences to support researchers in running pipelines of tools to manipulate data. Workflows in Galaxy can be stored, shared and published, and we hope this will also become a way for human communication science researchers to codify and exchange common analyses.

A number of the tools listed in Table 2 have been packaged as Python scripts, for instance NLTK based scripts to carry out part-of-speech tagging, stemming and parsing. Other tools are implemented in R, e.g. EMU/R and ParseEval. An API is provided to mediate access to data, ensuring that permissions are respected, and providing a way to access individual items, and 'mount' datasets for fast access (Steve Cassidy, Estival, Jones, Burnham, & Burghold, 2014). An instance of the Galaxy Workflow engine is run on a virtual machine in the NeCTAR Research Cloud, a secure platform for Australian research, funded by the same government program (https://www.nectar.org.au/research-cloud). Finally, a UIMA interface has been developed to enable the conversion of Alveo items, as well as their associated annotations, into UIMA CAS documents, for analysis in a conventional UIMA pipeline. Conversely annotations from a UIMA pipeline can be associated with a document in Alveo. Figure 1 gives an overview of the architecture.

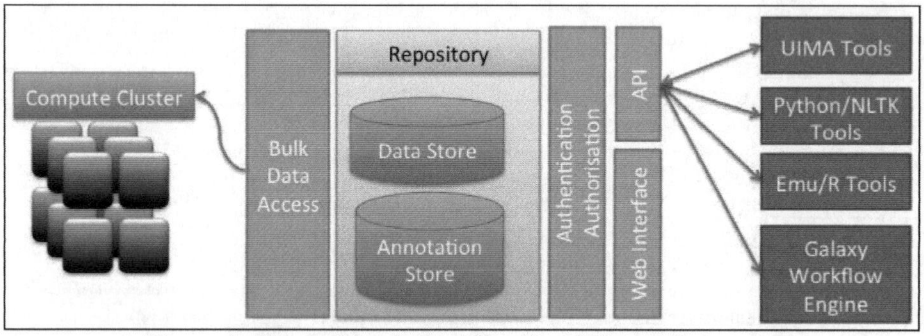

Figure 1: The architecture of the Alveo Virtual Laboratory

2.1 Annotations in Alveo

Annotations in Alveo are stored in a standoff format based on the model described in the ISO Linguistic Annotation Framework (ISO-LAF). Internally, annotations are represented as RDF using the DADA (Steve Cassidy, 2010). Each annotation is identified by a distinct URI and references into the source documents are stored as offsets either using character positions, times or frame counts for audio/video data. Annotations have an associated type attribute that denotes the kind of annotation (speaker turn, part of speech, phonetic segment) and a label that defines a simple string value associated with the annotation. Annotations may also have other properties defined as standard RDF properties and values.

The API exposes a direct interface to the annotation store in RDF via a SPARQL endpoint, but the normal mode of access is via the REST API where each item (document) has a corresponding URI that returns the collection of annotations on that item in a JSON-LD format. JSON-LD allows us to represent the full RDF namespaces of properties and values in a concise format that is easily processed using standard JSON tools. An example annotation delivered in this format is shown in Figure 2. The same JSON-LD format can be used to upload new annotations to be stored in Alveo.

```
{
 "@context": "https://app.alveo.edu.au/schema/json-ld",
 "commonProperties": {
    "alveo:annotates":"https://app…AusE08/document/GCSAusE07.mp3"
 },
 "alveo:annotations": [
 {
  "@id": "http://ns.ausnc.org.au/corpora/gcsause/annotation/535958",
  "type": "http://ns.ausnc.org.au/schemas/annotation/conversation/micropause",
  "@type": "dada:TextAnnotation",
  "end": "34",
  "start": "33"
 },
…}
```

Figure 2: An example of the Alveo JSON-LD annotation format

3 UIMA

3.1 Background

The Unstructured Information Management Architecture (UIMA) is an Apache open source project (http://uima.apache.org) (D. Ferrucci & Lally, 2004) that provides an architecture for developing applications involving analysis of large volumes of unstructured information. This framework allows development of modular pipelines for analysing the sorts of data available in Alveo, including speech, text and video. A number of groups around the world have adopted UIMA to enable easier interoperability and sharing of language technology components. This is true particularly in the biomedical natural language processing community; several groups have made tools available as UIMA modules. Most OpenNLP modules have been wrapped for use within UIMA, and the UIMA community more broadly has a range of language technology tools available in UIMA-compliant modules (David Ferrucci et al., 2010).

Each component in a UIMA application implements interfaces defined by the framework and provides self-describing metadata via XML descriptor files. The framework manages these components and the data flow between them. Since UIMA applications are defined in terms of descriptors that clearly specify both the component modules of the application and the configuration parameter settings for executing the application, they are "re-runnable, re-usable procedures" of the kind that Alveo aims to capture.

Given the objective of Alveo to facilitate access to analysis tools, and the UIMA objective of making such analysis tools interoperable, bringing the two frameworks together made sense. Thus the objective of the integration was to build a bidirectional translation layer between Alveo and any standard UIMA pipeline. In other words, the translation component was required to: 1) read corpus data including associated annotations stored in Alveo into a UIMA pipeline and 2) store annotations produced by a UIMA pipeline in Alveo.

3.2 Overview of the Conversion Layer Architecture

We opted for the most straightforward connection between the two frameworks, i.e. communicating directly with the Alveo REST API. The approach involves allowing annotations and documents to flow from Alveo, be processed externally to Alveo in a specially-configured UIMA pipeline, and then providing a mechanism for new annotations over the documents to be returned to Alveo for storage. The Alveo REST API provides access to item metadata, documents and annotations using a JSON-LD based interchange format. The API supports most actions that are available via the web interface including meta-data queries and retrieval of documents either individually or in batches.

We built the UIMA-Alveo conversion layer, denoted *Alveo-UIMA*. It allows reading a group of documents from Alveo, and converting the documents along with their associated annotations into UIMA *Common Annotation Structure* (CAS) instances. It also allows annotations produced by a UIMA *Collection Processing Engine* (CPE) pipeline on a set of CASes to be uploaded to an Alveo server. *Alveo-UIMA* is built on top of a native Java wrapper for the Alveo REST API. It is implemented in Java and is distributed as an open-source package.[2] The conversion layer exposes the Alveo data as native Java data structures and is also available as a standalone package,[3] providing, as a side effect, a method to access the Alveo REST API without needing to invoke the UIMA machinery. Similar packages are also available for Python and R in the Alveo repository.

The first component of the UIMA interface, for reading existing items, is implemented as UIMA *Collection Reader*. This takes as parameters an Alveo item list ID, corresponding to a user-created list of documents, and server credentials. It converts the Alveo items from that item list, as well as their associated annotations, into UIMA CAS documents, which can then be used as part of a conventional UIMA pipeline. The UIMA processing pipeline can then take advantage of the annotations downloaded from Alveo (e.g. by using a speaker turn annotation to demarcate a sentence).

---

[2] https://github.com/Alveo; https://github.com/Alveo/alveo-uima

[3] https://github.com/Alveo/alveo-java-rest-api

The second component is for the opposite direction, i.e. taking annotations from a UIMA pipeline and associating them with the document in Alveo. There is no capability yet to add new documents that derive from outside Alveo, as this is not currently possible using Alveo's REST API. This means that documents for which we are uploading UIMA annotations must have originated in Alveo and have come from the *Collection Reader*, ensuring that each document has appropriate identifying metadata for Alveo.

Annotations need to be converted from Alveo to UIMA and vice versa, since the annotation formats are not identical. Some attributes, such as textual character offsets, are directly convertible, while others require more work. Every document retrieved from the Alveo server has metadata (e.g. data source, recording date and language) and annotations (e.g. POS tags) associated with it. Converting metadata from Alveo to UIMA is straightforward, as the expected metadata fields can be directly mapped to a customised UIMA type. Converting annotations from between the frameworks requires more work, due to the required use of a type system in UIMA. This is discussed further below.

3.3 Conversion from Alveo to UIMA

An annotation in Alveo consists of a beginning and ending offset, which can correspond to a character span for textual data or a time span for audio-visual data, a human-readable plain-text *label* indicating additional attributes of the data, and a *type* (a URI indicating the kind of entity to which the annotation corresponds, e.g. "speaker-turn", "intonation" or "part-of-speech"). Since UIMA also encodes text annotations as character spans, these can be straightforwardly converted into the UIMA CAS (audio-visual data can be similarly treated, but we have focused on text in the current work).

UIMA allows the definition of custom data types with specific fields for storing salient values. We add a generic Alveo annotation type (inheriting from the standard UIMA *Annotation*, which means it still has spans attached). The label of the annotation in Alveo is a non-decomposable string, so this top-level type has a field to store the label as a string.

Handling annotation types requires more care. Types in Alveo are encoded as fully-qualified URIs, while types in UIMA are more strictly defined. In particular, UIMA has a notion of a fully-specified *type system* associated with each pipeline specification, including a full inheritance hierarchy up to a root type and features corresponding to attributes of each type. There are also minor differences between the encoding of the type names (instead of a URI, UIMA uses a 'big-endian' qualified type name similar to a Java package, such as `com.example.nlp.Sentence`).

In addition, UIMA component specification requires specifying in advance the type system to which all annotations represented within UIMA must conform. All these requirements are handled in a type system generation phase triggered when the *Alveo-UIMA* collection reader is created.[4] During this phase, the reader requests an enumeration of all known type URIs from the Alveo server. Since we have no explicit additional information about type inheritance from the URIs, we make as few assumptions as possible by having all types inherit from a generic Alveo annotation parent type. The Alveo URIs are automatically converted to UIMA types names, essentially by reversing the components of the domain name, and replacing the '/' character in the path component of the URI with '.', with some extra handling of non-alphanumeric characters, giving conversions such as the following:

`http://example.com/nlp/sentence` → `com.example.nlp.Sentence`

In addition, the type URI is stored as an attribute of the UIMA annotation, providing an explicit record of the original Alveo type. Because it is far more natural to work with UIMA types than comparing string values when manipulating and filtering annotations in a UIMA pipeline, the automatically generated type system is very beneficial.

We note that there have been proposals to simplify the internal UIMA type system through the use of a generic `Referent` type which refers to an external source of domain semantics (D. Ferrucci, Lally, Verspoor, & Nyberg, 2009) This would be a good strategy to pursue here, so that the UIMA annotations could refer explicitly to the Alveo URIs as an external type system. However, it has been noted previously that this representational choice has consequences for the indexing and reasoning over the semantics of annotations in UIMA analysis engines (Verspoor, Baumgartner Jr, Roeder, &

[4] If the framework users are using UIMA canonically, where the type systems are described by pre-existing XML descriptors, they can explicitly request generation of the appropriate XML. The wrapper was primarily developed using UIMAFit (https://uimafit.apache.org/uimafit), which allows a more dynamic approach.

Hunter, 2009). The current version of UIMA does not provide direct support for this model and hence our strategy is in line with current technical practice. These proposals aim to not replicate the full external type structure within the UIMA type system definition, and this is the practice we follow here, although since Alveo does not currently have a strong notion of type hierarchy this was not a significant consideration.

3.4 Conversion from UIMA to Alveo

The annotation upload component is implemented as a UIMA CAS Consumer, i.e. a component which accepts CASes and performs some action with them. To upload annotations, as noted above, we expect the supplied CAS to derive originally from the Alveo server, with annotations added to that CAS by UIMA processing components. The original metadata from Alveo is used to determine the URL of the original item, and otherwise ignored.

The first step in annotation upload is to retrieve the original source document and remove from the set of annotations to be uploaded those annotations which already appear in the version found on the server. In addition, since processing pipelines may produce a wide variety of annotations which may not all be appropriate or relevant for uploading to Alveo, the annotation type must occur in a preconfigured whitelist. Converting each annotation from UIMA to Alveo is in some ways the inverse of the operation described in the previous section, although there are some intricacies to the process.

The character spans can be directly converted as before; again the type and label require more work. For type conversion, some sensible default behaviours are used. A configurable list of UIMA features are inspected on the UIMA annotations, and the first match found is used as the Alveo annotation type. This list of features naturally includes the default feature for storing the type URI, ensuring that annotations which derive from Alveo originally can be matched back to the original annotation. If no matches are found, a type URI is inferred from the fully-qualified UIMA annotation type name, using the inverse operation to that described above.

Alveo annotations also have labels, as noted in the previous section. As with the annotation types, there is a similar list of UIMA feature names which can be used to populate the label attribute on the Alveo annotation, defaulting to the empty string if no feature name is found. If these strategies do not produce the desired behaviour when uploading, it is possible to customise them by implementing a Java interface. Alternatively, it is also possible to insert a custom UIMA component into the pipeline to convert the added UIMA annotations so that the Alveo conversion works as desired.

4 Alveo User Acceptance Testing

As it was a requirement of the funding agency for the project to provide evidence of User Acceptance Testing (UAT) and acceptance of the results of these tests by the project governing body (the Steering Committee), the project was organised from the start around these requirements, with all the partners bidding for participation in tests of specific components or versions of the system. A testing schedule was developed to accompany the system development, with the aim of gathering feedback from the project partners during development to provide targeted input for improvement. A sub-committee of the Steering Committee was designated to oversee the tests distributed to the testers, examine the reports summarising the results of those tests and recommend acceptance.

Alveo was designed and implemented in partnership with Intersect, a commercial software development company specialised in the support of academic eResearch. This partnership afforded extensive professional support during development, using the Agile process (Beck & al, 2001) as well as thorough regression testing and debugging. In other projects of this type, Intersect provided UAT or managed the UAT process in-house. For the Alveo project, since user testing was the main way in which the academic partners were involved in the project, UAT was organised by the academic partners with technical support from Intersect. The central team at the lead institution oversaw the creation of the tests (see section 4.2), distributed the tests and monitored the results.

4.1 The Alveo UAT process

During development, Alveo was deployed incrementally on separate servers. While the Production Server remained stable between versions, the Staging 1 server was reserved for UAT and only updated when new functionalities were added; the Staging 2 Server was used for development and frequently updated. This rarely caused problems, even with the distributed nature of the testing process.

Each partner site engaged High Degree Researchers (HDRs), generally Masters and Doctoral students but also Post-Doctoral Fellows or project members, who had an interest in a particular domain or tool, or who could provide critical comments about the functionalities. Some Testers were Linguistics students with no computing background, some were Computer Science students with limited linguistic knowledge. At some sites, the Testers were Research Assistants who had worked on the tools or corpora contributed by their institutions, while others were the tool developers themselves. This variety of backgrounds and skills ensured coverage of the main domains and functionalities expected of the Alveo Virtual Lab. Some sites had undertaken to conduct large amounts of testing throughout the development, while other partners only chose to perform limited or more targeted testing, with commitments varying from 10 to 200 hours. Over 30 Testers participated at various times during of the project and a total of more than 300 hours has been spent on testing during Phase I.

4.2 Evolution of the tests

For each version of the system during development (Prototype, Version 1, 2, and 3) a series of tests were developed and posted on a Google Form. To record the results, the Testers filled out a Google form which was monitored by the central team. The first tests developed were very directive, giving very specific instructions as to what actions the user was asked to perform and what results were expected for each action, as shown in Figure 3, one of the tests for Version 1.

Test 2 - Browsing COOEE

1. Login to the main website.
2. In the list of facets on the left, click Corpus, this should show a list of corpus names.
3. From the list of corpus names click cooee, the page should update to show 1354 results, listing the first 10 matching items from the COOEE corpus.
4. In the list of facets on the left click Created, this should show a list of decades.
5. From the list of decades click 1870-1879, the page should update to show 61 results which are COOEE items from the 1870s.
6. From the list of matching items, click on the first item, the page should update to show the details of this item. Verify that the Created date is within the 1870s and that the isPartOf field shows cooee.
7. Scroll down to the bottom of the page where you should see links to the documents in this item. Click on the document marked Text(Original), you should see the text of the document including some markup at the start and end of the file.
8. Use the Back button in your browser to return to the item display page, click on the document marked Text(Plain), you should see the text of the document with no markup.
9. Use the Back button in your browser to return to the item display page.
10. When you are finished, click on the HCSvLab logo on the top left of the page to return to the home page and reset your search.

Figure 3: Test for Alveo Version 1

Gradually the tests became more open-ended, giving less guidance and gathering more informative feedback. The latest round of testing asked Testers to log in and to carry out a small research task, as shown in Figure 4, the instructions for the open form testing of Version 3.

Based on your own research interests and based on what you've seen of the HCS vLab platform, please try to make use of the virtual lab to carry out a small research task. Use the form below to tell us about what you tried to do: the collections and tools that you used, a description of your task, the outcomes and any problems that you faced.

Figure 4: Open form test for Alveo Version 3

Some of the early tests, such as the one shown in Figure 3, have become tutorials provided on the Alveo web page and are now available as help from within the Virtual Lab.

4.3 UIMA Testing

In order to test the Alveo-UIMA implementation and provide an example of how it can be used, we created a tutorial application[5] available from the Alveo github repository. This tutorial shows an example of instantiating a UIMA CPE pipeline which reads documents from an Alveo item list, augments it with part-of-speech annotations and uploads them to the Alveo server. A UIMA pipeline consists of a collection reader, and one or more CAS annotators. The UIMA tutorial pipeline includes the standard *Collection Reader* from Alveo-UIMA, a basic POS-tagging CAS annotator from DKPro-Core,[6] and the annotation uploading CAS annotator from Alveo-UIMA. An advanced version also demonstrates implementing an interface which remaps the POS tag types from those automatically-derived from DKPro.outputs.

5 Discussion

5.1 Related Work

There are several frameworks that have been developed to enable development and evaluation of text processing workflows, and UIMA has been used as the backbone for a few such frameworks due to its support for processing module interoperability. The Argo web service (Rak, Rowley, & Ananiadou, 2012; Rak, Rowley, Carter, & Ananiadou, 2013) is a recent web application that enables development of UIMA-based text processing workflows through an on-line graphical interface. In contrast to Alveo, documents are uploaded to the system within an individual user space, and resulting annotations are not persisted outside of the UIMA data structures; although they can be serialised and stored for subsequent re-use in processing pipelines, or exported as RDF, they are not directly accessible within the framework itself. The repository contains a wide range of NLP components, e.g., modules to perform sentence splitting, POS tagging, parsing, and a number of information extraction tasks targeted to biomedical text.

The U-Compare system (Kano et al., 2009; Kano, Dorado, McCrohon, Ananiadou, & Tsujii, 2010) also supports evaluation and performance comparison of UIMA-based automated annotation tools. It was designed with UIMA in mind from the ground up, enabling UIMA workflow creation and execution through a GUI. Therefore it assumes that all analysis of collections is performed with a set of UIMA components, and indeed provides a substantial number of such components in their repository, although other components can be added. The system is launched locally via Java Web Start; given recent changes to how browsers interact with Java, this no longer works reliably and off-line use (after downloading and installing) is likely necessary, although interaction with web service based processing components is possible (Kontonasios, Korkontzelos, Kolluru, & Ananiadou, 2011).

A competing framework based on the GATE architecture (Cunningham, Maynard, Bontcheva, & Tablan, 2002) is the cloud-based AnnoMarket platform. This framework provides access to natural language processing (NLP) components, and a limited number of existing resources (one at the time of writing[7], with the facility to upload user-specific data) on a fee-for-service basis (passing along costs of using the Amazon cloud services). Results of NLP studies of this data can be downloaded, or indexed and made available for search. There are a wide array of annotation services and pre-configured pipelines available within the AnnoMarket that can be applied to a user's document collection, either directly through the on-line application or via a web service API.

5.2 Alternative strategies for UIMA integration with Alveo

There were several possible places where the UIMA-Alveo translation layer could have been inserted, and indeed several possible architectures were considered for integrating UIMA with Alveo.

Since Alveo was already working with the workflow engine Galaxy, one option was to create a compatibility layer to bridge UIMA with Galaxy, for instance to enable a pre-configured UIMA pipeline to be instantiated via a Galaxy wrapper. The technical details for accomplishing this were not immediately obvious, and it was decided that this approach would add substantial complexity to the conversion of annotations in the conversion layer.

[5] http://github.com/Alveo/alveo-uima-tutorial
[6] https://code.google.com/p/dkpro-core-asl/
[7] https://annomarket.com/dataSources, accessed 29 May 2014

Another option that was considered was to allow for dynamic construction of UIMA workflows from UIMA components directly through the Alveo web interface. UIMA is a workflow engine analogous to Galaxy, in that it enables dynamic configuration of pipelines from the available set of UIMA components set up in a given environment. In principle, therefore, it would be possible to enable specification, instantiation, and execution of UIMA pipelines from a set of UIMA components made available via Alveo. However, this would have required a substantial development effort specifically targeted towards hosting UIMA components and manipulating UIMA pipelines; it was decided that a more general approach to integrating a broader range of tools was more appropriate for Alveo. Given the recent availability of the Argo web application, an Alveo/Argo integration could be considered that would enable users to create UIMA workflows with Argo but execute them from Alveo, and on documents or corpora stored in Alveo (Rak et al., 2012; Rak et al., 2013). The current web service-based architecture of the *Alveo-UIMA* integration lends itself well to this possibility. This could be explored in future work.

The current implementation assumes that an Alveo user will have the knowledge to create and run UIMA pipelines externally to Alveo. A complementary strategy, possible now that the conversion layer is in place, would be to make complete, pre-configured UIMA pipelines available as tools that can be applied to Alveo corpora/data. A number of such services, e.g. services aimed at annotation of text with one of a set of biomedically-relevant entity types (diseases, genes, chemicals) have been built (MacKinlay & Verspoor, 2013). Each such service is run as a separate UIMA instance that is accessed via a web service. Text is passed in via the REST interface, handed over to the UIMA instance, processed, and annotations are returned. This basic model could be replicated for a number of UIMA pipelines that do standard text-related processing (e.g. split sentences, perform part of speech tagging and parsing, etc.) such that text extracted from Alveo could be processed by the UIMA-based service and annotations returned. This approach has been criticised for its inability to be extended or adapted (Tablan, Bontcheva, Roberts, Cunningham, & Dimitrov, 2013) although it is suitable where prepackaged pipelines can be applied to accomplish tasks of broad interest.

6 Conclusions

The development of Alveo presented a number of challenges, some technical, such as the integration of UIMA with the platform, and others more logistic, such as the distributed nature of testing during development. In this paper, we described the solution and the choices we made for the implementation of UIMA pipelines, given the constraints regarding the organisation of items, documents and their associated annotations in Alveo. One of the conditions of success of such a project is that the platform be used by researchers for their own projects and on their own data. The organisation of the User Acceptance Testing, requiring partners to contribute during the development, and providing exposure to the tools and the datasets to a large group of diverse researchers is expected to lead to a much wider uptake of Alveo as a platform for HCS research in Australia. We plan to open it to users outside the original project partners during Phase II (2014-2016). We will also continue to explore further interactions with complementary frameworks, such that the data and annotation storage available in Alveo can be enhanced via processing and tools from external services to supplement the functionality that is currently directly integrated.

Acknowledgements

We gratefully acknowledge funding from the Australian Government National eResearch Collaboration Tools and Resources (NeCTAR) and thank all our collaborating partners in the Alveo Virtual Laboratory project: University of Western Sydney, Macquarie University, RMIT, University of Melbourne, Australian National University, University of Western Australia, University of Sydney, University of New England, University of Canberra, Flinders University, University of New South Wales, University of La Trobe, University of Tasmania, ASSTA, AusNC Inc., NICTA, and Intersect.

References

Arka, I. W. (2012). *Developing a Deep Grammar of Indonesian within the ParGram Framework: Theoretical and Implementational Challenges* Paper presented at the 26th Pacific Asia Conference on Language,Information and Computation.

Beck, K., et al. (2001). Manifesto for Agile Software Development. http://agilemanifesto.org/

Bird, S., Klein, E., & Loper, E. (2009). *Natural Language Processing with Python - Analyzing Text with the Natural Language Toolkit*: O'Reilly Media.

Burnham, D., Estival, D., Fazio, S., Cox, F., Dale, R., Viethen, J., . . . Wagner, M. (2011). *Building an audio-visual corpus of Australian English: large corpus collection with an economical portable and replicable Black Box*. Paper presented at the Interspeech 2011, Florence, Italy.

Cabrera, D., Ferguson, S., & Schubert, E. (2007). *'Psysound3': Software for Acoustical and Psychoacoustical Analysis of Sound Recordings*. Paper presented at the International Community on Auditory Display.

Cassidy, S. (2010). *An RDF Realisation of LAF in the DADA Annotation Server*. Paper presented at the ISA-5, Hong Kong.

Cassidy, S., Estival, D., Jones, T., Burnham, D., & Burghold, J. (2014). *The Alveo Virtual Laboratory: A Web Based Repository API*. Paper presented at the 9th Language Resources and Evaluation Conference (LREC 2014), Reykjavik, Iceland.

Cassidy, S., & Harrington, J. (2000). Multi-level Annotation in the Emu Speech Database Management System. *Speech Communication, 33*, 61–77.

Cassidy, S., Haugh, M., Peters, P., & Fallu, M. (2012). *The Australian National Corpus : national infrastructure for language resources*. Paper presented at the LREC.

Charniak, E., & Johnson, M. (2005). *Coarse-to-fine n-best parsing and MaxEnt discriminative reranking*. Paper presented at the 43rd Annual Meeting on Association for Computational Linguistics.

Cunningham, H., Maynard, D., Bontcheva, K., & Tablan, V. (2002). *GATE: A Framework and Graphical Development Environment for Robust NLP Tools and Applications*. Paper presented at the 40th Anniversary Meeting of the Association for Computational Linguistics (ACL'02), Philadelphia, USA.

Estival, D., Cassidy, S., Sefton, P., & Burnham, D. (2013). *The Human Communication Science Virtual Lab*. Paper presented at the 7th eResearch Australasia Conference, Brisbane, Australia.

Ferrucci, D., Brown, E., Chu-Carroll, J., Fan, J., Gondek, D., Kalyanpur, A. A., . . . Welty, C. (2010). Building Watson: An Overview of the DeepQA Project. *AI Magazine, 31*(3), 59-79. doi: http://dx.doi.org/10.1609/aimag.v31i3.2303

Ferrucci, D., & Lally, A. (2004). UIMA: an architectural approach to unstructured information processing in the corporate research environme. *Natural Language Engineering, 10*(3-4), 327-348.

Ferrucci, D., Lally, A., Verspoor, K., & Nyberg, A. (2009). Unstructured Information Management Architecture (UIMA) Version 1.0 *Oasis Standard*.

Goecke, R., & Millar, J. B. (2004). *The Audio-Video Australian English Speech Data Corpus AVOZES*. Paper presented at the 8th International Conference on Spoken Language Processing (INTERSPEECH 2004 - ICSLP), Jeju, Korea.

Goecks, J., Nekrutenko, A., Taylor, J., & Team, T. G. (2010). Galaxy: a comprehensive approach for supporting accessible, reproducible, and transparent computational research in the life sciences. *Genome Biology, 11*(8), R86.

Kano, Y., Baumgartner, W. A., McCrohon, L., Ananiadou, S., Cohen, K. B., Hunter, L., & Tsujii, J. I. (2009). U-Compare: share and compare text mining tools with UIMA. *Bioinformatics, 25*(15), 1997-1998.

Kano, Y., Dorado, R., McCrohon, L., Ananiadou, S., & Tsujii, J. (2010). *U-Compare: An Integrated Language Resource Evaluation Platform Including a Comprehensive UIMA Resource Library*. Paper presented at the LREC. http://citeseerx.ist.psu.edu/viewdoc/download?doi=10.1.1.180.8878&rep=rep1&type=pdf

Kontonasios, G., Korkontzelos, I., Kolluru, B., & Ananiadou, S. (2011). *Adding text mining workflows as web services to the BioCatalogue*. Paper presented at the Proceedings of the 4th International Workshop on Semantic Web Applications and Tools for the Life Sciences (SWAT4LS '11).

MacKinlay, A., & Verspoor, K. (2013). *A Web Service Annotation Framework for CTD Using the UIMA Concept Mapper*. Paper presented at the Fourth BioCreative Challenge Evaluation Workshop. http://www.biocreative.org/media/store/files/2013/bc4_v1_14.pdf

Musgrave, S., & Haugh, M. (2009). *The AusNC Project: Plans, Progress and Implications for Language Technology*. Paper presented at the ALTA 2009, Sydney.

Rak, R., Rowley, A., & Ananiadou, S. (2012). *Collaborative Development and Evaluation of Text-processing Workflows in a UIMA-supported Web-based Workbench*. Paper presented at the LREC. http://www.lrec-conf.org/proceedings/lrec2012/pdf/960_Paper.pdf

Rak, R., Rowley, A., Carter, J., & Ananiadou, S. (2013). *Development and Analysis of NLP Pipelines in Argo*. Paper presented at the ACL. http://aclweb.org/anthology//P/P13/P13-4020.pdf

Shaw, J. A., & Gafos, A. I. (2010). *Quantitative evaluation of competing syllable parses*. Paper presented at the 11th Meeting of the Association for Computational Linguistics. Special Interest Group on Computational Morphology and Phonology, Uppsala, Sweden.

Tablan, V., Bontcheva, K., Roberts, I., Cunningham, H., & Dimitrov, M. (2013). *AnnoMarket: An Open Cloud Platform for NLP*. Paper presented at the 51st Annual Meeting of the Association for Computational Linguistics (ACL 2013), Sofia, Bulgaria.

Thieberger, N., Barwick, L., Billington, R., & Vaughan, J. (Eds.). (2011). *Sustainable data from digital research: Humanities perspectives on digital scholarship. A PARDISEC Conference*: Custom Book Centre. http://ses.library.usyd.edu.au/handle/2123/7890.

Verspoor, K., Baumgartner Jr, W., Roeder, C., & Hunter, L. (2009). Abstracting the types away from a UIMA type system *From Form to Meaning: Processing Texts Automatically* (pp. 249-256).

Towards Model Driven Architectures for Human Language Technologies

Alessandro Di Bari
IBM Center for
Advanced Studies of Trento
Povo di Trento
Piazza Manci 12
alessandro_dibari@it.ibm.com

Kateryna Tymoshenko
Trento RISE
Povo di Trento
Via Sommarive 18
k.tymoshenko@trentorise.eu

Guido Vetere
IBM Center for
Advanced Studies of Trento
Povo di Trento
Piazza Manci 12
guido_vetere@it.ibm.com

Abstract

Developing multi-purpose Human Language Technologies (HLT) pipelines and integrating them into the large scale software environments is a complex software engineering task. One needs to orchestrate a variety of new and legacy Natural Language Processing components, language models, linguistic and encyclopedic knowledge resources. This requires working with a variety of different APIs, data formats and knowledge models. In this paper, we propose to employ the Model Driven Development (MDD) approach to software engineering, which provides rich structural and behavioral modeling capabilities and solid software support for model transformation and code generation. These benefits help to increase development productivity and quality of HLT assets. We show how MDD techniques and tools facilitate working with different data formats, adapting to new languages and domains, managing UIMA type systems, and accessing the external knowledge bases.

1 Introduction

Modern architectures of knowledge-based computing (cognitive computing) require HLT components to interact with increasingly many sources and services, such as Open Data and APIs, which may not be known before the system is designed. IBM's Watson[1], for instance, works on textual documents to provide question answering and other knowledge-based services by integrating lexical resources, ontologies, encyclopaedic data, and potentially any available information source. Also, they combine a variety of analytical procedures, which may use search, reasoning services, database queries, to provide answers based on many kinds of evidence (IJRD, 2012). Development platforms such as UIMA[2] or GATE[3] facilitate the development of HLT components to a great extent, by providing tools for annotating texts, based on vocabularies and ontologies, training and evaluating pipeline components, etc. However, in general, they focus on working with specific analytical structures (annotations), rather than integrating distributed services and heterogeneous resources. Such integration requires great flexibility in the way linguistic and conceptual data are encoded and exchanged, since each independent service or resource may adopt different representations for notions whose standardization is still in progress. Therefore, developing HLT systems and working with them in such environments requires modeling, representing, mapping, manipulating, and exchanging linguistic and conceptual data in a robust and flexible way. Supporting these tasks with mature methodologies, representational languages, and development environments appears to be of paramount importance.

Since the early 90s, Computer Sciences have envisioned methodologies, languages, practices, and tools for driving the development of software architectures by models (Model Driven Architecture, MDA)[4]. The MDA approach starts from providing formal descriptions (models) of requirements, interactions, data structures, protocols and many other aspects of the desired system. Then, models are turned

[1] http://www.ibm.com/innovation/us/watson/

[2] http://uima.apache.org/

[3] https://gate.ac.uk/

[4] http://www.omg.org/mda/

Proceedings of the Workshop on Open Infrastructures and Analysis Frameworks for HLT, pages 23–33,
Dublin, Ireland, August 23rd 2014.

into technical resources (e.g. schemes and software modules) by means of programmable transformation procedures. Model-to-model transformations, both at schema and instance level, are also supported, based on model correspondence rules (mappings) that can be programmed in a declarative way.

As part of the development of UIMA-based NLP components, easily pluggable in services ecosystems, we are working on an open, flexible and interoperable pipeline, based on MDA. We want our platform to be language agnostic and domain independent, to facilitate its use across projects and geographies. To achieve this, we adopted the Eclipse Modeling Framework[5] as modeling and developing platform, and we generate UIMA resources (Type System) as a Platform Specific Model, by means of a specific transformation. We started by designing models of all the required components, and analyzed the way to improve usability and facilitate interoperability by providing appropriate abstraction and layering.

In the present paper we provide the motivation of our architectural choices, we illustrate the basic features, and discuss relevant issues. Also, we provide some example of how MDA facilitates the design and the implementation of open and easily adaptable HLT functionalities.

2 Model-driven Development and NLP

2.1 Model-driven Development

Generally speaking, we talk about a "modeling" language when it is possible to visually represent (or model) objects under construction (such as services and objects) from both a structural and behavioral point of view. The most popular (software) modeling language is the Unified Modeling Language (UML)(Rumbaugh et al., 2005). One of the strengths of such language is that it allows clear and transparent communication among different stakeholders and roles such as developers, architects, analyst, project managers and testers.

Model Driven Development (MDD) is a software development approach aimed at improving quality and productivity by raising the level of abstraction of services and related objects under development. Given an application domain, we usually have a "business" model that allows for fast and highly expressive representation of specific domain objects. Based on business models, the MDD tooling provides facilities to generate a variety of platform specific "executable models"[6]

2.2 Model-driven Architecture

Model Driven Architecture (MDA)(Miller and Mukerji, 2003) is a development approach, strictly based on formal specifications of information structures and behaviors, and their semantics. MDA is promoted by the Object Management Group (OMG)[7] based on several modeling standards such as: Unified Modeling Language (UML)[8], Meta-Object Facility (MOF[9]), XML Metadata Interchange (XMI) and others. The aim is to provide complex software environments with a higher level of abstraction, so that the application (or service) can be completely designed independently from the underlying technological platform. To this end, MDA defines three macro modeling layers:

- **Computation Independent Model** (CIM) abstract from any possible (software) automation; usually business processes are represented at this layer
- **Platform Independent Model** (PIM) represents any software automation (that supports the CIM) but this representation is really independent from any technological constraint such as the running platform or related middleware, or any third party software. Usually, the skeleton or structure of such a model is automatically generated from the CIM but it is expected to be further expanded for

[5]http://www.eclipse.org/modeling/emf/

[6]For a typical MDD approach, there are two different possible implementation strategies: the first one is to customize generic modeling languages (such as UML) by providing specific profiles (representing the business domain) for the language (UML is very generic and it offers several extensibility mechanisms such as profiles); the second one is a stronger approach that leads to what we call a DSL (Domain Specific Language), a fully specified, vertical language for a particular domain. Such a language is usually built in order to allow business experts to directly work on it, without the need of technological skills.

[7]`http://omg.org/`

[8]`http://www.uml.org/`

[9]`http://www.omg.org/mof/`

a fully specification. PIM can be expressed in UML (Rumbaugh et al., 2005) or EMF[10] but also in any peculiar DSL (domain specific language).

- **Platform Specific Model** (PSM) can be completely generated from the PIM. Among other things, this requires PIM to be able to represent every aspect of the solution under development: both structural and behavioral parts have to be fully specified at this level.

2.3 Eclipse Modeling Framework (EMF)

We chose to adopt EMF as the underlying modeling framework and tooling for our model-driven approach. EMF is an Eclipse[11]-based modeling framework and code generation facility. Ecore is the core meta-model for EMF. Ecore represents the reference implementation of OMG's EMOF (Essential Meta-Object Facility). EMF is at the heart of several important tools and applications and it is often used to represent meta-models and their instances (models) management. Just as an example, UML open source implementation defines its meta-model in terms of EMF-Ecore. Applications or tools that use Ecore to represent their meta model can leverage the EMF tooling to accomplish several goals such as the code generation for model management, diagramming and editing of models, transformations visual development and so on.

2.4 Model-driven NLP

We considered the main features of the Model Driven approach as a powerful way to handle the complexity of modern HLT use cases (Di Bari et al., 2013). In adopting this approach, we chose UIMA[12] as a standardized and well supported tool to deploy our Platform Specific models.

With respect to the basic features of the UIMA platform, we wanted to enhance:

- The representation, visualization and management of complex linguistic and conceptual models
- The use of many kinds of data specifications
- The interaction with many kinds of platforms and services

Therefore, we decided to design a set of models in EMF, considering this as our PIM layer. From these models, we can generate PSM components to support a variety of tasks, including:

- A UIMA Type System for implementing NLP pipelines
- A set of data format transformations for working with linguistic corpora
- A set of basic interfaces to access linguistic and knowledge services
- A Business Object Model (BOM) to work with rule engines (business rules management systems)

3 Modeling NLP with EMF and UIMA

3.1 Working with data formats

In order to train our statistical parser based on OpenNLP[13] and UIMA, we had to adapt different corpora formats, (such as PENN[14] and CONLL[15]), because OpenNLP requests them for different analysis classes (such as named entity, part-of-speech, chunking, etc.). In fact, we had to transform available corpora from standard formats to OpenNLP specific ones. We represented standard formats with EMF (an Ecore model for each one) and we created specific transformations using Java Emitter Templates (JET)[16], a

[10] http://www.eclipse.org/modeling/emf/
[11] http://eclipse.org/
[12] http://uima.apache.org/
[13] http://opennlp.apache.org/
[14] http://www.cis.upenn.edu/~treebank/
[15] http://ilk.uvt.nl/conll/#dataformat
[16] http://www.eclipse.org/modeling/m2t/?project=jet

framework for fast code generation based on EMF. This solution gives us a lot of flexibility: if the parser or corpora formats change, we just have to adapt EMF models and/or JET templates consistently. For a better understanding, we show here an example of the JET template used for transforming from CONLL to OpenNLP POSTag format:

```
<c:setVariable select="/contents" var="root"/>
<c:iterate select="$root/sentence" var="sentence">
    <c:iterate select="$sentence/token" var="token">
        <c:get select="$token/@FORM"/>_<c:get select="$token/@CPOSTAG"/>
    </c:iterate>
</c:iterate>
```

Having the simple CONLL Ecore model (in Figure 1) available, this template is the only artifact realizing the needed transformation. This template simply iterates over all sentences of a document (`root`), then over all tokens of a `sentence` and print out the `form` and its `postag` in the requested format. Other format conversions are done with the same technique. Notice that this tool allows to write (even complex) transformation without requiring programming skills, thus ensuring a greater maintainability and lowering the overall cost of the project.

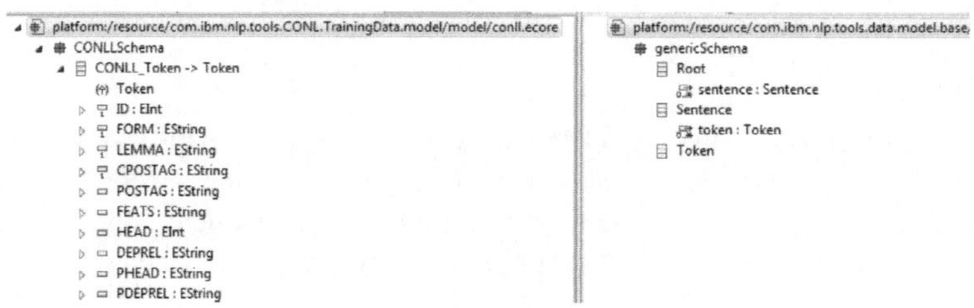

Figure 1: A simple EMF model representing CONLL format

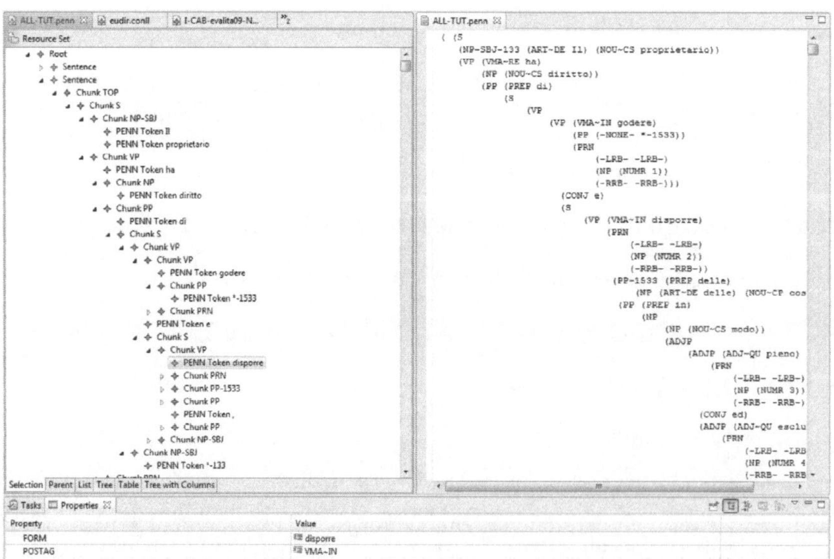

Figure 2: A sentence represented in PENN format (EMF editor on the left)

Further, as we can notice from the Figure 2, EMF provides very powerful MDD capabilities also from the modeling instantiation and editing point of view. Notice that these are two view of the very same resource (a PENN file). This is done by "teaching" the EMF framework how to parse the underlying persisted data, by providing an implementation (that can be done manually or using some parser generation tool in its turn) through a specific EMF extension point. From that point on, the framework will always be able to open and manage PENN resources as instances (with all semantic constraints and validation available) of the PENN Ecore model. Furthermore, the editor and all the specific model management tooling are automatically generated by the EMF platform. This way, all instance management (and editing) tasks are transferred to the EMF framework, which reduces costs and helps developers focusing on NLP tasks.

3.2 Managing the UIMA Type System

In order to manage a (complex enough) UIMA Type System, we fully leveraged the EMF/UIMA interoperability provided by the UIMA framework. UIMA already provides simple transformations from EMF to a UIMA type system and viceversa; furthermore, UIMA provides the XMI serialization so that an instance of a type system can be read as an instance of the corresponding EMF model. However, we had to modify the transformation from EMF to UIMA (type system) in order to reach our "model driven" goals and also to handle several dependent, but separated EMF modules. Specifically, our model is organized around the following modules (packages):

- **Text**. A model of linguistic occurrences in their context, which are given to the parser (token, sentences, named entities, parse) and get annotated by the underlying document analysis framework (e.g. UIMA).
- **Linguistics** A model that abstracts the linguistic apparatus, including categories, morphological and syntactic features, and relationships. This is the key for the multilinguality we walk through in the next section. We can see a fragment of this model in Figure 3
- **Ontology** An abstract representation of any entity and concept, along with a uniform interface to a variety of existing knowledge bases
- **Mapping** A model that allows bridging any tag-set, also explained in next section.

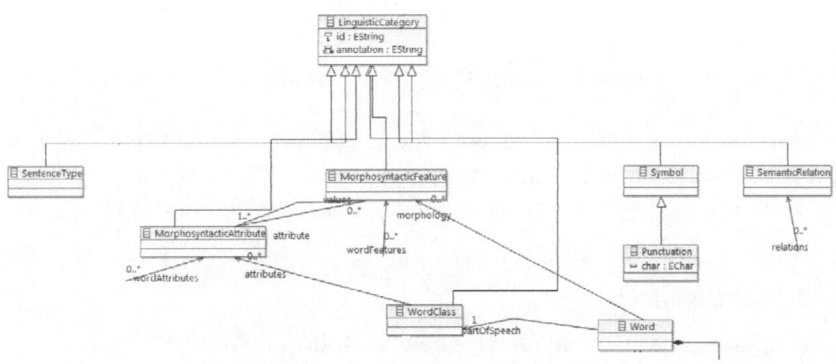

Figure 3: A fragment of the Linguistic model

3.3 Adapting to new languages and domains

Given this basis, we can now illustrate how we are able to incorporate new linguistic resources (such as vocabularies, ontologies, training corpora with different formats, tag-sets, etc) obtaining UIMA-based pipeline components. Given an (untrained) statistical library for parsing (such as OpenNLP or others) and a new natural language to represent, we do the following:

1. Analyze the format requested for the training corpora by the NLP parsing library versus the available training data for the new language. Most likely the training data will be in some standard format (e.g. CONLL, PENN, IOB) that is already represented by a suitable Ecore (EMF) model. If not yet present, we have to write a transformation (usually a simple JET template) from the standard to the specific one requested by the parser.

2. Train the parser for the specific language and tag-set.

3. Given the linguistic knowledge for the new language, and the task at hand, we adopt/modify/extend a suitable `Linguistics` model. If needed, we generate the UIMA Type System portion corresponding to the requested features.[17]

4. In case of a new business domain also, we adopt/modify/extend the ontology. If needed, we wrap business knowledge bases where the ontology is instantiated.[18]

5. Given the tag-set in use, we represent the mapping with the linguistic model, by instantiating a suitable `Mapping` model. At run-time, the (UIMA-based) parser asks (the mapping manager) to get a Linguistic Category (see Figure 4) of a given tag (the `key` feature in the `Mapping` model).

Given the workflow above, we can figure out how the `Linguistics` and `Mapping` model are playing a key role for achieving a multi-language solution. Just as an example, for the Italian language, the `Linguistics` model defines 55 Word Classes (part of speech), 6 morpho-syntactic attributes composed by 22 morpho-syntactic features and 27 syntactic dependencies. The mapping model for the EVALITA[19]tagset, contains 115 mapping elements.

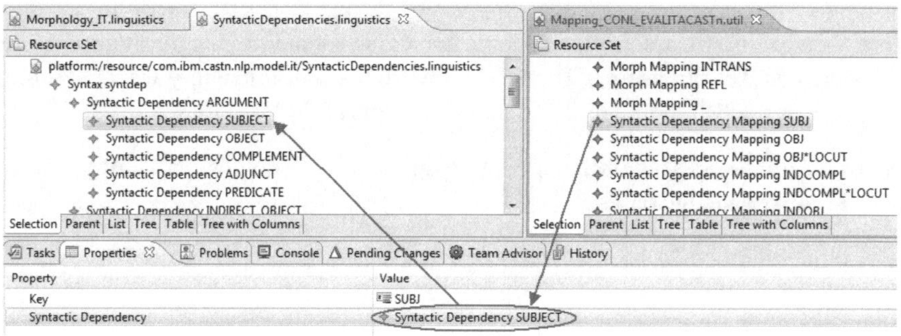

Figure 4: A fragment of the mapping between tag-set and the Linguistic model

We can now prove how the specific language knowledge has been encapsulated in the suitable model so that for example, the code that manages the parser results and creates UIMA annotations does not change for a new language. Correspondingly, no programming skills are needed to represent this linguistic knowledge.

3.4 Benefits for NLP development

To show the benefits of our approach, we summarize here the following remarks:

- Whereas we consider UIMA the reference framework for document management and annotation, we also leveraged the features of a mature and stable modeling framework such as EMF. For instance, we could exploit diagramming, model and instance management and code generation. In sum, we saved significant development time by means of higher level of abstraction that allowed us to easily create transformations, create mapping models, smoothly use different format for the same data and so on.

- Having an additional level of abstraction can lead in thinking there is an additional cost; however, as stated above, this is not the case for transforming from EMF to UIMA. The only, real additional cost is represented by the effort of developing transformations. Nevertheless, this is quickly absorbed as soon as the transformation is re-used. In our case, just for data conversions, we re-used the same

[17]Steps 2, 3, 4 are done through our Eclipse-based tooling.
[18]The benefit of abstracting semantic information from the Type System has been illustrated in (Verspoor et al., 2009)
[19]`http://www.evalita.it/`

EMF models (and their underlying data parsing capabilities we implemented) several times. Each time we wanted to change a parser library, or new corpora were available, we reused the same EMF models and techniques.

- The abstraction introduced by the `Linguistic` model, allowed us to create a language-independent parsing software layer. Furthermore, the same model was leveraged in order to allow interoperability between different parsers that were using different tagsets.

4 Using an External Knowledge Base

State-of-the-art NLP algorithms frequently employ semantic knowledge about entities or concepts, mentioned in the text being processed. This kind of knowledge is typically extracted from the external lexicons and knowledge bases (KB)[20], e.g. WordNet (Fellbaum, 1998) or Wikipedia[21]. Therefore, in our NLP stack, we have to model extraction, usage and representation of semantic knowledge from the external KBs each of which might have different structure and access protocols. Moreover, we may need to plug new KBs into our software environment, with the least effort. Finally, in complex services ecosystems, we might also need to use the KB outside of the NLP system, e.g. in a remote reasoning system, and we should be able to reuse the same model for these purposes.

MDD allows us to define the a single ontology/knowledge base (KB) abstraction, i.e. KB PIM, based on the high-level requirements of our software system, regardless of the actual implementation details of the KBs to be used. In contrast to UIMA type systems, which are limited to type hierarchies and type feature structures with the respective getters and setters, MDD allows to specify also functionalities, i.e. methods, such as querying and updating the KB. Figure 5 demonstrates a diagram of a KB abstraction that we employ in the `Ontology` module. In this abstraction *KnowledgeBase* is a collection of *Individuals* and *Concepts*, *Relationships* and *Roles*, which all are subclasses of the *Entity* abstraction. The figure contains also the visualizations of some components from the `Text` module, which show how we model annotating text with references to the KB elements. For this purpose we have a special kind of *TextUnit* called *EntityToken* used to encode the fact that a certain span in a text denotes a specific *Entity*. Note that this is a high-level abstract schema without any platform-related details. This KB PIM may be invoked in the various parts of the full system PIM model, not necessarily within the NLP stack. We can use this schema to generate different PSMs depending on our needs.

One of the core benefits of MDD are the transformations. After we have defined our high-level KB PIM conceptual model we may define a set of transformations which will convert it to the PSM models, which contain the implementation details of the conceptual model within a specific platform. For example, it can be Jena TDB[22], a framework for storing and managing structured knowledge models, or a SQL relational database. PIM-to-PSM transformations can be defined programmatically, by means of special tools such as IBM Rational Software Architect[23], or by means of a specific modeling language, e.g. *ATL Transformation Language* (Jouault et al., 2006). Finally, we can use a number of tools for code generation from the PSM model, thus facilitating and speeding up the software development process.

Depending on the task, our `Ontology` PIM may be instantiated both as an UIMA PSM or as a PSM for another platform. More specifically, we have the following scenarios for the KB usage.

Within NLP stack. This may be required, for example, if some annotators in the NLP UIMA pipeline, such as a relation extractor or a coreference resolver, require knowledge about types of the individuals (entities) mentioned in a text. In such case, in order to annotate the text with information about individuals and their classes from an external KB we can transform the PIM model to a UIMA Type System (TS). We define a transformation which converts *TextUnit* to a subclass of *UIMA Annotation*[24], and the *Entity* element in `Ontology` to a direct subclass of *UIMA TOP*[25]. Therefore, for example, within our model

[20] Here we use the term "knowledge base" to refer to any external resource containing structured semantic knowledge
[21] `http://en.wikipedia.org/`
[22] `http://jena.apache.org/documentation/tdb/index.html`
[23] `http://www-03.ibm.com/software/products/en/ratisoftarch`
[24] `https://uima.apache.org/d/uimaj-2.6.0/apidocs/org/apache/uima/jcas/tcas/Annotation.html`
[25] `https://uima.apache.org/d/uimaj-2.6.0/apidocs/org/apache/uima/jcas/cas/TOP.html`

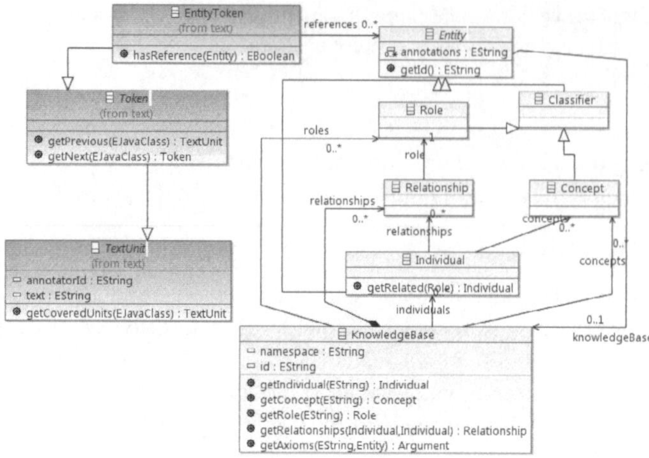

Figure 5: Fragments of the Ontology and Text models

illustrated in Figure 5, *Individual* abstraction, which is a subclass of *Entity*, becomes a subclass of *UIMA TOP*. The *EntityToken* annotations from `Text` are converted to a subclass of *UIMA Annotation* and are used to mark the spans of the *Individual*'s mentions in a text. In the original PIM model *EntityTokens* have property *references* which is a collection of pointers to the respective entities. In UIMA PSM this property is converted to a UIMA TS feature.

KnowledgeBase is an abstraction for an external KB resource to be plugged into the UIMA NLP stack. UIMA contains a mechanism for plugging in external resources[26] such as KBs. Each resource is defined by its name, location and a name of the class which implements handling this resource. MDA and PIM-to-PSM transformations can simplify modeling the resource implementations for different platforms, and EMF tools can further help with automatic code generation. We can define a transformation which would convert platform independent *KnowledgeBase* model elements to a platform-specific models, for instance a class diagram for implementing a *KnowledgeBase* within Jena TDB platform. Then we can use code generation tools for further facilitation of software development.

Within a reasoning component of a QA system. We may need to use both the output of the NLP stack and information stored in a KB within some reasoning platform. For instance, this could be needed within a Question Answering system which provides an answer to the input question based on both text evidence coming from the UIMA pipeline, e.g. syntactic parse information, and a KB. In this case, the PIM representations of linguistic annotations (`Text` and `Linguistics` packages) and KB knowledge (`Ontology` package) may be instantiated as PSMs relative to the specific reasoning (rule- or statistic-based) framework. UIMA annotations previously obtained within the UIMA can be converted to the format required by the reasoning framework by means of model-to-model transformations.

5 Related Work

In the recent years, a number of approaches to modeling annotations and language in NLP software systems and increasing interoperability of distinct NLP components have been proposed (Hellmann et al., 2013; Ide and Romary, 2006; McCrae et al., 2011).

The most widely-accepted solutions for assembling NLP pipelines are UIMA and the GATE (Cunningham et al., 2011) frameworks. They both use annotation models based on referential and feature structures and allow to define custom language models called *UIMA type system (TS)* or *GATE annotation schema* in an XML descriptor file. There are ongoing efforts to develop all-purpose UIMA-based

[26]`http://uima.apache.org/downloads/releaseDocs/2.1.0-incubating/docs/html/tutorials_and_users_guides/tutorials_and_users_guides.html#ugr.tug.aae.accessing_external_resource_files`

NLP toolkits , such as DKPro[27] or ClearTK (Ogren et al., 2009), with TSs describing a variety of linguistic phenomena. UIMA is accompanied with a UIMAfit toolkit (Ogren and Bethard, 2009), which contains a set of utilities that facilitate construction and testing of UIMA pipelines. The two frameworks are compatible, and GATE provides means to integrate GATE with UIMA and vice versa by using XML mapping files to reconcile the annotation schemes and software wrappers to integrate the components[28]. From the MDA perspective, UIMA and GATE type/annotation systems are platform specific models. Defining a language model as a platform independent EMF model results in greater expressivity. For example, in UIMA TS one can model only type class hierarchy and type features, while in EMF model we can also encode the types behavior, i.e. their methods. Moreover, MDA allows to model the usage of the annotation produced by an NLP pipeline within a larger system. For instance, this could be a question answering system which uses both information extracted from text (e.g. question parse) and information extracted from a knowledge base (e.g. query results) and provides tools to facilitate the code generation.

Certain effort has been made on reconciling the different annotation formats. For example, Ide et al. (2003) and Ide and Suderman (2007) proposed Linguistic Annotation Framework (LAF), a graph-based annotation model, and its extension, Graph Annotation Format (GrAF), an XML serialization of LAF, for representing various corpora annotations. It can be used as a pivot format to run the transformations between different annotation models that adhere to the *abstract data model*. The latter contains *referential structures* for associating annotations with the original data and uses feature structure graphs to describe the annotations. Ide and Suderman (2009) show how one may perform GrAF-UIMA-GrAF and GrAF-GATE-GrAF transformations and provide the corresponding software. However, in GrAF representation feature values are strings, and additionally, it is not possible to derive information about annotations types hierarchy from the GrAF file only, therefore, the resulting UIMA TS would be shallow and with all feature values types being string, unless additional information is provided (Ide and Suderman, 2009). At the same time, MDD tools like EMF provide a both a modeling language with high expressiveness and solid support to any transformation. We show how MDD facilitates conversion between different formats in Section 3.1. Additionaly, MDD tools like EMF have a solid sofware support for complex model visualization, this helps to facilitate understanding and managing large models.

After the emergence of the Semantic Web, RDF/OWL formalisms have been used to describe language and annotation models (Hellmann et al., 2013; McCrae et al., 2011; Liu et al., 2012). For instance, NLP Interchange Format, NIF, (Hellmann et al., 2013) is intended to allow various NLP tools to interact on web in a decentralized manner. Its annotation model, *NIF Core Ontology*, encoded in OWL, provides means to describe strings, documents, spans, and their relations. Choice of a language model depends on the developers of the NLP tools, however, they are recommended to reuse existing ontologies, e.g. Ontologies of Linguistic Annotations (OLiA) (Chiarcos, 2012). Another effort, Lemon (McCrae et al., 2011), is a common RDF meta-model for describing lexicons for ontologies and linking them with ontologies. Its core element is a lexical entry which has a number of properties, e.g. semantic roles or morpho-syntactic properties. There has also been research on converting UIMA type systems to the OWL format (Liu et al., 2012). OWL is highly expressive, and a number of tools exists for reasoning upon OWL/RDF models or visualizing them, e.g. Protégé[29], or for aligning them (Volz et al., 2009). Expressiveness of UML, which is typically used to encode the PIM models in MDD, is comparable to that of the ontology description languages (Guizzardi et al., 2004), and it may be reasoned upon (Calvanese et al., 2005). However, differently from the OWL models, there is a number of software solutions which are able to generate code on top of UML representations. Therefore, when using MDD we benefit both from the high expressiveness of the modeling language and the solid software engineering support provided by the MDD tools.

[27] `http://www.ukp.tu-darmstadt.de/software/dkpro-core/`
[28] `http://gate.ac.uk/sale/tao/splitch21.html`
[29] `http://protege.stanford.edu/`

6 Conclusion

Model Driven Development and Architecture is a successful paradigm for tackling the complexity of modern software infrastructures, well supported by tools and standards. We have discussed how the basic principles behind MDD/A are relevant for Human Language Technologies, when approaching the coming era of high-level cognitive functionalities delivered by interconnected software services, and grounded on open data. Model-to-model transformations, supported by specific tools, offer the possibility to rapidly integrate different platforms, and to work with many kinds of data representations. To get the best of this approach, it is important to carefully analyze the layering and interconnections of different models, and to provide them with a suitable design. In our work, we are learning the benefit of modeling aspects such as morpho-syntax and semantics separately, to foster adaptability across languages and domains. A complete and principled analysis of such general design is yet to come. Here we have presented some preliminary result of our experiences, and shared what we achieved so far.

Acknowledgements

This research is partially supported by the EU FP7 / Marie Curie Industry-Academia Partnerships and Pathways schema / PEOPLE Work Programme (Grant agreement no.: 286348, K-Drive project) and by the IBM Center for Advanced Studies of Trento, Italy.

References

D. Calvanese, G. De Giacomo, D. Lembo, M. Lenzerini, and R. Rosati. 2005. DL-Lite: Tractable description logics for ontologies. In *AAAI*, pages 602–607.

C. Chiarcos. 2012. Ontologies of linguistic annotation: Survey and perspectives. In *LREC*, pages 303–310.

H. Cunningham, D. Maynard, K. Bontcheva, V. Tablan, N. Aswani, I. Roberts, G. Gorrell, A. Funk, A. Roberts, D. Damljanovic, T. Heitz, M. A. Greenwood, H. Saggion, J. Petrak, Y. Li, and W. Peters. 2011. *Text Processing with GATE (Version 6).* University of Sheffield Department of Computer Science.

A. Di Bari, A. Faraotti, C. Gambardella, and G. Vetere. 2013. A Model-driven approach to NLP programming with UIMA. In *3rd Workshop on Unstructured Information Management Architecture*, pages 2–9.

C. Fellbaum. 1998. *WordNet: An electronic lexical database*. The MIT press.

G. Guizzardi, G. Wagner, and H. Herre. 2004. On the foundations of uml as an ontology representation language. In E. Motta, N. Shadbolt, A. Stutt, and N. Gibbins, editors, *EKAW*, volume 3257 of *Lecture Notes in Computer Science*, pages 47–62. Springer.

S. Hellmann, J. Lehmann, S. Auer, and M. Brümmer. 2013. Integrating NLP using Linked Data. In *ISWC*.

N. Ide and L. Romary. 2006. Representing linguistic corpora and their annotations. In *LREC*.

N. Ide and K. Suderman. 2007. GrAF: A graph-based format for linguistic annotations. In *Proceedings of the Linguistic Annotation Workshop*, pages 1–8. Association for Computational Linguistics.

N. Ide and K. Suderman. 2009. Bridging the gaps: interoperability for GrAF, GATE, and UIMA. In *Third Linguistic Annotation Workshop*, pages 27–34. Association for Computational Linguistics.

N. Ide, L. Romary, and E. de la Clergerie. 2003. International standard for a linguistic annotation framework. In *HLT-NAACL workshop on Software engineering and architecture of language technology systems*, pages 25–30. Association for Computational Linguistics.

IJRD. 2012. This is Watson [Special issue]. *IBM Journal of Research and Development, editor Clifford A. Pickover*, 56(3.4).

F. Jouault, F. Allilaire, J. Bézivin, I. Kurtev, and P. Valduriez. 2006. ATL: a QVT-like transformation language. In *Companion to the 21st ACM SIGPLAN symposium on Object-oriented programming systems, languages, and applications*, pages 719–720. ACM.

H. Liu, S. Wu, C. Tao, and C. Chute. 2012. Modeling UIMA type system using web ontology language: towards interoperability among UIMA-based NLP tools. In *2nd international workshop on Managing interoperability and compleXity in health systems*, pages 31–36. ACM.

J. McCrae, D. Spohr, and P. Cimiano. 2011. Linking lexical resources and ontologies on the semantic web with lemon. In *The Semantic Web: Research and Applications*, pages 245–259. Springer.

J. Miller and J. Mukerji. 2003. MDA Guide Version 1.0.1. Technical report, Object Management Group (OMG).

P. Ogren and S. Bethard. 2009. Building test suites for UIMA components. In *Workshop on Software Engineering, Testing, and Quality Assurance for Natural Language Processing*, pages 1–4. Association for Computational Linguistics, June.

P. V. Ogren, P.G. Wetzler, and S. J. Bethard. 2009. ClearTK: a framework for statistical natural language processing. In *Unstructured Information Management Architecture Workshop at the Conference of the German Society for Computational Linguistics and Language Technology*.

J. Rumbaugh, I. Jacobson, and G. Booch. 2005. *The Unified Modeling Language Reference Manual.* Addison-Wesley, Boston, MA, 2 edition.

K. Verspoor, W. Baumgartner Jr, C. Roeder, and L. Hunter. 2009. Abstracting the types away from a UIMA type system. *From Form to Meaning: Processing Texts Automatically. Tübingen:Narr*, pages 249–256.

J. Volz, C. Bizer, M. Gaedke, and G. Kobilarov. 2009. Silk - A Link Discovery Framework for the Web of Data. In *LDOW*.

The Language Application Grid Web Service Exchange Vocabulary

Nancy Ide
Department of Computer Science
Vassar College
Poughkeepsie, New York USA
ide@cs.vassar.edu

James Pustejovsky
Department of Computer Science
Brandeis University
Waltham, Massachusetts USA
jamesp@cs.brandeis.edu

Keith Suderman
Department of Computer Science
Vassar College
Poughkeepsie, New York USA
suderman@anc.org

Marc Verhagen
Department of Computer Science
Brandeis University
Waltham, Massachusetts USA
marc@cs.brandeis.edu

Abstract

In the context of the Linguistic Applications (LAPPS) Grid project, we have undertaken the definition of a Web Service Exchange Vocabulary (WS-EV) specifying a terminology for a core of linguistic objects and features exchanged among NLP tools that consume and produce linguistically annotated data. The goal is not to define a new set of terms, but rather to provide a single web location where terms relevant for exchange among NLP tools are defined and provide a "sameAs" link to all known web-based definitions that correspond to them. The WS-EV is intended to be used by a federation of six grids currently being formed but is usable by any web service platform. Ultimately, the WS-EV could be used for data exchange among tools in general, in addition to web services.

1 Introduction

There is clearly a demand within the community for some sort of standard for exchanging annotated language data among tools.[1] This has become particularly urgent with the emergence of web services, which has enabled the availability of language processing tools that can and should interact with one another, in particular, by forming pipelines that can branch off in multiple directions to accomplish application-specific processing. While some progress has been made toward enabling *syntactic interoperability* via the development of standard representation formats (e.g., ISO LAF/GrAF (Ide and Suderman, 2014; ISO-24612, 2012), NLP Interchange Format (NIF) (Hellmann et al., 2013), UIMA[2] Common Analysis System (CAS)) which, if not identical, can be trivially mapped to one another, *semantic interoperability* among NLP tools remains problematic (Ide and Pustejovsky, 2010). A few efforts to create repositories, type systems, and ontologies of linguistic terms (e.g., ISOCat[3], OLiA[4], various repositories for UIMA type systems[5], GOLD[6], NIF Core Ontology[7]) have been undertaken to enable (or provide) a mapping among linguistic terms, but none has yet proven to include all requisite terms and relations or be easy to use and reference. General repositories such as Dublin Core[8], schema.org, and the Friend of a Friend

[1]See, for example, proceedings of the recent LREC workshop on "Language Technology Service Platforms: Synergies, Standards, Sharing" (http://www.ilc.cnr.it/ltsp2014/).
[2]https://uima.apache.org/
[3]http://www.isocat.org
[4]http://nachhalt.sfb632.uni-potsdam.de/owl/
[5]E.g., http://www.julielab.de/Resources/Software/UIMA+type+system-p-91.html
[6]http://linguistics-ontology.org
[7]http://persistence.uni-leipzig.org/nlp2rdf/ontologies/nif-core/nif-core
[8]http://dublincore.org

Proceedings of the Workshop on Open Infrastructures and Analysis Frameworks for HLT, pages 34–43, Dublin, Ireland, August 23rd 2014.

project[9] include some relevant terms, but they are obviously not designed to fully cover the kinds of information found in linguistically annotated data.

In the context of the Linguistic Applications (LAPPS) Grid project (Ide et al., 2014), we have undertaken the definition of a Web Service Exchange Vocabulary (WS-EV) specifying a terminology for a core of linguistic objects and features exchanged among NLP tools that consume and produce linguistically annotated data. The work is being done in collaboration with ISO TC37 SC4 WG1 in order to ensure full community engagement and input. The goal is not to define a new set of terms, but rather to provide a single web location where terms relevant for exchange among NLP tools are defined and provide a "sameAs" link to all known web-based definitions that correspond to them. A second goal is to define relations among the terms that can be used when linguistic data are exchanged. The WS-EV is intended to be used by a federation of grids currently being formed, including the Kyoto Language Grid[10], the Language Grid Jakarta Operation Center[11], the Xinjiang Language Grid, the Language Grid Bangkok Operation Center[12], LinguaGrid[13], MetaNET/Panacea[14], and LAPPS, but is usable by any web service platform. Ultimately, the WS-EV could be used for data exchange among tools in general, in addition to web services.

This paper describes the LAPPS WS-EV, which is currently under construction. We first describe the LAPPS project and then overview the motivations and principles for developing the WS-EV. Because our goal is to coordinate with as many similar projects and efforts as possible to avoid duplication, we also describe existing collaborations and invite other interested groups to provide input.

2 The Language Application Grid Project

The Language Application (LAPPS) Grid project is in the process of establishing a framework that enables language service discovery, composition, and reuse, in order to promote sustainability, manageability, usability, and interoperability of natural language Processing (NLP) components. It is based on the service-oriented architecture (SOA), a more recent, web- oriented version of the pipeline architecture that has long been used in NLP for sequencing loosely-coupled linguistic analyses. The LAPPS Grid provides a critical missing layer of functionality for NLP: although existing frameworks such as UIMA and GATE provide the capability to wrap, integrate, and deploy language services, they do not provide general support for service discovery, composition, and reuse.

The LAPPS Grid is a collaborative effort among US partners Brandeis University, Vassar College, Carnegie-Mellon University, and the Linguistic Data Consortium at the University of Pennsylvania, and is funded by the US National Science Foundation (NSF). The project builds on the foundation laid in the NSF-funded project SILT (Ide et al., 2009), which established a set of needs for interoperability and developed standards and best practice guidelines to implement them. LAPPS is similar in its scope and goals to ongoing projects such as The Language Grid[15], PANACEA/MetaNET[16], LinguaGrid[17], and CLARIN[18], which also provide web service access to basic NLP processing tools and resources and enable pipelining these tools to create custom NLP applications and composite services such as question answering and machine translation, as well as access to language resources such as mono- and multilingual corpora and lexicons that support NLP. The transformative aspect of the LAPPS Grid is therefore not the provision of a suite of web services, but rather that it orchestrates access to and deployment of language resources and processing functions available from servers around the globe, and enables users to easily add their own language resources, services, and even service grids to satisfy their particular needs.

[9] http://www.foaf-project.org
[10] http://langrid.nict
[11] http://langrid.portal.cs.ui.ac.id/langrid/
[12] http://langrid.servicegrid-bangkok.org
[13] http://www.linguagrid.org/
[14] http://www.panacea-lr.eu
[15] http://langrid.nict
[16] http://panacea-lr.eu/
[17] http://www.linguagrid.org/
[18] http://www.clarin.eu/

The most distinctive innovation in the LAPPS Grid that is not included in other projects is the provision of an open advancement (OA) framework (Ferrucci et al., 2009a) for component- and application-based evaluation of NLP tools and pipelines. The availability of this type of evaluation service will provide an unprecedented tool for NLP development that could, in itself, take the field to a new level of productivity. OA involves evaluating *multiple possible solutions* to a problem, consisting of different configurations of component tools, resources, and evaluation data, to find the optimal solution among them, and enabling rapid identification of frequent error categories, together with an indication of which module(s) and error type(s) have the greatest impact on overall performance. On this basis, enhancements and/or modifications can be introduced with an eye toward achieving the largest possible reduction in error rate (Ferrucci et al., 2009; Yang et al., 2013). OA was used in the development of IBM's Watson to achieve steady performance gains over the four years of its development (Ferrucci et al., 2010); more recently, the open-source OAQA project has released software frameworks which provide general support for open advancement (Garduno et al., 2013; Yang et al., 2013), which has been used to rapidly develop information retrieval and question answering systems for bioinformatics (Yang et al., 2013; Patel et al., 2013).

The fundamental system architecture of the LAPPS Grid is based on the Open Service Grid Initiative's Service Grid Server Software[19] developed by the National Institute of Information and Communications Technology (NICT) in Japan and used to implement Kyoto University's Language Grid, a service grid that supports multilingual communication and collaboration. Like the Language Grid, the LAPPS Grid provides three main functions: language service registration and deployment, language service search, and language service composition and execution. As noted above, the LAPPS Grid is instrumented to provide relevant component-level measures for standard metrics, given gold-standard test data; new applications automatically include instrumentation for component-level and end-to-end measurement, and intermediate (component-level) I/O is logged to support effective error analysis.[20] The LAPPS Grid also implements a dynamic licensing system for handling license agreements on the fly[21], provides the option to run services locally with high-security technology to protect sensitive information where required, and enables access to grids other than those based on the Service Grid technology.

We have adopted the JSON-based serialization for Linked Data (JSON-LD) to represent linguistically annotated data for the purposes of web service exchange. The JavaScript Object Notation (JSON) is a lightweight, text-based, language-independent data interchange format that defines a small set of formatting rules for the portable representation of structured data. Because it is based on the W3C Resource Definition Framework (RDF), JSON-LD is trivially mappable to and from other graph-based formats such as ISO LAF/GrAF and UIMA CAS, as well as a growing number of formats implementing the same data model. Most importantly, JSON- LD enables services to reference categories and definitions in web-based repositories and ontologies or any suitably defined concept at a given URI.

The LAPPS Grid currently supports SOAP services, with plans to support REST services in the near future. We provide two APIs: `org.lappsgrid.api.DataSource`, which provides data to other services, and `org.lappsgrid.api.WebService`, for tools that annotate, transform, or otherwise manipulate data from a datasource or another web service. All LAPPS services exchange `org.lappsgrid.api.Data` objects consisting of a discriminator (type) that indicates how to interpret the payload, and a payload (typically a utf-8 string) that consists of the JSON-LD representation. Data converters included in the LAPPS Grid Service Engines map from commonly used formats to the JSON-LD interchange format; converters are automatically invoked as needed to meet the I/O requirements of pipelined services. Some LAPPS services are pre-wrapped to produce and consume JSON-LD. Thus, JSON-LD provides *syntactic interoperability* among services in the LAPPS Grid; *semantic inter-*

[19] http://servicegrid.net

[20] Our current user interface provides easy (re-)configuration of single pipelines; we are currently extending the interface to allow the user to specify an entire range of pipeline configurations using configuration descriptors (ECD; (Yang et al., 2013) to define a space of possible pipelines, where each step might be achieved by multiple components or services and each component or service may have configuration parameters with more than one possible value to be tested. The system will then automatically generate metrics measurements plus variance and statistical significance calculations for each possible pipeline, using a service-oriented version of the Configuration Space Exploration (CSE) algorithm (Yang et al., 2013).

[21] See (Cieri et al., 2014) for a description of how licensing issues are handled in the LAPPS Grid.

operability is provided by the LAPPS Web Service Exchange Vocabulary, described in the next section.

3 LAPPS Web Service Exchange Vocabulary

3.1 Motivation

The WS-EV addresses a relatively small but critical piece of the overall LAPPS architecture: it allows web services to communicate about the content they deliver, such that the *meaning*–i.e., exactly what to do with and/or how to process the data–is understood by the receiver. As such it performs the same function as a UIMA type system performs for tools in a UIMA pipeline that utilize that type system, or the common annotation labels (e.g., "Token", "Sentence", etc.) required for communication among pipelined tools in GATE: these mechanisms provide semantic interoperability among tools as long as one remains in either the UIMA or GATE world. To pipeline a tool whose output follows GATE conventions with a tool that expects input that complies with a given UIMA type system, some mapping of terms and structures is likely to be required.[22] This is what the WS-EV is intended to enable; effectively, it is a *meta-type-system* for mapping labels assigned to linguistically annotated data so that they are understood and treated consistently by tools that exchange them in the course of executing a pipeline or workflow. Since web services included in LAPPS and federated grids may use any i/o semantic conventions, the WS-EV allows for communication among any of them–including, for example, between GATE and UIMA services[23]

The ability to pipeline components from diverse sources is critical to the implementation of the OA development approach described in the previous section, it must be possible for the developer to "plug and play" individual tools, modules, and resources in order to rapidly re-configure and evaluate new pipelines. These components may exist on any server across the globe, consist of modules developed within frameworks such as UIMA and GATE, and or be user-defined services existing on a local machine.

3.2 WS-EV Design

The WS-EV was built around the following design principles, which were compiled based on input from the community:

1. The WS-EV will not reinvent the wheel. Objects and features defined in the WS-EV will be linked to definitions in existing repositories and ontologies wherever possible.

2. The WS-EV will be designed so as to allow for easy, one-to-one mapping from terms designating linguistic objects and features commonly produced and consumed by NLP tools that are wrapped as web services. It is not necessary for the mapping to be object-to-object or feature-to-feature.

3. The WS-EV will provide a *core* set of objects and features, on the principle that "simpler is better", and provide for (principled) definition of additional objects and features beyond the core to represent more specialized tool input and output.

4. The WS-EV is not LAPPS-specific; it will not be governed by the processing requirements or preferences of particular tools, systems, or frameworks.

5. The WS-EV is intended to be used *only* for interchange among web services performing NLP tasks. As such it can serve as a "pivot" format to which user and tool-specific formats can be mapped.

6. The web service provider is responsible for providing wrappers that perform the mapping from internally-used formats to and/or from the WS-EV.

7. The WS-EV format should be compact to facilitate the transfer of large datasets.

[22]Within UIMA, the output of tools conforming to different type systems may themselves require conversion in order to be used together.

[23]Figure 5 shows a pipeline in which both GATE and UIMA services are called; GATE-to-GATE and UIMA-to-UIMA communication does not use the WS-EV, but it is used for communication between GATE and UIMA services, as well as other services.

8. The WS-EV format will be chosen to take advantage, to the extent possible, of existing technological infrastructures and standards.

As noted in the first principle, where possible the objects and features in the WS-EV are drawn from existing repositories such as ISOCat and the NIF Core Ontology and linked to them via the **owl:sameAs** property[24] or, where appropriate, **rdfs:subClassOf**[25]. However, many repositories do not include some categories and objects relevant for web service exchange (e.g., "token" and other segment descriptors), do include multiple (often very similar) definitions for the same concept, and/or do not specify relations among terms. We therefore attempted to identify a set of (more or less) "universal" concepts by surveying existing type systems and schemas – for example, the Julie Lab and DARPA GALE UIMA type systems and the GATE schemas for linguistic phenomena – together with the I/O requirements of commonly used NLP software (e.g., the Stanford NLP tools, OpenNLP, etc.). Results of the survey for token and sentence identification and part-of-speech labeling[26] showed that even for these basic categories, no existing repository provides a suitable set of categories and relations.

Perhaps more problematically, sources that do specify relations among concepts, such as the various UIMA type systems and GATE's schemas, vary widely in their choices of what is an object and what is a feature; for example, some treat "token" as an object (label) and "lemma" and "POStag" as associated features, while others regard "lemma" and/or "POStag" as objects in their own right. Decisions concerning what is an object and what is a feature are for the most part arbitrary; no one scheme is right or wrong, but a consistent organization is required for effective web service interchange. The WS-EV therefore defines an organization of objects and features for the purposes of interchange only. Where possible, the choices are principled, but they are otherwise arbitrary. The WS-EV includes *sameAs* and *similarTo* mappings that link to like concepts in other repositories where possible, thus serving primarily to group the terms and impose a structure of relations required for web service exchange in one web-based location.

In addition to the principles above, the WS-EV is built on the principle of orthogonal design, such that there is one and only one definition for each concept. It is also designed to be very lightweight and easy to find and reference on the web. To that end we have established a straightforward web site (the Web Service Exchange Vocabulary Repository[27]), similar to *schema.org*, in order to provide web-addressable terms and definitions for reference from annotations exchanged among web services. Our approach is bottom-up: we have adopted a minimalist strategy of adding objects and features to the repository only as they are needed as services are added to the LAPPS Grid. Terms are organized in a shallow ontology, with inheritance of properties, as shown in Figure 1.

4 WS-EV and JSON-LD

References in the JSON-LD representation used for interchange among LAPPS Grid web services point to URIs providing definitions for specific linguistic categories in the WS-EV. They also reference documentation for processing software and rules for processes such as tokenization, entity recognition, etc. used to produce a set of annotations, which are often left unspecified in annotated resources (see for example (Fokkens et al., 2013)). While not required for web service exchange in the LAPPS Grid, the inclusion of such references can contribute to the better replication and evaluation of results in the field. Figure 3 shows the information for Token, which defines the concept, identifies application types that produce objects of this type, cross-references a similar concept in ISOCat, and provides the URI for use in the JSON-LD representation. It also specifies the common properties that can be specified for a set of Token objects, and the individual properties that can be associated with a Token object. There is no requirement to use any or all of the properties in the JSON-LD representation, and we foresee that many web services will require definition of objects and properties not included in the WS-EVR or elsewhere.

[24] http://www.w3.org/TR/2004/REC-owl-semantics-20040210/#owl_sameAs

[25] http://www.w3.org/TR/owl-ref/#subClassOf-def

[26] Available at `http://www.anc.org/LAPPS/EP/Meeting-2013-09-26-Pisa/ep-draft.pdf`

[27] http://vocab.lappsgrid.org

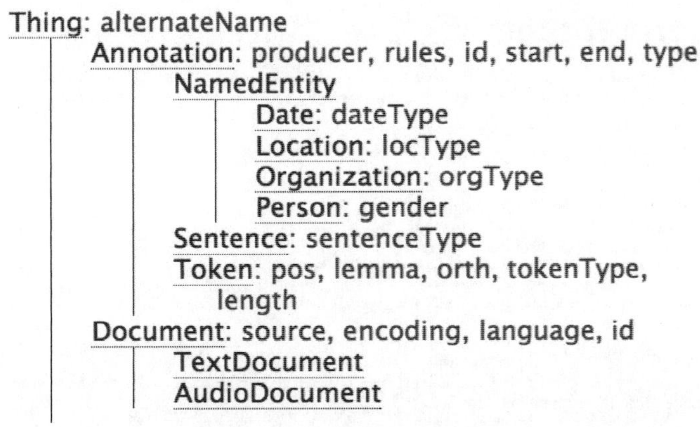

Figure 1: Fragment of the WS-EV ontology (associated properties in gray)

We therefore provide mechanisms for (principled) definition of objects and features beyond the WS-EVR. Two options exist: users can provide a URI where a new term or other documentation is defined, or users may add a definition to the WS-EVR. In the latter case, service providers use the name space automatically assigned to them at the time of registration, thereby avoiding name clashes and providing a distinction between general categories used across services and more idiosyncratic categories.

Figure 2 shows a fragment of the JSON-LD representation that references terms in the WS-EV. The *context* statement at the top identifies the URI that is to be prefixed to any unknown name in order to identify the location of its definition. For the purposes of the example, the text to be processed is given inline. Our current implementation includes results from each step in a pipeline, where applicable, together with metadata describing the service applied in each step (here, org.anc.lapps.stanford.SATokenizer:1.4.0) and identified by an internally defined type (stanford). The annotations include references to the objects defined in the WS-EV, in this example, Token (defined at http://vocab.lappsgrid.org/Token) with (inherited) features *id, start, end* and specific feature *string*, defined at http://vocab.lappsgrid.org/Token#id, http://vocab.lappsgrid.org/Token#start, http://vocab.lappsgrid.org/Token#end, and http://vocab.lappsgrid.orgToken/#string, respectively. The web page defining these terms is shown in Figure 3.


```
"@context" : "http://vocab.lappsgrid.org/",
"metadata" : { },
"text" : {
    "@value" : "Some of the strongest critics of our welfare system..." }
"steps" : [ {
    "metadata" : {
          "contains" : {
          "Token" : {
          "producer" : "org.anc.lapps.stanford.SATokenizer:1.4.0",
          "type" : "stanford"
        }
      }
    },
    "annotations" : [ {
      "@type" : "Token",
      "id" : "tok0",
      "start" : 18,
      "end" : 22,
      "features" : {
        string" : "Some" }
    },
```


Figure 2: JSON-LD fragment referencing the LAPPS Grid WS-EV

Thing>Annotation>Token

Definition	A string of one or more characters that serves as an indivisible unit for the purposes of morpho-syntactic labeling (part of speech tagging).
Producer type(s)	tokenizer, POStagger
sameAs	http://persistence.uni-leipzig.org/nlp2rdf/ontologies/nif-core#Word
similarTo	http://www.isocat.org/datcat/DC-1403
URI	http://vocab.lappsgrid.org/Token

Properties	Expected Type	Description
Metadata (Common Properties) from Token		
posTagset	URI	The POS tagset used for morpho-syntactic tagging.
Properties from Token		
pos	String or URI	Part-of-speech tag associated with the token.
lemma	String or URI	The root (base) form associated with the token. URI may point to a lexicon entry.
tokenType	String or URI	Sub-type such as word, punctuation, abbreviation, number, symbol, etc. Ideally a URI referencing a pre-defined descriptor.
orth	String or URI	Orthographic properties of the token such as LowerCase, UpperCase, UpperInitial, etc. Ideally a URI referencing a pre-defined descriptor.
length	Integer	Length of the token.
Metadata (Common Properties) from Annotation		
producer	List of URI	The software that produced the annotations.
rules	List of URI	The documentation for the rules that were used to identify the annotations.
Properties from Annotation		
id	String	A unique identifier associated with the annotation.
start	Integer	The starting offset (0-based) in the primary data.
end	Integer	The ending offset (0-based) in the primary data.
Properties from Thing		
alternateName	String	An alias for the item.

Figure 3: Token definition in the LAPPS WS-EVR

4.1 Mapping to JSON-LD

As noted above in Section 1, existing schemes and systems for organizing linguistic information exchanged by NLP tools vary considerably. Figure 4 shows some variants for a few commonly used NLP tools, which differ in terminology, structure, and physical format. To be used in the LAPPS Grid, tools such as those in the list are wrapped so that their output is in JSON-LD format, which provides syntactic interoperability, terms are mapped to corresponding objects in the WS-EV, and the object-feature relations reflect those defined in the WS-EV. Correspondingly, wrappers transduce the JSON-LD/WS-EV representation to the format used internally by the tool on input. This way, the tools use their internal format as usual and map to JSON-LD/WS-EV for exchange only.

Name	Input	Form	Output	Form	Example
Stanford tagger	pt	n/a	word_pos	opl	box_NN1
	XML	n/a	XML	inline	<word id="0" pos="VB">Let</word>
NaCTeM tagger	pt	n/a	word/pos	inline	box/NN1
CLAWS (1)	pt	n/a	word_pos	inline	box_NN1
CLAWS (2)	pt	n/a	XML	inline	<w id="2" pos="NN1">Type</w>
CST Copenhagen	pt	n/a	word/pos	inline	box/NN1
TreeTagger	pt?	n/a	word pos lem	opl	The DT the
TnT	token	opl	word pos	opl	der ART
			word (pos pr)+	opl	Falkenstein NE 8.00 NN 1.99
Twitter NLP	pt	opl	word pos conf	opl	smh G 0.9406
NLTK	pt	s, bls	[('word', 'pos')]	inline	[('At', 'IN'), ('eight', 'CD'),]
OpenNLP splitter	pt	n/a	sentences	ospl	I can't tell you if he's here.
OpenNLP tokenizer	sent	ospl	tokens	wss, ospl	I can 't tell you if he 's here .
OpenNLP tagger	token	wss, ospl	word_pos	ospl	At_IN eight_CD o'clock_JJ on_IN

pt = plain text	opl = one per line	wss = white space separated
	ospl = one sentence per line	bps = blank line separated

Figure 4: I/O variants for common splitters, tokenizers, and POS taggers

For example, the Stanford POS tagger XML output format produces output like this:

```
<word id="0" pos="VB">Let</word>
```

This maps to the following JSON-LD/WS-EV representation:

```
{
   "@type" : "Token",
   "id" : 0",
   "start" : 18,
   "end" : 21,
   "features" : {
     "string" : "Let",
     "pos"    : "VB"
   }
}
```

The Stanford representation uses the term "word" as an XML element name, gives an id and pos as attribute-value pairs, and includes the string being annotated as element content. For conversion to JSON-LD/WS-EV, "word" is mapped to "Token", the attributes *id* and *pos* map to features of the Token object with the same names, and the element content becomes the value of the *string* feature. Because the JSON-LD representation uses standoff annotation, the attributes *start* and *end* are added in order to provide the offset location of the string in the original data.

Services that share a format other than JSON-LD need not map into and out of JSON-LD/WS-EV when pipelined in the LAPPS Grid. For example, two GATE services would exchange GATE XML documents, and two UIMA services would exchange UIMA CAS, as usual. This avoids unnecessary conversion and at the same time allows including services (consisting of individual tools or composite workflows) from other frameworks. Figure 5 gives an example of the logical flow in the LAPPS Grid, showing conversions into and out of JSON-LD/WS-EV where needed.

Each service in the LAPPS Grid is required to provide metadata that specifies what kind of input is required and what kind of output is produced. For example, any service as depicted in the flow diagram in Figure 5 can require input of a particular format (gate, uima, json-ld) with specific content (tokens, sentences, etc.). The LAPPS Grid uses the notion of *discriminators* to encode these requirements, and the pipeline composer can use these discriminators to determine if conversions are needed and/or input requirements are met. The discriminators refer to elements of the vocabulary.

5 Collaborations

The LAPPS Grid project is collaborating with several other projects in an attempt to harmonize the development of web service platforms, and ultimately to participate in a federation of grids and service platforms throughout the world. Existing and potential projects across the globe are beginning to

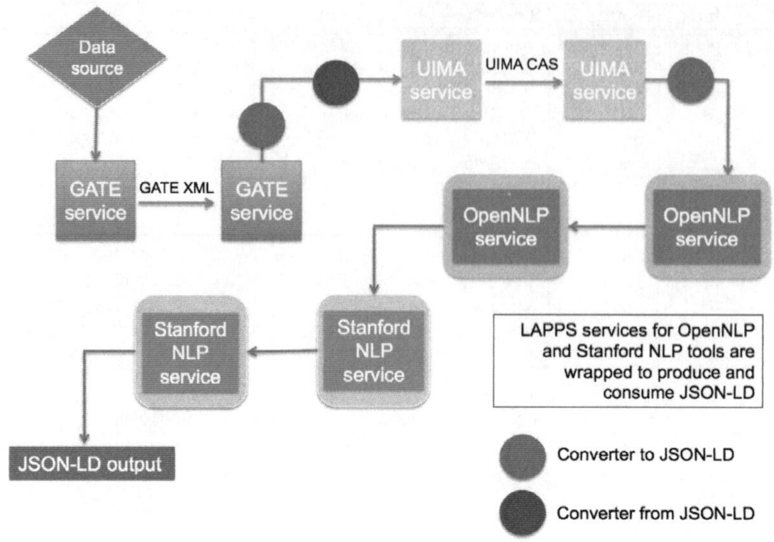

Figure 5: Logical flow through the LAPPS Grid (client-server communication not represented)

converge on common data models, best practices, and standards, and the vision of a comprehensive infrastructure supporting discovery and deployment of web services that deliver language resources and processing components is an increasingly achievable goal. Our vision is therefore not for a monolithic grid, but rather a heterogeneous configuration of federated grids that implement common strategies for managing and inter-changing linguistic information, so that services on all of these grids are mutually accessible.

To this end, the LAPPS Grid project has established a multi-way international collaboration among the US partners and institutions in Asia, Australia, and Europe. The basis is a formal federation among the LAPPS Grid, the Language Grid (Kyoto University, Japan), NECTEC (Thailand), grids operated by the University of Indonesia and Xinjiang University (China), and LinguaGrid[28], scheduled for implementation in January 2015. The connection of these six grids into a single federated entity will enable access to all services and resources on any of these grids by users of any one of them and, perhaps most importantly, facilitate adding additional grids and service platforms to the federation. Currently, the European META-NET initiative is committed to joining the federation in the near future.

In addition to the projects listed above, we are also collaborating with several groups on technical solutions to achieve interoperability and in particular, on development of the WS-EV, the JSON-LD format, and a corollary development of an ontology of web service types. These collaborators include the Alveo Project (Macquarie University, Australia) (Cassidy et al., 2014), the Language Grid project, and the Lider project[29]. We actively seek collaboration with others in order to move closer to achieving a "global laboratory" for language applications.

6 Conclusion

In this paper, we have given a brief overview of the LAPPS Web Service Exchange Vocabulary (WS-EV), which provides a terminology for a core of linguistic objects and features exchanged among NLP tools that consume and produce linguistically annotated data. The goal is to bring the field closer to achieving semantic interoperability among NLP data, tools, and services. We are actively working to both engage with existing projects and teams and leverage available resources to move toward convergence of terminology in the field for the purposes of exchange, as well as promote an environment (the LAPPS Grid) within which the WS-EV can help achieve these goals.

[28] http://www.linguagrid.org/

[29] http://www.lider-project.eu

Acknowledgements

This work was supported by National Science Foundation grants NSF-ACI 1147944 and NSF-ACI 1147912.

References

Steve Cassidy, Dominique Estival, Timothy Jones, Denis Burnham, and Jared Burghold. 2014. The Alveo Virtual Laboratory: A Web based Repository API. In *Proceedings of the Ninth International Conference on Language Resources and Evaluation (LREC'14)*, Reykjavik, Iceland, may. European Language Resources Association (ELRA).

Christopher Cieri, Denise DiPersio, , and Jonathan Wright. 2014. Intellectual property rights management with web services. In *Proceedings of the Workshop on Open Infrastructures and Analysis Frameworks for HLT*, Dublin, Ireland, August.

David Ferrucci, Eric Nyberg, James Allan, Ken Barker, Eric Brown, Jennifer Chu-Carroll, Arthur Ciccolo, Pablo Duboue, James Fan, David Gondek, Eduard Hovy, Boris Katz, Adam Lally, Michael McCord, Paul Morarescu, Bill Murdock, Bruce Porter, John Prager, Tomek Strzalkowski, Chris Welty, and Wlodek Zadrozny. 2009. Towards the Open Advancement of Question Answering Systems. Technical report, IBM Research, Armonk, New York.

David A. Ferrucci, Eric W. Brown, Jennifer Chu-Carroll, James Fan, David Gondek, Aditya Kalyanpur, Adam Lally, J. William Murdock, Eric Nyberg, John M. Prager, Nico Schlaefer, and Christopher A. Welty. 2010. Building Watson: An overview of the DeepQA project. *AI Magazine*, 31(3):59–79.

Antske Fokkens, Marieke van Erp, Marten Postma, Ted Pedersen, Piek Vossen, and Nuno Freire. 2013. Offspring from reproduction problems: What replication failure teaches us. In *Proceedings of the 51st Annual Meeting of the Association for Computational Linguistics (Volume 1: Long Papers)*, pages 1691–1701, Sofia, Bulgaria, August. Association for Computational Linguistics.

Elmer Garduno, Zi Yang, Avner Maiberg, Collin McCormack, Yan Fang, and Eric Nyberg. 2013. CSE Framework: A UIMA-based Distributed System for Configuration Space Exploration Unstructured Information Management Architecture. In Peter Klgl, Richard Eckart de Castilho, and Katrin Tomanek, editors, *UIMA@GSCL*, CEUR Workshop Proceedings, pages 14–17. CEUR-WS.org.

Sebastian Hellmann, Jens Lehmann, Sören Auer, and Martin Brümmer. 2013. Integrating nlp using linked data. In *12th International Semantic Web Conference, 21-25 October 2013, Sydney, Australia.*

Nancy Ide and James Pustejovsky. 2010. What Does Interoperability Mean, Anyway? Toward an Operational Definition of Interoperability. In *Proceedings of the Second International Conference on Global Interoperability for Language Resources*. ICGL.

Nancy Ide and Keith Suderman. 2014. The Linguistic Annotation Framework: A Standard for Annotation Interchange and Merging. *Language Resources and Evaluation*.

Nancy Ide, James Pustejovsky, Nicoletta Calzolari, and Claudia Soria. 2009. The SILT and FlaReNet international collaboration for interoperability. In *Proceedings of the Third Linguistic Annotation Workshop, ACL-IJCNLP*, August.

Nancy Ide, James Pustejovsky, Christopher Cieri, Eric Nyberg, Di Wang, Keith Suderman, Marc Verhagen, and Jonathan Wright. 2014. The language application grid. In *Proceedings of the Ninth International Conference on Language Resources and Evaluation (LREC'14)*, Reykjavik, Iceland, may. European Language Resources Association (ELRA).

ISO-24612. 2012. Language Resource Management - Linguistic Annotation Framework. ISO 24612.

Alkesh Patel, Zi Yang, Eric Nyberg, and Teruko Mitamura. 2013. Building an optimal QA system automatically using configuration space exploration for QA4MRE'13 tasks. In *Proceedings of CLEF 2013.*

Zi Yang, Elmer Garduno, Yan Fang, Avner Maiberg, Collin McCormack, and Eric Nyberg. 2013. Building optimal information systems automatically: Configuration space exploration for biomedical information systems. In *Proceedings of the CIKM'13.*

Significance of Bridging Real-world Documents and NLP Technologies

Tadayoshi Hara **Goran Topić** **Yusuke Miyao** **Akiko Aizawa**
National Institute of Informatics
2-1-2 Hitotsubashi, Chiyoda-ku, Tokyo 101-8430, Japan
{harasan, goran_topic, yusuke, aizawa}@nii.ac.jp

Abstract

Most conventional natural language processing (NLP) tools assume plain text as their input, whereas real-world documents display text more expressively, using a variety of layouts, sentence structures, and inline objects, among others. When NLP tools are applied to such text, users must first convert the text into the input/output formats of the tools. Moreover, this awkwardly obtained input typically does not allow the expected maximum performance of the NLP tools to be achieved. This work attempts to raise awareness of this issue using XML documents, where textual composition beyond plain text is given by tags. We propose a general framework for data conversion between XML-tagged text and plain text used as input/output for NLP tools and show that text sequences obtained by our framework can be much more thoroughly and efficiently processed by parsers than naively tag-removed text. These results highlight the significance of bridging real-world documents and NLP technologies.

1 Introduction

Recent advances in natural language processing (NLP) technologies have allowed us to dream about applying these technologies to large-scale text, and then extracting a wealth of information from the text or enriching the text itself with various additional information. When actually considering the realization of this dream, however, we are faced with an inevitable problem. Conventional NLP tools usually assume an ideal situation where each input text consists of a plain word sequence, whereas real-world documents display text more expressively using a variety of layouts, sentence structures, and inline objects, among others. This means that obtaining valid input for a target NLP tool is left completely to the users, who have to program pre- and postprocessors for each application to convert their target text into the required format and integrate the output results into their original text. This additional effort reduces the viability of technologies, while the awkwardly obtained input does not allow the expected maximum benefit of the NLP technologies to be realized.

In this research, we raise awareness of this issue by developing a framework that simplifies this conversion and integration process. We assume that any textual composition beyond plain text is captured by tags in XML documents, and focus on the data conversion between XML-tagged text and the input/output formats of NLP tools. According to our observations, the data conversion process is determined by the textual functions of the XML-tags utilized in the target text, of which there seem to be only four types. We therefore devise a conversion strategy for each of the four types. After all tags in the XML tagset of the target text have been classified by the user into the four types, data conversion and integration can be executed automatically using our strategies, regardless of the size of the text (see Figure 1).

In the experiments, we apply our framework to several types of XML documents, and the results show that our framework can extract plain text sequences from the target XML documents by classifying only 20% or fewer of the total number of tag types. Furthermore, with the obtained sequences, two typical parsers succeed in processing entire documents with a much greater coverage rate and using much less parsing time than with naively tag-removed text.

Proceedings of the Workshop on Open Infrastructures and Analysis Frameworks for HLT, pages 44–52,
Dublin, Ireland, August 23rd 2014.

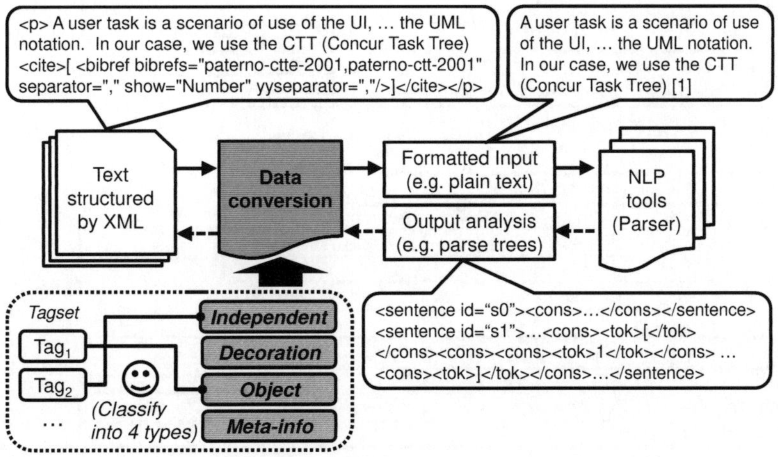

Figure 1: Proposed data conversion framework for applying NLP tools to text structured as XML

Tag type	Criteria for classification	Strategies for data conversion
Independent	To represent a region syntactically independent from the surrounding text	Remove the tag and tagged region → (apply tools to the tagged region independently) → recover the (analyzed) tagged region after applying the tools
Decoration	To set the display style of the tagged region at the same level as the surrounding text	Remove only the tag → recover the tag after applying the tools
Object	To represent the minimal object unit that should be handled in the the same level as the surrounding text	Replace the tag (and the tagged region) with a plain word → (do not process the tagged region further) → recover the tag (and region) after applying the tools
Meta-info	To describe the display style setting or additional information	Remove the tag and tagged region → (do not process the tagged region further) → recover the tag and region after applying the tools

Table 1: Four types of tags and the data conversion strategy for each type

The contribution of this work is to demonstrate the significance of bridging real-world documents and NLP technologies in practice. We show that, if supported by a proper framework, conventional NLP tools already have the ability to process real-world text without significant loss of performance. We expect the demonstration to promote further discussion on real-world document processing.

In Section 2, some related research attempts are introduced. In Section 3, the four types of textual functions for XML tags and our data conversion strategies for each of these are described and implemented. In Section 4, the efficiency of our framework and the adequacy of the obtained text sequences for use in NLP tools are examined using several types of documents.

2 Related Work

To the best of our knowledge, no significant work on a unified methodology for data conversion between target text and the input/output formats of NLP tools has been published. Some NLP tools provide scripts for extracting valid input text for the tools from real-world documents; however, even these scripts assume specific formats for the documents. For example, deep syntactic parsers such as the C&C Parser (Clark and Curran, 2007) and Enju (Ninomiya et al., 2007) assume POS-tagged sentences as input, and therefore the distributed packages for the parsers[1] contain POS-taggers together with the parsers. The POS-taggers assume plain text sentences as their input.

As the work most relevant to our study, UIMA (Ferruci et al., 2006) deals with various annotations in an integrated framework. However, in this work, the authors merely proposed the framework and did

[1] [C&C Parser]: http://svn.ask.it.usyd.edu.au/trac/candc/wiki / [Enju]: http://kmcs.nii.ac.jp/enju/

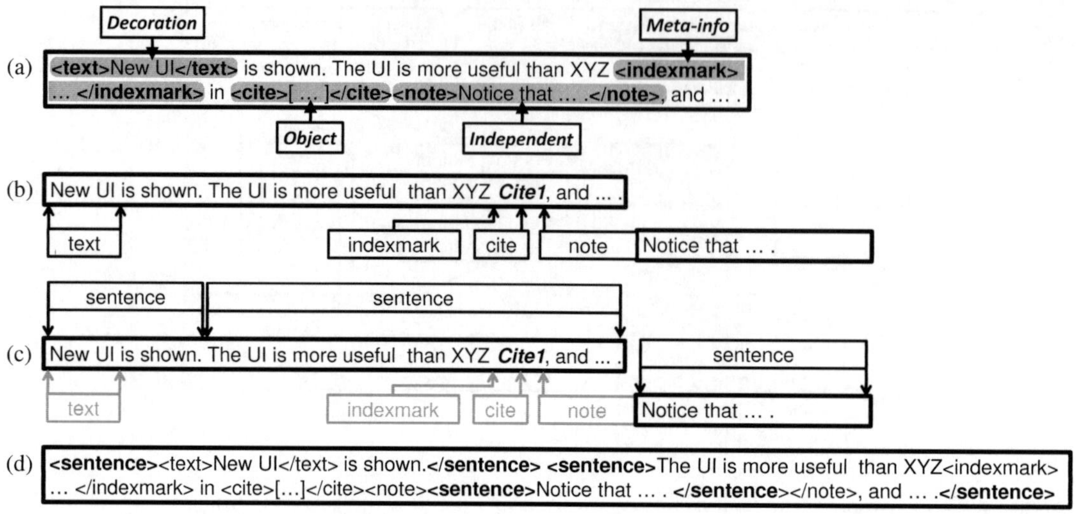

Figure 2: Example of executing our strategy

not explain how the given text can be used in a target annotation process such as parsing. Some projects based on the UIMA framework, such as RASP4UIMA (Andersen et al., 2008), U-compare (Kano et al., 2011), and Kachako (Kano, 2012)[2], have developed systems where the connections between various documents and various tools are already established. Users, however, can utilize only the text and tool pairs that have already been integrated into the systems. GATE (Cunningham et al., 2013) is based on a similar concept to UIMA; it supports XML documents as its input, while the framework also requires integration of tools into the systems.

In our framework, although availability of XML documents is assumed, a user can apply NLP tools to the documents without modifying the tools; instead, this is achieved by merely classifying the XML-tags in the documents into a small number of functional types.

3 Data Conversion Framework

We designed a framework for data conversion between tagged text and the input/output formats of NLP tools based on the four types of textual functions of tags. First, we introduce the four tag types and the data conversion strategy for each. Then, we introduce the procedure for managing the entire data conversion process using the strategies.

3.1 Strategies for the Four Tag Types

The functions of the tags are classified into only four types, namely, Independent, Decoration, Object, and Meta-info, and for each of these types, a strategy for data conversion is described, as given in Table 1. This section explains the types and their strategies using a simple example where we attempt to apply a sentence splitter to the text given in Figure 2(a). The target text has four tags, "*<note>*", "*<text>*", "*<cite>*", and "*<indexmark>*", denoting, respectively, Independent, Decoration, Object, and Meta-info tags. We now describe each of the types.

Regions enclosed by Independent tags contain syntactically independent text, such as *titles*, *sections*, and so on. In some cases, a region of this type is inserted into the middle of another sentence, like the "*<note>*" tags in the example, which represent footnote text. The data conversion strategy for text containing these tags is to split the enclosed region into multiple subregions and apply the NLP tools separately to each subregion.

[2] [U-compare]: http://u-compare.org/ / [Kachako]: http://kachako.org/kano/

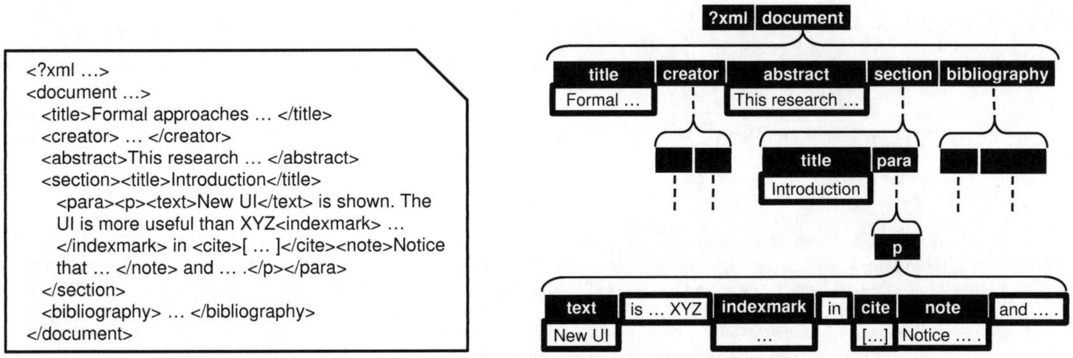

(a) XML document (b) Structure of XML document

Figure 3: Example XML document

Decoration tags, on the other hand, do not necessarily guarantee the independence of the enclosed text regions, and are utilized mainly for embossing the regions visually, such as *changing the font or color of the text* ("<*text*>" in the example), *paragraphing sections*[3], and so on. The data conversion strategy for text containing these tags is to remove the tags before inputting the text into the NLP tools, and then to recover the tags afterwards[4].

Regions enclosed by Object tags contain special descriptions for representing objects treated as single syntactic components in the surrounding text. The regions do not consist of natural language text, and therefore cannot be analyzed by NLP tools[5]. The data conversion strategy for text containing this tag is to replace the enclosed region with some proper character sequence before inputting the text into NLP tools, and then to recover the replaced region afterwards.

Regions enclosed by Meta-info tags are not targets of NLP tools, mainly because the regions are not displayed, but utilized for other purposes, such as creating index pages (like this "<*indexmark*>")[6]. The data conversion strategy for text containing these tags is to delete the tagged region before inputting the text into NLP tools, and then to recover the region afterwards.

According to the above strategies, which are summarized in Table 1, conversion of the example text in Figure 2(a) is carried out as follows. In the first step, tags are removed from the text, whilst retaining their offsets in the resulting tag-less sequence shown in (b). "Cite1" in the sequence is a plain word utilized to replace the "<*cite*>" tag region. For the "<*note*>" tag, we recursively apply our strategies to its inner region, with two plain text regions "New UI ..." and "Notice that ..." consequently input into the sentence splitter. Thereafter, sentence boundary information is returned as shown in (c), and finally, using the retained offset information of the tags, the obtained analysis and original tag information are integrated to produce the XML-tagged sequence shown in (d).

3.2 Procedure for Efficient Tag Classification and Data Conversion

In actual XML documents as shown in Figure 3(a), a number of tags are introduced and tagged regions are multi-layered as illustrated in Figure 3(b) (where black and white boxes represent, respectively, XML tags and plain text regions, and regions enclosed by tags are placed below the tags in the order they appear.). We implemented a complete data conversion procedure for efficiently classifying tags in text documents into the four types and simultaneously obtaining plain text sequences from such documents,

[3] In some types of scientific articles, one sentence can be split into two *paragraph* regions. It depends on the target text whether a *paragraph* tag is classified as Independent or Decoration.

[4] The tags may imply that the enclosed regions constitute chunks of text, which may be suitable for use in NLP tools.

[5] In some cases, natural language text is used for parts of the descriptions, for example, *itemization* or *tables* in scientific articles. How the inner textual parts are generally associated with the surrounding text would be discussed in our future work. For the treatment of list structures, we can learn more from Aït-Mokhtar et al. (2003).

[6] If the tagged region contains analyzable text, it depends on the user policy whether NLP tools should be applied to the region, that is, whether to classify the tag as Independent.

```
@plain_text_sequences = ();  # plain text sequences input to NLP tools
@recovery_info = ();         # information for recovering original document after applying NLP tools
@unknown = ();               # unknown tags

function data_convert ($target_sequence, $seq_ID) {

  if ($target_sequence contains any tags) {  # process one instance of tag usage in a target sequence
    $usage = (pick one instance of top-level tag usage in $target_sequence);
    $tag = (name of the top-level tag in $usage);
    @attributes = (attributes and their values for the top-level tag in $usage);
    $region = (region in $target_sequence enclosed by tag $tag in $usage);
    $tag_and_region =  (region in $target_sequence consisting of $region & tag $tag enclosing it);

    if ($tag ∈ @independent)        { remove $tag_and_region from $target_sequence;
                                      add ["independent", $tag, @attributes, $seq_ID, $seq_ID + 1,
                                          (offset in $target_sequence where $tag_and_region should be inserted) ] to @recovery_info;
                                      data_convert($region, $seq_ID + 1); } # process the tagged region separately
    else if ($tag ∈ @decoration)    { remove only tag $tag enclosing $region from $target_sequence;
                                      add ["decoration", $tag, @attributes,
                                          (offsets in $target_sequence where $region begans and ends)] to @recovery_info; }
    else if ($tag ∈ @object)        { replace $tag_and_region in $target_sequence with a unique plain word $uniq;
                                      add ["object", $uniq, $tag_and_region] to @recovery_info; }
    else if ($tag ∈ @meta_info)     { remove $tag_and_region from $target_sequence;
                                      add ["meta_info", $tag_and_region,
                                          (offset in $target_sequence where $tag_and_region should be inserted)] to @recovery_info; }
    else                            { replace $tag_and_region in $target_sequence with a unique plain word $uniq;
                                      add ["unknown", $uniq, $tag_and_region] to @recovery_info;
                                      if ($tag ∉ @unknown) { add $tag to @unknown; } }

    data_convert($target_sequence, $seq_ID); # process the remaining tags
  }
  else {  # a plain text sequence is obtained
    add [$seq_id, $target_sequence] to @plain_text_sequences;
  }
}

function main ($XML_document) {
  data_convert ($XML_document, 0);
  return @plain_text_sequences, @recovery_info, @unknown;
}
```

Figure 4: Pseudo-code algorithm for data conversion from XML text to plain text for use in NLP tools

as given by the pseudo-code algorithm in Figure 4. In the remainder of this section, we explain how the algorithm works.

Our data conversion procedure applies the strategies for the four types of tags recursively from the top-level tags to the lower tags. The $@independent$, $@decoration$, $@object$ and $@meta\_info$ lists contain, respectively, Independent, Decoration, Object, and Meta-info tags, which have already been classified by the user. When applied to a target document, the algorithm uses the four lists and strategies given in the previous section in its first attempt at converting the document into plain text sequences, storing unknown (and therefore unprocessed) tags, if any, in $@unknown$. After the entire document has been processed for the first time, the user classifies any reported unknown tags. This process is repeated until no further unknown tags are encountered.

In the first iteration of processing the document in Figure 3(a) the algorithm is applied to the target document with the four tag lists empty. In the function "*data_convert*", top-level tags in the document, "*<?xml>*" and "*<document>*", are detected as yet-to-be classified tags and added to $@unknown$. The tags and their enclosed regions in the target document are replaced with unique plain text such as "UN1" and "UN2", and the input text thus becomes a sequence consisting of only plain words like "UN1 UN2". The algorithm then adds the sequence to $@plain\_text\_sequences$ and terminates. The user then classifies the reported yet-to-be classified tags in $@unknown$ into the four tag lists, and the algorithm

Article type	# articles	# total tags (# types)	# classified tags (# types)					#obtained seq.
			I	D	O	M	Total	
PMC	1,000	1,357,229(421)	32,109(12)	62,414(8)	48205(9)	33,953(56)	176,681(85)	25,679
ArX.	300	1,969,359(210*)	5,888(15)	46,962(12)	60,194(8)	7,960(17)	121,004(52)	4,167
ACL	67	130,861(66*)	3,240(24)	14,064(29)	4,589(15)	2,304(19)	24,197(87)	2,293
Wiki.	300	223,514(60*)	3,530(12)	11,197(8)	1,470(28)	11,360(67)	27,557(115)	2,286

(**ArX.**: arXiv.org, **Wiki.**: Wikipedia, I: Independent, D: Decoration, O: Object, M: Meta-info)

Table 2: Classified tags and obtained sequences for each type of article

Article type	Treated tag classes	Parsing with Enju parser				Parsing with Stanford parser			
		* # sentences	** Time (s)	Avg. (**/*)	# failures (rate)	* # sentences	** Time (s)	Avg. (**/*)	# failures (rate)
PMC	**None**	159,327	209,783	1.32	4,721 (2.96%)	170,999	58,865	0.39	18,621 (10.89%)
	O/M	112,285	135,752	1.21	810 (0.72%)	126,176	50,741	0.44	11,881 (9.42%)
	All	126,215	132,250	1.05	699 (0.55%)	139,805	63,295	0.49	11,338 (8.11%)
ArX.	**None**	74,762	108,831	1.46	2,047 (2.74%)	75,672	27,970	0.43	10,590 (13.99%)
	O/M	41,265	89,200	2.16	411 (1.00%)	48,666	24,630	0.57	5,457 (11.21%)
	All	43,208	87,952	2.04	348 (0.81%)	50,504	26,360	0.58	5,345 (10.58%)
ACL	**None**	19,571	15,142	0.77	115 (0.59%)	17,166	5,047	0.29	1,095 (6.38%)
	O/M	9,819	9,481	0.97	63 (0.64%)	11,182	4,157	0.37	616 (5.51%)
	All	11,136	8,482	0.76	39 (0.35%)	12,402	4,871	0.39	587 (4.73%)
Wiki.	**None**	10,561	14,704	1.39	1,161 (10.99%)	14,883	3,114	0.24	1,651 (11.09%)
	O/M	5,026	6,743	1.34	67 (1.33%)	6,173	2,248	0.38	282 (4.57%)
	All	6,893	6,058	0.88	61 (0.88%)	8,049	2,451	0.31	258 (3.21%)

(**ArX.**: arXiv, **Wiki.**: Wikipedia, O/M: Object and Meta-info)

Table 3: Impact on parsing performance of plain text sequences extracted using classified tags

starts its second iteration[7].

In the case of Independent/Decoration tags, the algorithm splits the regions enclosed by the tags/removes only the tags from the target text, and recursively processes the obtained text sequence(s) according to our strategies. In the splitting/removal operation, the algorithm stores in $@recovery\_info$, the locations (offsets) in the obtained text where the tags should be inserted in order to recover the tags and textual structures after applying the NLP tools. In the case of Object/Meta-info tags, regions enclosed by these tags are replaced with unique plain text/omitted from the target text, which means that the inner regions are not unpacked and processed (with relevant information about the replacement/omitting process also stored in $@recovery\_info$). This avoids unnecessary classification tasks for tags that are utilized only in the regions, and therefore minimizes user effort.

When no further unknown tags are reported, sufficient tag classification has been done to obtain plain text sequences for input into NLP tools, with the sequences already stored in $@plain\_text\_sequences$. After applying NLP tools to the obtained sequences, $@recovery\_info$ is used to integrate the annotated output from the tools into the original XML document by merging the offset information[8], and consequently to recover the structure of the original document.

4 Experiments

We investigated whether the algorithm introduced in Section 3.2 is robustly applicable to different types of XML documents and whether the obtained text sequences are adequate for input into NLP tools. The results of this investigation highlight the significance of bridging real-world text and NLP technologies.

4.1 Target Documents

Our algorithm was applied to four types of XML documents: three types of scientific articles, examples of which were, respectively, downloaded from PubMed Central (PMC) (http://www.ncbi.nlm.nih.gov/pmc/tools/ftp/), arXiv.org (http://arxiv.org/) and ACL Anthology

[7]The user can delay the classification for some tags to later iterations.

[8]When crossover of tag regions occur, the region in the annotated output is divided into subregions at the crossover point.

(http://anthology.aclweb.org/)[9], and a web page type, examples of which were downloaded from Wikipedia (http://www.wikipedia.org/). The articles obtained from PMC were originally given in an XML format, while those from arXiv.org and ACL Anthology were given in XHTML (based on XML), and those from Wikipedia were given in HTML, with the HTML articles generated via intermediate XML files. These four types of articles were therefore more or less based on valid XML (or XML-like) formats. For our experiments, we randomly selected 1,000 PMC articles, randomly selected 300 arXiv.org articles, collected 67 (31 long and 36 short) ACL 2014 conference papers without any conversion errors (see Footnote 9), and randomly downloaded 300 Wikipedia articles.

Each of the documents contained a variety of textual parts; we decided to apply the NLP tools to the titles of the articles and sections, abstracts, and body text of the main sections in the scientific articles, and to the titles of the articles, body text headings, and the actual body text of the Wikipedia articles. According to these policies, we classified the tags appearing in all articles of each type.

4.2 Efficiency of Tag Classification

Table 2 summarizes the classified tags and obtained sequences for each type of document. The second to ninth columns give the numbers of utilized articles, tags (in tokens and types) in the documents, each type of tag actually classified and processed, and obtained text sequences, respectively[10]. Using simple regular-expression matching, we found no remaining tagged regions in the obtained sequences. From this we concluded that our framework at least succeeded in converting XML-tagged text into plain text.

For the PMC articles, we obtained plain text sequences by classifying only a fifth or less of the total number of tag types, that is, focusing on less than 15% of the total tag occurrences in the documents (comparing the third and eighth columns). This is because the tags within the regions enclosed by Object and Meta-info tags were not considered by our procedure. For each of the arXiv.org, ACL and Wikipedia articles, a similar effect was implied by the fact that the number of classified tags was less than 20% of the total occurrences of all tags.

4.3 Adequacy of Obtained Sequences for Use in NLP Tools

We randomly selected several articles from each article type, and confirmed that the obtained text sequences consisted of valid *sentences*, which could be directly input into NLP tools and which thoroughly covered the content of the original articles. Then, to evaluate the impact of this adequacy in a more practical situation, we input the obtained sequences (listed in Table 2) into two typical parsers, namely, the Enju parser for deep syntactic/semantic analysis, and the Stanford parser (de Marneffe et al., 2006)[11] for phrase structure and dependency analysis[12]. Table 3 compares the parsing performance on three types of plain text sequences obtained by different strategies: simply removing all tags, processing Object and Meta-info tags using our framework and removing the remaining tags, and processing all the tags using our framework. For each combination of parser and article type, we give the number of detected sentences[13], the total parsing time, the average parsing time per sentence[14], and the number/ratio of sentences that could not be parsed[15].

For all article types, the parsers, especially the Enju parser, succeeded in processing the entire article with much higher coverage (see the fourth column for each parser) and in much less time (see the third

[9] The XHTML version of 178 ACL 2014 conference papers were available at ACL Anthology. Each of the XHTML files was generated by automatic conversion of the original article using LaTeXML (http://dlmf.nist.gov/LaTeXML/).

[10] For Wikipedia, arXiv.org and ACL articles, since HTML/XHTML tag names represent more abstract textual functions, the number of different tag types was much smaller than for PMC articles (see * in the table). To better capture the textual functions of the tagged regions, we used the combination of the tag name and its selected attributes as a single tag. The number of classified tags for Wikipedia, arXiv.org and ACL given in the table reflects this decision.

[11] http://nlp.stanford.edu/software/lex-parser.shtml

[12] The annotated output from the parsers was integrated into the original XML documents by merging the offset information, and the structures of the original documents were consequently recovered. The recovered structures were input to *xmllint*, a UNIX tool for parsing XML documents, and the tool succeeded in parsing the structures without detecting any error.

[13] For the Enju parser, we split each text sequence into sentences using GeniaSS [http://www.nactem.ac.uk/y-matsu/geniass/].

[14] For the Enju parser, the time spent parsing failed sentences was also considered.

[15] For the Stanford parser, the maximum sentence length was limited to 50 words using the option settings because several sentences caused parsing failures, even after increasing the memory size from 150 MB to 2 GB, which terminated the whole process.

column for each parser) using the text sequences obtained by treating some (Object and Meta-info) or all tags with our framework than with those sequences obtained by merely removing the tags. This is mainly because the text sequences obtained by merely removing the tags contained some embedded inserted sentences (specified by Independent tags), bare expressions consisting of non natural language (non-NL) principles (specified by Object tags), and sequences not directly related to the displayed text (specified by Meta-info tags), which confused the parsers. In particular, treating Object and Meta-info tags drastically improved parsing performance, since non-NL tokens were excluded from the analysis.

Compared with treating Object/Meta-info tags, treating all tags, that is, additionally treating Independent tags and removing the remaining tags as Decoration tags, increased the number of detected sentences. This is because Independent tags provide solid information for separating text sequences into shorter sequences and thus prompting the splitting of sequences into shorter sentences, which decreased parsing failure by preventing a lack of search space for the Enju parser and by increasing target (≤ 50 word) sentences for the Stanford parser. Treating all tags increased the total time for the Stanford parser since a decrease in failed (> 50 word) sentences directly implied an increase in processing cost, whereas, for the Enju parser, the total time decreased since the shortened sentences drastically narrowed the required search space.

4.4 Significance of Bridging Real-world Documents and NLP Technologies

As demonstrated above, the parsers succeeded in processing the entire article with much higher coverage and in much less time with the text sequences obtained by our framework than with those sequences obtained by merely removing the tags. Then, what does such thorough and efficient processing bring about? If our target is shallow analysis of documents which can be achieved by simple approaches such as counting words, removing tags will suffice; embedded sentences do not affect word count, and non-NL sequences can be canceled by a large amount of valid sequences in the target documents.

Such shallow approaches, however, cannot satisfy the demands on more detailed or precise analysis of documents: discourse analysis, translation, grammar extraction, and so on. In order to be sensitive to subtle signs from the documents, information uttered even in small parts of text cannot be overlooked, under the condition that sequences other than body text are excluded.

This process of plain text extraction is a well-established procedure in NLP research; in order to concentrate on precise analysis of natural language phenomena, datasets have been arranged in the format of plain text sequences, and, using those datasets, plenty of remarkable achievements have been reported in various NLP tasks while brand-new tasks have been found and tackled.

But what is the ultimate goal of these challenges? Is it to just parse carefully arranged datasets? We all know this to be just a stepping stone to the real goal: to parse real-world, richly-formatted documents. As we demonstrated, if supported by a proper framework, conventional NLP tools already have the ability to process real-world text without significant loss of performance. Adequately bridging target real-world documents and NLP technologies is thus a crucial task for taking advantage of full benefit brought by NLP technologies in ubiquitous application of NLP.

5 Conclusion

We proposed a framework for data conversion between XML-tagged text and input/output formats of NLP tools. In our framework, once each tag utilized in the XML-tagged text has been classified as one of the four types of textual functions, the conversion is automatically done according to the classification. In the experiments, we applied our framework to several types of documents, and succeeded in obtaining plain text sequences from these documents by classifying only a fifth of the total number of tag types in the documents. We also observed that with the obtained sequences, the target documents were much more thoroughly and efficiently processed by parsers than with naively tag-removed text. These results emphasize the significance of bridging real-world documents and NLP technologies.

We are now ready for public release of a tool for conversion of XML documents into plain text sequences utilizing our framework. We would like to share further discussion on applying NLP tools to various real-world documents for increased benefits from NLP.

Acknowledgements

This research was partially supported by "Data Centric Science: Research Commons" at the Research Organization of Information and Systems (ROIS), Japan.

References

Salah Aït-Mokhtar, Veronika Lux, and Éva Bánik. 2003. Linguistic parsing of lists in structured documents. In *Proceedings of Language Technology and the Semantic Web: 3rd Workshop on NLP and XML (NLPXML-2003)*, Budapest, Hungary, April.

Ø. Andersen, J. Nioche, E.J. Briscoe, and J. Carroll. 2008. The BNC parsed with RASP4UIMA. In *Proceedings of the 6th Language Resources and Evaluation Conference (LREC 2008)*, pages 865–869, Marrakech, Morocco, May.

Stephen Clark and James R. Curran. 2007. Wide-coverage efficient statistical parsing with CCG and log-linear models. *Computational Linguistics*, 33(4):493–552.

H. Cunningham, V. Tablan, A. Roberts, and K. Bontcheva. 2013. Getting more out of biomedical documents with GATE's full lifecycle open source text analytics. *PLoS Comput Biol*, 9(2).

Marie-Catherine de Marneffe, Bill MacCartney, and Christopher D. Manning. 2006. Generating typed dependency parses from phrase structure parses. In *Proceedings of the 5th Language Resources and Evaluation Conference (LREC 2006)*, pages 449–454, Genoa, Italy, May.

David Ferruci, Adam Lally, Daniel Gruhl, Edward Epstein, Marshall Schor, J. William Murdock, Andy Frenkiel, Eric W. Brown, Thomas Hampp, Yurdaer Doganata, Christopher Welty, Lisa Amini, Galina Kofman, Lev Kozakov, and Yosi Mass. 2006. Towards an interoperability standard for text and multi-modal analytics. Technical Report RC24122, IBM Research Report.

Yoshinobu Kano, Makoto Miwa, Kevin Cohen, Larry Hunter, Sophia Ananiadou, and Jun'ichi Tsujii. 2011. U-Compare: a modular NLP workflow construction and evaluation system. *IBM Journal of Research and Development*, 55(3):11:1–11:10.

Yoshinobu Kano. 2012. Kachako: a hybrid-cloud unstructured information platform for full automation of service composition, scalable deployment and evaluation. In *Proceedings in the 1st International Workshop on Analytics Services on the Cloud (ASC), the 10th International Conference on Services Oriented Computing (ICSOC 2012)*, Shanghai, China, November.

Takashi Ninomiya, Takuya Matsuzaki, Yusuke Miyao, and Jun'ichi Tsujii. 2007. A log-linear model with an n-gram reference distribution for accurate HPSG parsing. In *Proceedings of the 10th International Conference on Parsing Technologies (IWPT'07)*, Prague, Czech Republic, June.

A Conceptual Framework of Online Natural Language Processing Pipeline Application

Chunqi Shi, Marc Verhagen, James Pustejovsky
Brandeis University
Waltham, United States
{shicq, jamesp, marc}@cs.brandeis.edu

Abstract

This paper describes a conceptual framework that enables online NLP pipelined applications to solve various interoperability issues and data exchange problems between tools and platforms; e.g., tokenizers and part-of-speech taggers from GATE, UIMA, or other platforms. We propose a restful wrapping solution, which allows for universal resource identification for data management, a unified interface for data exchange, and a light-weight serialization for data visualization. In addition, we propose a semantic mapping-based pipeline composition, which allows experts to interactively exchange data between heterogeneous components.

1 Introduction

The recent work on open infrastructures for human language technology (HLT) research and development has stressed the important role that interoperability should play in developing Natural Language Processing (NLP) pipelines. For example, GATE (Cunningham et al., 2002), UIMA (Ferrucci and Lally, 2004), and NLTK (Loper and Bird, 2002) all allow integrating components from different categories based on common XML, or object-based (e.g., Java or Python) data presentation. The major categories of components included in these capabilities include: Sentence Splitter, Phrase Chunker, Tokenizer, Part-of-Speech (POS) Tagger, Shallow Parser, Name Entity Recognizer (NER), Coreference Solution, etc. Pipelined NLP applications can be built by composing several components; for example, a text analysis application such as "relationship analysis from medical records" can be composed by Sentence Splitter, Tokenizer, POS Tagger, NER, and Coreference Resolution components.

In addition to interoperability, the very availability of a component can also play an important role in building online application based on distributed components, especially in tasks such as online testing and judging new NLP techniques by comparing to existing components. For example, the Language Grid (Ishida, 2006) addresses issues relating to accessing components from different locations or providers based on Service-Oriented Architecture (SOAs) models. In this paper, we explore structural, conceptual interoperability, and availability issues, and provide a conceptual framework for building online pipelined NLP applications.

The conventional view of structural interoperability is that a common set of data formats and communication protocols should be specified by considering data management, data exchange, and data visualization issues. Data management determines how to access, store and locate sources of data. For example, GATE provides pluggable document readers or writers and XML (with meta-data configuration) serialization of reusable objected-based data. UIMA provides document or database readers and writers and XMI serialization of common object-based data structures. The Language Grid provides Java object serialization of data collections. Data exchange strategies describe how components communicate their data. For example, GATE provides CREOLE (Collection of REusable Objects for Language Engineering) data collections for data exchange. UIMA provides CAS (Common Analysis Structure), and NLTK provides API modules for each component type. Similarly, the Language Grid provides LSI

Proceedings of the Workshop on Open Infrastructures and Analysis Frameworks for HLT, pages 53–59,
Dublin, Ireland, August 23rd 2014.

(Language Service Interface) for a concrete ontology for a given language infrastructure. Data visualization facilitates manual reading, editing and adjudication. For example, GATE and UIMA provide XML-based viewers for selection, searching, matching and comparison functionality.

The conventional view of conceptual interoperability is that expert knowledge should be used in bridging heterogeneous components. For example, GATE provides integration plugins for UIMA, OpenNLP, and Stanford NLP, where experts have already engineered the specific knowledge on conversion strategies among these components. This leaves open the question of how one would ensure the interoperable pipelining of new or never-before-seen heterogeneous components, for which experts have not encoded bridge protocols.

In order to achieve an open infrastructure of online pipelined applications, we will argue two points regarding the conceptual design, considering both interoperability and availability:

- Universal resource identification, a SQL-like data management, and a light-weight data serialization should be added with structural interoperability in online infrastructure of distributed components.

- By verifying and modifying inconsistent ontology mappings, experts can interactively learn conceptual interoperability for online heterogeneous components pipelines.

2 Data, Tool and Knowledge Types

Interoperability in building pipelined NLP applications is intended ensure the exchange of information between the different NLP tools. For this purpose, existing infrastructures like GATE or UIMA have paid a lot of attention to common entity based data exchanges between the tools. When exchanging data between heterogeneous tools (e.g., the GATE tokenizer pipelined with the NLTK POS tagger), the knowledge of how these different entity based NLP tools can work together becomes much more important, because there might be exchange problems between heterogeneous data or tool information, and we may need specific knowledge to fix them. Thus, when considering interoperability, the main flow of information should be exchanged in the open infrastructure consisting of source data information, NLP tools information, and the knowledge that allows the tools to work together.

What are the main entity types of data and tools in designing an open infrastructure for online NLP pipeline applications? From an abstract view of how linguistic analysis is related to human knowledge, there are the following: Morphological, Lexical, Syntactic, Semantic, Pragmatic tool classifications; and Utterance, Phoneme, Morpheme, Token, Syntactic Structure, Semantic Interpretation, and Pragmatic Interpretation data classifications. (Manaris, 1998; Pustejovsky and Stubbs, 2013). From a concrete application perspective, where tools are available for concrete text mining for communities such as OpenNLP, Stanford CoreNLP and NLTK, there are classification tools such as Sentence Splitter, Tokenizer, POS Tagger, Phrase Chunker, Shallow Parser, NER, Lemmatizer, Coreference; and data classifications such as Document, Sentence, Annotation, and Feature (Cunningham et al., 2002).

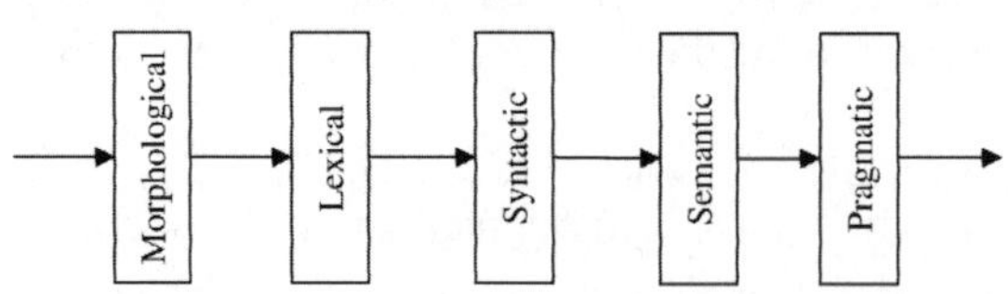

Figure 1: A NLP pipeline can be a (sub)-process of an abstract five-step process

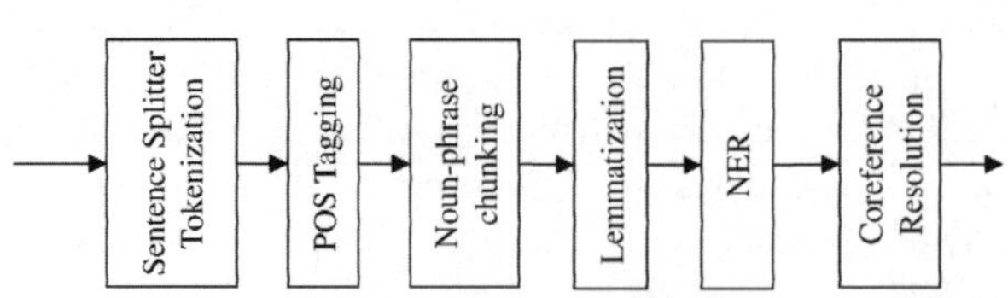

Figure 2: An example NLP pipeline of a concrete six-step process

The knowledge types needed for designing an open infrastructure also can be seen abstractly or concretely. Abstractly, an NLP pipeline should be part of the process of morphological, lexical, syntactic, semantic to pragmatic processing (see Figure 1). From a concrete view, each component of an NLP pipeline should have any requisite preprocessing. For example, tokenization is required preprocessing for POS tagging (see Figure 2). Such knowledge for building NLP pipelines can be interactively determined by the NLP expert or preset as built-in pipeline models.

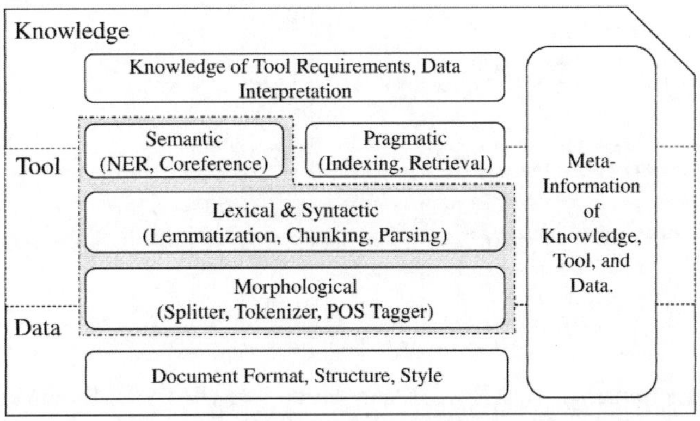

Figure 3: Information for NLP pipeline application description

We can put the above analyzed data, tool, and knowledge types with their meta-information together as the information required for describing an NLP pipeline application (see Figure 3). Regarding the document format, structure and style, for example, the Text Encoding Initiative (TEI)[1] provides one standard for text encoding and interchange, which also enables meta-information description. Concerning the main part (see dashdotted-line part of Figure 3), it is generally referred to as the model of **annotation**. For example, GATE has its own single unified model of annotation, which is organized in annotation graphs. The arcs in the graph have a start node and an end node, an identifier, a type and a set of features (Bontcheva et al., 2004). One standardization effort (Ide and Romary, 2004), the Linguistic Annotation Framework (LAF) architecture is designed so that a pivot format, such as GrAF (Ide and Suderman, 2007), can bridge various annotation collections. Another standardization effort, the Syntactic Annotation Framework (SynAF) (Declerck, 2006), has evolved into the Morpho-syntactic annotation framework (MAF) (Declerck, 2008), which is based on the TEI and designed as the XML serialization for morpho-syntactic annotations. A NLP processing middleware, the Heart of Gold, treats XML standoff annotations for natively XML support, and provides XSLT-based online integration mechanism of various annotation collections (Schäfer, 2006). The UIMA specifies a UML-based data model of annotation, which also has a unified XML serialization (Hahn et al., 2007). Differently from Heart of Gold's XSLT-based mechanism, the conversion tools that bridge GATE annotation and UIMA annotation use GrAF as a pivot and are provided as GATE plugins and UIMA modules (Ide and Suderman, 2009).

Thus, while a pivot standard annotation model like GrAF seems very promising, popular annotation models like those provided by GATE annotations (see Figure 4) or UIMA annotations (see Figure 4) will continue to exist and evolve for a long time. As a result, more bridge strategies, like the conversion plugin (module) of GATE (UIMA) and the XSLT-based middleware mechanism, will continue to be necessary. In the following sections, we consider the issue of the continuing availability of such conversion functions, and whether the current realization of those two conversion strategies is sufficient to bridge the various annotations made available by linguistic experts, without further substantial engineering work.

3 Towards A Conceptual Design of Online Infrastructure

In this section, we discuss the conceptual design of online infrastructure, focusing on both the interoperability and availability of the tools. Concerning the latter, the Service-oriented architecture (SOA) is

[1]http://www.tei-c.org/

```xml
<!-- GATE -->
<GateDocument>
<TextWithNodes>
<Node id="15"/>Sonnet<Node id="21"/>
</TextWithNodes>
<AnnotationSet>
<Annotation Id="18" Type="Token"
StartNode="15" EndNode="21">
<Feature>
 <Name className="java.lang.String">length</Name>
 <Value className="java.lang.String">6</Value>
</Feature>
<Feature>
 <Name className="java.lang.String">category</Name>
 <Value className="java.lang.String">NNP</Value>
</Feature>
<Feature>
 <Name className="java.lang.String">kind</Name>
 <Value className="java.lang.String">word</Value>
</Feature>
<Feature>
  <Name className="java.lang.String">string</Name>
  <Value className="java.lang.String">Sonnet</Value>
</Feature>
</Annotation>
</AnnotationSet>
</GateDocument>
```

```xml
<!-- UIMA -->
<xmi:XMI
xmlns:xmi="http://www.omg.org/XMI"
xmlns:opennlp=
"http:///org/apache/uima/examples/opennlp.ecore"
xmlns:cas="http:///uima/cas.ecore"
xmi:version="2.0">

<cas:Sofa
xmlns:cas="http:///uima/cas.ecore"
xmi:id="1" sofaNum="1" sofaID="_InitialView"
mimetype="text"
sofaString="Sonnet." />

<opennlp:Token
xmi:id="18" sofa="1"
begin="0" end="6"
posTag="NNP" />

<cas:View sofa="1"
members="18"/>

</xmi:XMI>
```

Figure 4: Examples of GATE XML annotation and UIMA XML annotation

a promising approach. For example, while the Language Grid infrastructure makes NLP tools highly available (Ishida, 2006), it can still have limitations regarding interoperability issues. Generally, service interfaces can be either *operation-oriented* which allows flexible operations with simple input/output data, or *resource-oriented* which allows flexible input/output data with simple operations. The NLP processing services of Language Grid are more or less *operation-oriented*, and lack a certain structural flexibility for composing with each other. We present a *resource-oriented* view of NLP tools, which should have universal resource identification for distributed reference, an SQL-like data management, and a light-weight data serialization for online visualization. We propose Restful wrapping both data and tools into Web services for this purpose.

Restful wrapping makes both data and tools easy-to-access and with a unified interface, enabling structural interoperability between heterogeneous tools, assuming standoff annotation from various NLP tools is applied. For example, if the NLP tools are wrapped into Restful services so that they are operated through HTTP GET protocol, and the XML serialization of UIMA annotation is applied for input and output, each NLP components will have the same interface and data structure.

Once an internationalized resource identifier (IRI) is given, all the input and output of tools can be distributed and ubiquitously identified. Moreover, a PUT/GET/POST/DELETE protocol of restful data management is equivalent to an SQL-like CRUD data management interface. For example, an IRI can be defined by a location identifier and the URL of the data service (Wright, 2014).

In addition, a lightweight serialization of stand-off annotation can benefit the online visualization of data, which will be easy for experts to read, judge, or edit. For example, the XML serialization of UIMA annotation can be transferred into JSON serialization, which is preferred for online reading or editing.

NLP tool services will be available by applying restful wrapping (see Figure 5). However, structural interoperability based on the restful wrapping is not enough for conceptual interoperability. For example, if an OpenNLP tokenizer is wrapped using HTTP GET protocol and GATE annotation, but a Stanford NLP POS tagger is wrapped using UIMA annotation, it will raise conceptual interoperability issues. Based on the previously mentioned bridging strategies, a conversion service from GATE annotation to UIMA annotation should work, or a transformation interaction with a XSLT-like service should work. We would like to assume that the interaction and contribution of linguistic experts without online support by engineers can solve this issue. But how can we design the interaction to take advantage of such expert knowledge?

We present a semantic mapping-based composer for building an NLP pipeline application (see Fig-

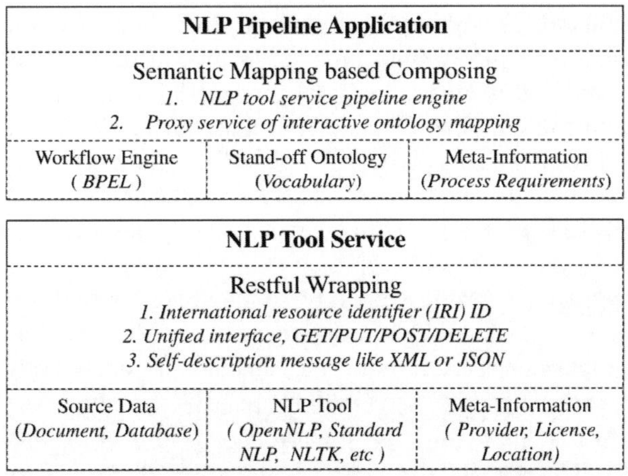

Figure 5: Conceptual design of online NLP pipeline application

ure 5). Conceptual interoperability requires the same vocabularies for the same concept of a standoff annotation. Once we have the standoff ontology of annotation, we can perform automatic semantic mapping from NLP tool output to that ontology. The interaction from experts will be triggered once the automatic semantic mapping has failed (see Figure 6). For example, both GATE and UIMA XML annotations could be transformed into JSON formation, which is easy to present as tree structure entities. Based on these tree structure entities, automatic ontology mapping tools like UFOme, which identifies correspondences among entities in different ontologies (Pirró and Talia, 2010), can be applied to build up various mapping solutions. Knowledge from experts can also be applied interactively, and successful mapping solutions can be stored for further reference and use.

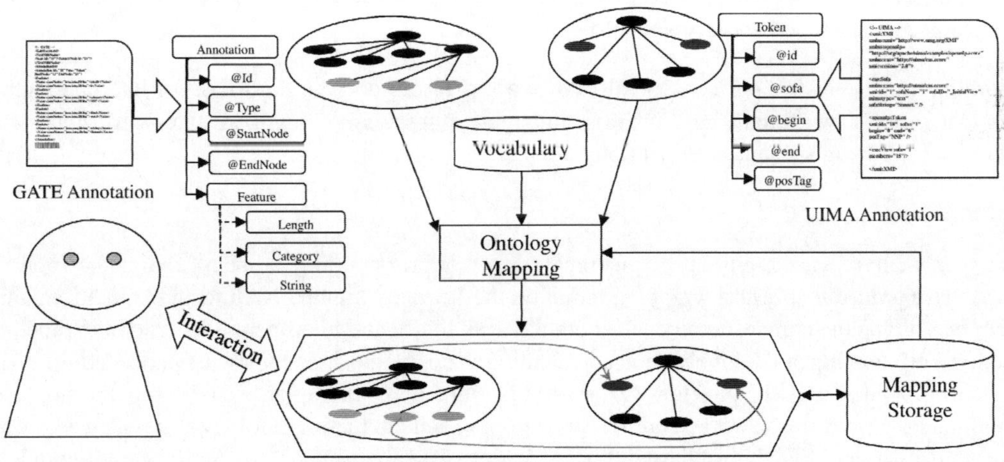

Figure 6: Interactive ontology mapping of two different annotations of NLP tools (Tree structures are learned from XML annotations in Figure 4)

The semantic mapping will be interactively created by the experts, when heterogeneous components with different data models are used in the NLP pipeline created by the end-users, who create the NLP pipeline without consideration of components interoperability. It means that this semi-automatically created semantic mapping separates acquiring the knowledge of tool requirements from end-users and acquiring the knowledge of data interpretation from experts (see Figure 3). For example, the end-users chooses two POS Taggers (OpenNLP and NLTK) and two NER tools (OpenNLP and Stanford NLP) components in the NLP application of "relationship analysis from medical records". When NLTK POS

Tagger output are serialized in to JSON formats but cannot be directly used as the input of Stanford NLP NER component which requires the UIMA annotation, a semantic mapping issue will be automatically created and reported to experts. This NLTK POS Tagger JSON format output will be mapped into the standoff ontology of annotation of POS Tagger. After that, this output will bridge with the UIMA annotation of the Stanford NLP NER. This particular semantic mapping between JSON serialization of a NLTK POS Tagger and the standoff ontology of annotation of POS Tagger, and between the standoff ontology of annotation of POS Tagger and the UIMA annotation of Stanford NLP NER will be reused in the NLP application created by other end-users.

Our conceptual framework does not exclusively rely on the above interoperability design. Our conceptual framework (see Figure 5) should integrate existing knowledge of various annotation frameworks, for example, the alignment knowledge from the Open Annotation models (Verspoor and Livingston, 2012) and the pivot bridge knowledge from the GrAF (Ide and Suderman, 2007) under the Linguistic Annotation Framework (LAF). Thus, existing pivot conversion solutions and XSLT-based middleware solutions can also be applied. Our interactive ontology mapping design provides a more flexible choice for linguistic experts to build up NLP pipeline applications on top of heterogeneous components, without online help from engineers. Below we present varying levels of online NLP applications, according to what kind of extra support would be needed for composing different NLP components:

- Components are interoperable without extra data exchange issues. For example, tools are from the same community (e.g., only using OpenNLP tools).

- Components are interoperable with existing solutions of data exchange issues. For example, tools are from popular communities such as GATE plugins or UIMA modules.

- Components are interoperable with extra knowledge from experts. For example, tools are both from popular communities and personal developments or inner group software.

- Components are interoperable with considerable effort from both experts and engineers. For example, tools are developed under novel ontology designs.

According to these levels, our conceptual framework is targeted at the third level of interoperability issues. Our proposal will generate a ontology mapping storage (see Figure 6), which we hope will contribute to improving a standard annotation ontology.

4 Conclusion

In this paper, we have tried to present a conceptual framework for building online NLP pipeline applications. We have argued that restful wrapping based on the Service-Oriented Architecture and a semantic mapping based pipeline composition benefit both the availability and interoperability of online pipeline applications. By looking at the information surrounding the data, tools, and knowledge needed for NLP components pipelines, we explained how experts can be limited in building online NLP pipeline applications without help from engineers, and our restful wrapping and interactive ontology mapping design can help in such situations. Finally, we have described various levels of support needed for building online NLP pipelines, and we believe that this study can contribute to further online implementations of NLP applications.

Acknowledgements

This work was supported by National Science Foundation grants NSF-ACI 1147944.

References

Kalina Bontcheva, Valentin Tablan, Diana Maynard, and Hamish Cunningham. 2004. Evolving gate to meet new challenges in language engineering. *Nat. Lang. Eng.*, 10(3-4):349–373, September.

Hamish Cunningham, Diana Maynard, Kalina Bontcheva, and Valentin Tablan. 2002. GATE: A Framework and Graphical Development Environment for Robust NLP Tools and Applications. In *Proceedings of the 40th Anniversary Meeting of the Association for Computational Linguistics (ACL'02)*.

Thierry Declerck. 2006. Synaf: Towards a standard for syntactic annotation. In *Proceedings of the Fifth International Conference on Language Resources and Evaluation (LREC'06)*. European Language Resources Association (ELRA).

Thierry Declerck. 2008. A framework for standardized syntactic annotation. In Bente Maegaard Joseph Mariani Jan Odijk Stelios Piperidis Daniel Tapias Nicoletta Calzolari (Conference Chair), Khalid Choukri, editor, *Proceedings of the Sixth International Conference on Language Resources and Evaluation (LREC'08)*, Marrakech, Morocco, may. European Language Resources Association (ELRA). http://www.lrec-conf.org/proceedings/lrec2008/.

David Ferrucci and Adam Lally. 2004. Uima: An architectural approach to unstructured information processing in the corporate research environment. *Nat. Lang. Eng.*, 10(3-4):327–348, September.

Udo Hahn, Ekaterina Buyko, Katrin Tomanek, Scott Piao, John McNaught, Yoshimasa Tsuruoka, and Sophia Ananiadou. 2007. An annotation type system for a data-driven nlp pipeline. In *Proceedings of the Linguistic Annotation Workshop*, LAW '07, pages 33–40, Stroudsburg, PA, USA. Association for Computational Linguistics.

Nancy Ide and Laurent Romary. 2004. International standard for a linguistic annotation framework. *Nat. Lang. Eng.*, 10(3-4):211–225, September.

Nancy Ide and Keith Suderman. 2007. Graf: A graph-based format for linguistic annotations. In *Proceedings of the Linguistic Annotation Workshop*, LAW '07, pages 1–8, Stroudsburg, PA, USA. Association for Computational Linguistics.

Nancy Ide and Keith Suderman. 2009. Bridging the gaps: Interoperability for graf, gate, and uima. In *Proceedings of the Third Linguistic Annotation Workshop*, ACL-IJCNLP '09, pages 27–34, Stroudsburg, PA, USA. Association for Computational Linguistics.

T. Ishida. 2006. Language grid: an infrastructure for intercultural collaboration. In *Applications and the Internet, 2006. SAINT 2006. International Symposium on*, pages 5 pp.–100, Jan.

Edward Loper and Steven Bird. 2002. Nltk: The natural language toolkit. In *Proceedings of the ACL-02 Workshop on Effective Tools and Methodologies for Teaching Natural Language Processing and Computational Linguistics - Volume 1*, ETMTNLP '02, pages 63–70, Stroudsburg, PA, USA. Association for Computational Linguistics.

Bill Manaris. 1998. Natural language processing: A human-computer interaction perspective.

Giuseppe Pirró and Domenico Talia. 2010. Ufome: An ontology mapping system with strategy prediction capabilities. *Data Knowl. Eng.*, 69(5):444–471, May.

James Pustejovsky and Amber Stubbs. 2013. *Natural language annotation for machine learning*. O'Reilly Media, Sebastopol, CA.

Ulrich Schäfer. 2006. Middleware for creating and combining multi-dimensional nlp markup. In *Proceedings of the 5th Workshop on NLP and XML: Multi-Dimensional Markup in Natural Language Processing*, NLPXML '06, pages 81–84, Stroudsburg, PA, USA. Association for Computational Linguistics.

Karin Verspoor and Kevin Livingston. 2012. Towards adaptation of linguistic annotations to scholarly annotation formalisms on the semantic web. In *Proceedings of the Sixth Linguistic Annotation Workshop*, LAW VI '12, pages 75–84, Stroudsburg, PA, USA. Association for Computational Linguistics.

Jonathan Wright. 2014. Restful annotation and efficient collaboration. In Nicoletta Calzolari (Conference Chair), Khalid Choukri, Thierry Declerck, Hrafn Loftsson, Bente Maegaard, Joseph Mariani, Asuncion Moreno, Jan Odijk, and Stelios Piperidis, editors, *Proceedings of the Ninth International Conference on Language Resources and Evaluation (LREC'14)*, Reykjavik, Iceland, may. European Language Resources Association (ELRA).

Command-line utilities for managing and exploring annotated corpora

Joel Nothman and **Tim Dawborn** and **James R. Curran**
ə-lab, School of Information Technologies
University of Sydney
NSW 2006, Australia
`{joel.nothman,tim.dawborn,james.r.curran}@sydney.edu.au`

Abstract

Users of annotated corpora frequently perform basic operations such as inspecting the available annotations, filtering documents, formatting data, and aggregating basic statistics over a corpus. While these may be easily performed over flat text files with stream-processing UNIX tools, similar tools for structured annotation require custom design. Dawborn and Curran (2014) have developed a declarative description and storage for structured annotation, on top of which we have built generic command-line utilities. We describe the most useful utilities – some for quick data exploration, others for high-level corpus management – with reference to comparable UNIX utilities. We suggest that such tools are universally valuable for working with structured corpora; in turn, their utility promotes common storage and distribution formats for annotated text.

1 Introduction

Annotated corpora are a mainstay of language technology, but are often stored or transmitted in a variety of representations. This lack of standardisation means that data is often manipulated in an *ad hoc* manner, and custom software may be needed for even basic exploration of the data, which creates a bottleneck in the engineer or researcher's workflow. Using a consistent storage representation avoids this problem, since generic utilities for rapid, high-level data manipulation can be developed and reused.

Annotated text processing frameworks such as GATE (Cunningham et al., 2002) and UIMA (Lally et al., 2009) provide a means of implementing and combining processors over collections of annotated documents, for which each framework defines a serialisation format. Developers using these frameworks are aided by utilities for basic tasks such as searching among annotated documents, profiling processing costs, and generic processing like splitting each document into many. Such utilities provide a means of quality assurance and corpus management, as well as enabling rapid prototyping of complex processors.

The present work describes a suite of command-line utilities – summarised in Table 1 – designed for similar ends in a recently released document representation and processing framework, DOCREP (Dawborn and Curran, 2014). DOCREP represents annotation layers in a binary, streaming format, such that process pipelining can be achieved through UNIX pipes. The utilities have been developed organically as needed over the past two years, and are akin to UNIX utilities (`grep`, `head`, `wc`, etc.) which instead operate over flat file formats. The framework and utilities are free and open source (MIT Licence) and are available at `https://github.com/schwa-lab/libschwa`.

Some of our tools are comparable to utilities in UIMA and GATE, while others are novel. A number of our tools exploit the evaluation of user-supplied Python functions over each document, providing great expressiveness while avoiding engineering overhead when exploring data or prototyping.

Our utilities make DOCREP a good choice for UNIX-style developers who would prefer a quick scripting language over an IDE, but such modalities should also be on offer in other frameworks. We believe that a number of these utilities are applicable across frameworks and would be valuable to researchers and engineers working with manually and automatically annotated corpora. Moreover, we argue, the availability of tools for rapid corpus management and exploration is an important factor in encouraging users to adopt common document representation and processing frameworks.

Proceedings of the Workshop on Open Infrastructures and Analysis Frameworks for HLT, pages 60–65,
Dublin, Ireland, August 23rd 2014.

2 Utilities for managing structured data

Data-oriented computing tends to couple data primitives with a declarative language or generic tools that operate over those primitives. UNIX provides tools for operating over paths, processes, streams and textual data. Among them are `wc` to count lines and words, and `grep` to extract passages matched by a regular expression; piped together, such utilities accomplish diverse tasks with minimal development cost. Windows PowerShell extends these notions to structured .NET objects (Oakley, 2006); Yahoo! Pipes (Yahoo!, 2007) provides equivalent operations over RSS feeds; SQL transforms relational data; and XSLT (Clark, 1999) or XQuery (Chamberlin, 2002) make XML more than mere markup.

Textual data with multiple layers of structured annotation, and processors over these, are primitives of natural language processing. Such nested and networked structures are not well represented as flat text files, limiting the utility of familiar UNIX utilities. By standardising formats for these primitives, and providing means to operate over them, frameworks such as GATE and UIMA promise savings in development and data management costs. These frameworks store annotated corpora with XML, so users may exploit standard infrastructure (e.g. XQuery) for basic transformation and aggregation over the data. Generic XML tools are limited in their ability to exploit the semantics of a particular XML language, such that expressing queries over annotations (which include pointers, spatial relations, etc.) can be cumbersome. LT-XML (Thompson et al., 1997) implements annotators using standard XML tools, while Rehm et al. (2008) present extensions to an XQuery implementation specialised to annotated text.

Beyond generic XML transformation, UIMA and GATE and their users provide utilities with broad application for data inspection and management, ultimately leading to quality assurance and rapid development within those frameworks. Both GATE and UIMA provide sophisticated graphical tools for viewing and modifying annotations; for comparing parallel annotations; and for displaying a concordance of contexts for a term across a document collection (Cunningham et al., 2002; Lally et al., 2009). Both also provide means of profiling the efficiency of processing pipelines. The Eclipse IDE serves as a platform for tool delivery and is comparable to the UNIX command-line, albeit more graphical, while providing further opportunities for integration. For example, UIMA employs Java Logical Structures to yield corpus inspection within the Eclipse debugger (Lally et al., 2009).

Generic processors in these frameworks include those for combining or splitting documents, or copying annotations from one document to another. The community has further built tools to export corpora to familiar query environments, such as a relational database or Lucene search engine (Hahn et al., 2008). The uimaFIT library (Ogren and Bethard, 2009) simplifies the creation and deployment of UIMA processors, but to produce and execute a processor for mere data exploration still has some overhead.

Other related work includes utilities for querying or editing treebanks (e.g. Kloosterman, 2009), among specialised annotation formats; and for working with binary-encoded structured data such as Protocol Buffers (e.g. protostuff[1]). Like these tools and those within UIMA and GATE, the utilities presented in this work reduce development effort, with an orientation towards data management and evaluation of arbitrary functions from the command-line.

3 Common utility structure

For users familiar with UNIX tools to process textual streams, implementing similar tools for working with structured DOCREP files seemed natural. Core utilities are developed in C++, while others are able to exploit the expressiveness of interpreted evaluation of Python. We describe a number of the tools according to their application in the next section; here we first outline common features of their design.

Invocation and API Command-line invocation of utilities is managed by a dispatcher program, `dr`, whose operation may be familiar from the `git` versioning tool: an invocation of `dr` *`cmd`* delegates to a command named `dr-`*`cmd`* where found on the user's `PATH`. Together with utility development APIs in both C++ and Python, this makes it easy to extend the base set of commands.[2]

[1] `https://code.google.com/p/protostuff/`

[2] Note that DOCREP processing is not limited in general to these languages. As detailed in Dawborn and Curran (2014) APIs are currently available in C++, Java and Python.

Command	Description	Required input	Output	Similar in UNIX
dr count	Aggregate	stream or many	tabular	wc
dr dump	View raw annotations	stream	JSON-like	less / hexdump
dr format	Excerpt	stream + expression	text	printf / awk
dr grep	Select documents	stream + expression	stream	grep
dr head	Select prefix	stream	stream	head
dr sample	Random documents	stream + proportion	stream	shuf -n
dr shell	Interactive exploration	stream + commands	mixed	python
dr sort	Reorder documents	stream + expression	stream	sort
dr split	Partition	stream + expression	files	split
dr tail	Select suffix	stream	stream	tail

Table 1: Some useful commands and comparable UNIX tools, including required input and output types.

Streaming I/O As shown in Table 1, most of our DOCREP utility commands take a single stream of documents as input (defaulting to `stdin`), and will generally output either plain text or another DOCREP stream (to `stdout` by default). This parallels the UNIX workflow, and intends to exploit its constructs such as pipes, together with their familiarity to a UNIX user. This paradigm harnesses a fundamental design decision in DOCREP: the utilisation of a document *stream*, rather than storing a corpus across multiple files.

Self-description for inspection Generic command-line tools require access to the *schema* as well as the data of an annotated corpus. DOCREP includes a description of the data schema along with the data itself, making such tools possible with minimal user input. Thus by reading from a stream, fields and annotation layers can be referenced by name, and pointers across annotation layers can be dereferenced.[3]

Extensions to this basic schema may also be useful. For many tools, a Python class (on file) can be referenced that provides *decorations* over the document: in-memory fields that are not transmitted on the stream, but are derived at runtime. For example, a document with pointers from dependent to governor may be decorated with a list of dependents on each governor. Arbitrary Python accessor functions (*descriptors*) may similarly be added. Still, for many purposes, the self-description is sufficient.

Custom expression evaluation A few of our utilities rely on the ability to evaluate a function given a document. The suite currently supports evaluating such functions in Python, providing great flexibility and power.[4] Their input is an object representing the document, and its offset (0 for the first document in a stream, 1 for the second, etc.). Its output depends on the purpose of the expression, which may be for displaying, filtering, splitting or sorting a corpus, depending on the utility in use, of which examples appear below. Often it is convenient to specify an anonymous function on the command-line, a simple Python expression such as `len(doc.tokens) > 1000`, into which local variables `doc` (document object) and `ind` (offset index) are injected as well as built-in names like `len`. (Python code is typeset in blue.) In some cases, the user may want to predefine a library of such functions in a Python module, and may then specify the path to that function on the command-line instead of an expression.

4 Working with DOCREP on the command-line

Having described their shared structure, this section presents examples of the utilities available for working with DOCREP streams. We consider three broad application areas: quality assurance, managing corpora, and more specialised operations.

[3]This should be compared to UIMA's Type System Descriptions, and uimaFIT's automatic detection thereof.

[4]`dr grep` was recently ported to C++ with a custom recursive descent parser and evaluator, which limits expressiveness but promises faster evaluation. In terms of efficiency, we note that some of the Python utilities have performed more than twice as fast using the JIT compilation of PyPy, rather than the standard CPython interpreter.

4.1 Debugging and quality assurance

Validating the input and output of a process is an essential part of pipeline development in terms of quality assurance and as part of a debugging methodology. Basic quality assurance may require viewing the raw content contained on a stream: schema, data, or both. This could ensure, for instance, that a user has received the correct version of a corpus from a correspondent, or that a particular field was used as expected. Since DOCREP centres on a binary wire format, `dr dump` (cf. UNIX's `hexdump`) provides a decoded textual view of the raw content on a stream. Optionally, it can provide minimal interpretation of schema semantics to improve readability (e.g. labelling fields by name rather than number), or can show schema details to the exclusion of data.

For an aggregate summary of the contents of a stream, `dr count` is a versatile tool. It mirrors UNIX's `wc` in providing the basic statistics over a stream (or multiple files) at different granularities. Without any arguments, `dr count` outputs the total number of documents on standard input, but the number of annotations in each store (total number of tokens, sentences, named entities, etc.) can be printed with flag `-a`, or specific stores with `-s`. The same tool can produce per-document (as distinct from per-stream) statistics with `-e`, allowing for quick detection of anomalies, such as an empty store where annotations were expected. `dr count` also doubles as a progress meter, where its input is the output of a concurrent corpus processor, as in the following example:

```
my-proc < /path/to/input | tee /path/to/output | dr count -tacv 1000
```

Here, the options `-acv`*n* output cumulative totals over all stores every *n* documents, while `-t` prefixes each row of output with a timestamp.

Problems can often be identified from only a small sample of documents. `dr head` (cf. UNIX's `head`) extracts a specified number of documents from the beginning of a stream, defaulting to 1. `dr sample` provides a stochastic alternative, employing reservoir sampling (Vitter, 1985) to efficiently draw a specified fraction of the entire stream. Its output can be piped to processing software for smoke testing, for instance. Such tools are obviously useful for a binary format; yet it is not trivial to split on document boundaries even for simple text representations like the CONLL shared task format.

4.2 Corpus management

Corpora often need to be restructured: they may be heterogeneous, or need to be divided or sampled from, such as when apportioning documents to manual annotators. In other cases, corpora or annotations from many sources should be combined.

As with the UNIX utility of the same name, `dr grep` has many uses. Here it might be used to extract a particular document, or to remove problematic documents. The user provides a function that evaluates to a Boolean value; where true, an input document is reproduced on the output stream. Thus it might extract a particular document by its identifier, all documents with a minimum number of words, or those referring to a particular entity. Note, however, that like its namesake, it performs a linear search, while a non-streaming data structure could provide fast indexed access; each traversed document is (at least partially) deserialised, adding to the computational overhead.[5] `dr grep` is often piped into `dr count`, to print the number of documents (or sub-document annotations) in a subcorpus.

`dr split` moves beyond such binary filtering. Like UNIX's `split`, it partitions a file into multiple, using a templated filename. In `dr split`, an arbitrary function may determine the particular output paths, such as to split a corpus whose documents have one or more category label into a separate file for each category label. Thus `dr split -t /path/to/{key}.dr py 'doc.categories'` evaluates each document's `categories` field via a Python expression, and for each key in the returned list will write to a path built from that key. In a more common usage, `dr split k 10` will assign documents by round robin to files named `fold000.dr` through `fold009.dr`, which is useful to derive a *k*-fold cross-validation strategy for machine learning. In order to stratify a particular field across

[5]Two commands that are not featured in this paper may allow for faster access: `dr subset` extends upon `dr head` to extract any number of documents with minimal deserialisation overhead, given their offset indices in a stream. `dr offsets` outputs the byte offset *b* of each document in a stream, such that C's `fseek(`b`)` or UNIX's `tail -c+(`$b+1$`)` can be used to skip to a particular document. An index may thus be compiled in conjunction with `dr format` described below. Making fast random access more user friendly is among future work.

the partitions for cross-validation, it is sufficient to first sort the corpus by that field using `dr split k`. This is one motivation for `dr sort`, which may similarly accept a Python expression as the sort key, e.g. `dr sort py doc.label`. As a special case, `dr sort random` will shuffle the input documents, which may be useful before manual annotation or order-sensitive machine learning algorithms.

The inverse of the partitioning performed by `dr split` is to concatenate multiple streams. Given DOCREP's streaming design, UNIX's `cat` suffices; for other corpus representations, a specialised tool may be necessary to merge corpora.

While the above management tools partition over documents, one may also operate on portions of the annotation on each document. Deleting annotation layers, merging annotations from different streams (cf. UNIX's `cut` and `paste`), or renaming fields would thus be useful operations, but are not currently available as a DOCREP command-line utility. Related tasks may be more diagnostic, such as identifying annotation layers that consume undue space on disk; `dr count --bytes` shows the number of bytes consumed by each store (cf. UNIX's `du`), rather than its cardinality.

4.3 Exploration and transformation

Other tools allow for more arbitrary querying of a corpus, such as summarising each document. `dr format` facilitates this by printing a string evaluated for each document. The tool could be used to extract a concordance, or enumerate features for machine learning. The following would print each document's `id` field and its first thirty tokens, given a stream on standard input:

```
dr format py '"{}\t{}".format(doc.id, " ".join(tok.norm for tok in
                                          doc.tokens[:30]))'
```

We have also experimented with specialised tools for more particular, but common, formats, such as the tabular format employed in CoNLL shared tasks. `dr conll` makes assumptions about the schema to print one token per line with sentences separated by a blank line, and documents by a specified delimiter. Additional fields of each token (e.g. part of speech), or fields derived from annotations over tokens (e.g. IOB-encoded named entity recognition tags) can be added as additional columns using command-line flags. However, the specification of such details on the command-line becomes verbose and may not easily express all required fields, such that developing an *ad hoc* script to undertake this transformation may often prove a more maintainable solution.

Our most versatile utility makes it easy to explore or modify a corpus in an interactive Python shell. This functionality is inspired by server development frameworks (such as Django) that provide a shell specially populated with data accessors and other application-specific objects. `dr shell` reads documents from an input stream and provides a Python iterator over them named `docs`. If an output path is specified on the command-line, a function `write_doc` is also provided, which serialises its argument to disk. The user would otherwise have the overhead of opening input and output streams and initialising the de/serialisation process; the time saved is small but very useful in practice, since it makes interactive corpus exploration cheap. This in turn lowers costs when developing complex processors, as interactive exploration may validate a particular technique. The following shows an interactive session in which the user prints the 100 lemmas with highest document frequency.

```
$ dr shell /path/to/input.dr
>>> from collections import Counter
>>> df = Counter()
>>> for doc in docs:
...     doc_lemmas = {tok.lemma for tok in doc.tokens}
...     df.update(doc_lemmas)
...
>>> for lemma, count in df.most_common(100):
...     print("{:5d}\t{}".format(count, lemma))
```

Finally, `dr shell -c` can execute arbitrary Python code specified on the command-line, rather than interactively. This enables rapid development of *ad hoc* tools employing the common read-process-write paradigm (whether writing serialised documents or plain text), in the vein of `awk` or `sed`.

5 Discussion

DOCREP's streaming model allows the reuse of existing UNIX components such as `cat`, `tee` and pipes. This is similar to the way in which choosing an XML data representation means users can exploit standard XML tools. The specialised tools described above are designed to mirror the functionality if not names of familiar UNIX counterparts, making it simple for UNIX users to adopt the tool suite.

No doubt, many users of Java/XML/Eclipse find command-line tools unappealing, just as a "UNIX hacker" might be put off by monolithic graphical interfaces and unfamiliar XML processing tools. Ideally a framework should appeal to a broad user base; providing tools in many modalities may increase user adoption of a document processing framework, without which it may seem cumbersome and confining.

In this vein, a substantial area for future work within DOCREP is to provide more graphical tools, and utilities such as concordancing or database export that are popular within other frameworks. Further utilities might remove existing fields or layers from annotations; select sub-documents; set attributes on the basis of evaluated expressions; merge annotations; or compare annotations.

We have described utilities developed in response to a new document representation and processing framework, DOCREP. Similar suites deserve attention as an essential adjunct to representation frameworks, and should encompass expressive tools and various paradigms of user interaction. When performing basic corpus manipulation, these utilities save substantial user effort, particularly by adopting a familiar interface. Such boons highlight the benefit of using a consistent annotated corpus representation.

References

Donald D. Chamberlin. 2002. XQuery: An XML query language. *IBM Systems Journal*, 41(4):597–615.

James Clark. 1999. XSL transformations (XSLT). W3C Recommendation, 16 November.

Hamish Cunningham, Diana Maynard, Kalina Bontcheva, and Valentin Tablan. 2002. GATE: A framework and graphical development environment for robust NLP tools and applications. In *Proceedings of the 40th Annual Meeting of the Association for Computational Linguistics (ACL)*, pages 168–175.

Tim Dawborn and James R. Curran. 2014. docrep: A lightweight and efficient document representation framework. In *Proceedings of the 25th International Conference on Computational Linguistics*.

Udo Hahn, Ekaterina Buyko, Rico Landefeld, Matthias Mühlhausen, Michael Poprat, Katrin Tomanek, and Joachim Wermter. 2008. An overview of JCoRe, the JULIE lab UIMA component repository. In *Proceedings of LREC'08 Workshop 'Towards Enhanced Interoperability for Large HLT Systems: UIMA for NLP'*, pages 1–7.

Geert Kloosterman. 2009. *An overview of the Alpino Treebank tools*. `http://odur.let.rug.nl/vannoord/alp/Alpino/TreebankTools.html`. Last updated 19 December.

Adam Lally, Karin Verspoor, and Eoric Nyberg. 2009. *Unstructured Information Management Architecture (UIMA) Version 1.0*. OASIS Standard, 2 March.

Andy Oakley. 2006. *Monad (AKA PowerShell): Introducing the MSH Command Shell and Language*. O'Reilly Media.

Philip Ogren and Steven Bethard. 2009. Building test suites for UIMA components. In *Proceedings of the Workshop on Software Engineering, Testing, and Quality Assurance for Natural Language Processing (SETQA-NLP 2009)*, pages 1–4.

Georg Rehm, Richard Eckart, Christian Chiarcos, and Johannes Dellert. 2008. Ontology-based XQuery'ing of XML-encoded language resources on multiple annotation layers. In *Proceedings of the Sixth International Conference on Language Resources and Evaluation (LREC'08)*.

Henry S. Thompson, Richard Tobin, David McKelvie, and Chris Brew. 1997. LT XML: Software API and toolkit for XML processing. `http://www.ltg.ed.ac.uk/software/`.

Jeffrey S. Vitter. 1985. Random sampling with a reservoir. *ACM Transactions on Mathematical Software (TOMS)*, 11(1):37–57.

Yahoo! 2007. Yahoo! Pipes. `http://pipes.yahoo.com/pipes/`. Launched 7 February.

SSF: A Common Representation Scheme for Language Analysis for Language Technology Infrastructure Development

Akshar Bharati
Akshar Bharati Group
Hyderabad
sangal@iiit.ac.in

Rajeev Sangal
IIT (BHU), Varanasi
sangal@iiit.ac.in

Dipti Sharma
IIIT, Hyderabad
dipti@iiit.ac.in

Anil Kumar Singh
IIT (BHU), Varanasi
nlprnd@gmail.com

Abstract

We describe a representation scheme and an analysis engine using that scheme, both of which have been used to develop infrastructure for HLT. The Shakti Standard Format is a readable and robust representation scheme for analysis frameworks and other purposes. The representation is highly extensible. This representation scheme, based on the blackboard architectural model, allows a very wide variety of linguistic and non-linguistic information to be stored in one place and operated upon by any number of processing modules. We show how it has been successfully used for building machine translation systems for several language pairs using the same architecture. It has also been used for creation of language resources such as treebanks and for different kinds of annotation interfaces. There is even a query language designed for this representation. Easily wrappable into XML, it can be used equally well for distributed computing.

1 Introduction

Building infrastructures for human language technology is a non-trivial task. There can be numerous issues that have to be addressed, whether linguistic or non-linguistic. Unless carefully managed, the overall complexity can easily get out of control and seriously threaten the sustainability of the system. This may apply to all large software systems, but the complexities associated with humans languages (both within and across languages) only add to the problem. To make it possible to build various components of an infrastructure that scales within and across languages for a wide variety of purposes, and to be able to do it by re-using the representation(s) and the code, deserves to be considered an achievement.

GATE[1] (Cunningham et al., 2011; Li et al., 2009), UIMA[2] (Ferrucci and Lally, 2004; Bari et al., 2013; Noh and Padó, 2013) and NLTK[3] (Bird, 2002) are well known achievements of this kind. This paper is about one other such effort that has proved to be successful over the last decade or more.

2 Related Work

GATE is designed to be an architecture, a framework and a development environment, quite like UIMA, although the two differ in their realization of this goal. It enables users to develop and deploy robust language engineering components and resources. It also comes bundled with several commonly used baseline Natural Language Processing (NLP) applications. It makes strict distinction between data, algorithms, and ways of visualising them, such that algorithms + data + GUI = applications. Consequently, it has three types of components: language resources, processing resources and visual resources.GATE uses an annotation format with stand-off markup.

UIMA is a middleware architecture for processing unstructured information (UIM) (Ferrucci and Lally, 2004), with special focus on NLP. Its development originated in the realization that the ability to quickly discover each other's results and rapidly combine different technologies and approaches accelerates scientific advance. It has powerful search capabilities and a data-driven framework for the

[1]http://gate.ac.uk/
[2]https://uima.apache.org/
[3]http://www.nltk.org/

Proceedings of the Workshop on Open Infrastructures and Analysis Frameworks for HLT, pages 66–76, Dublin, Ireland, August 23rd 2014.

development, composition and distributed deployment of analysis engines. More than the development of independent UIM applications, UIMA aims to enable accelerated development of integrated and robust applications, combining independent applications in diverse sub-areas of NLP, so as to accelerate the research cycle as well as the production time. In UIMA, The original document and its analysis are represented in a structure called the Common Analysis Structure, or CAS. Annotations in the CAS are maintained separately from the document itself to allow greater flexibility than inline markup. There is an XML specification for the CAS and it is possible to develop analysis engines that operate on and output data in this XML format, which also (like GATE and NLTK) uses stand-off markup.

The Natural Language Toolkit (NLTK) is a suite of modules, data sets and tutorials (Bird, 2002). It supports many NLP data types and can process many NLP tasks. It has a rich collection of educational material (such as animated algorithms) for those who are learning NLP. It can also be used as a platform for prototyping of research systems.

SSF and the Shakti Analyzer are similar to the above three but have a major difference when compared with them. SSF is a "powerful" notation for representing the NLP analysis, at all stages, whether morphological, part-of-speech level, chunk level, or sentence level parse. The notation is so designed that it is flexible, as well as readable. The notation can be read by human beings and can also be loaded in memory, so that it can be used efficiently. It also allows the architecture to consist of modules which can be configured easily under different settings. The power of the notation and the flexibility of the resulting architecture gives enormous power to the system framework.

The readability of the format allows it to be used directly with any plain text editors, without requiring the use of any special tools or editors. Many users prefer the data in plain text format as it allows them to use the editors they are familiar with. Such readability and simplicity has turned out, in our experience, to be an advantage even for experts like software developers and (computer savvy) linguists.

It would be an interesting exercise to marry SSF notation and the Shakti way of doing things with the GATE and UIMA architecture. Our own feeling is that the resulting system/framework with a powerful notation like SSF and the comprehensive framework like UIMA/GATE would lead to a new even more powerful framework with a principled notation.

3 Shakti Standard Format

Shakti Standard Format (SSF) is a representation scheme (along with a corresponding format) that can be used for most kinds of linguistically analyzed data. It allows information in a sentence to be represented in the form of one or more *trees* together with a set of *attribute-value* pairs with nodes of the trees. The attribute-value pairs allow features or properties to be specified with every node. *Relations* of different types across nodes can also be specified using an attribute-value like representation. The representation is specially designed to allow different levels and kinds of linguistic analyses to be stored. The developers use APIs to store or access information regarding structure of trees and attribute-value pairs.

If a module is successful in its task, it adds a new analysis using trees and attribute values to the representation. Thus, even though the format is fixed, it is extensible in terms of attributes or analyses. This approach allows ready-made packages (such as, POS tagger, chunker, and parser) to be incorporated easily using a wrapper (or a pair of converters). In order to interface such pre-existing packages to the system, all that is required is to convert from (input) SSF to the input format required by that package and, the output of the package to SSF. The rest of the modules of the system continue to operate seamlessly.

The format allows both in-memory representation as well as stream (or text) representation. They are inter-convertible using a *reader* (stream to memory) and *printer* (memory to stream). The in-memory representation is good in speed of processing, while the stream is good for portability, heterogenous machines, and flexibility, in general.

SSF promotes the dictum: "Simplify globally, and if unavoidable, complicate only locally." Even if the number of modules is large and each module does a small job, the local complexity (of individual modules) remains under tight control for most of the modules. At worst, complexity is introduced only locally, without affecting the global simplicity.

3.1 Text Level SSF

In SSF, a text or a document has a sequence of sentences with some structure such as paragraphs and headings. It also includes meta information related to title, author, publisher, year and other information related to the origin of the text or the document. Usually, there is also the information related to encoding, and version number of the tagging scheme, etc. The text level SSF has two parts, header and body:

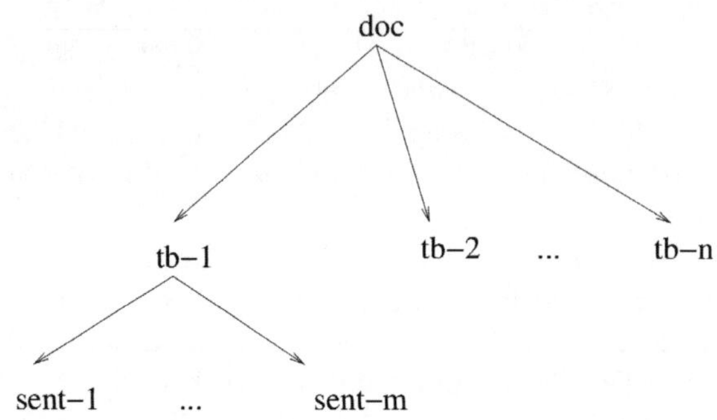

Figure 1: Document Structure in SSF

```
<document docid="..." docnumber="...">
<header>
...
</header>
<body>
...
</body>
```

The header contains meta information about the title, author, publisher, etc. as contained in the CML (Corpus Markup Language) input[4]. The body contains sentences, each in SSF. The body of a text in SSF contains text blocks given by the tag *tb*.

```
<body encode= ... >
<tb>
...
</tb>
...
</body>
```

A text block (tb) contains a sequence of sentences. Each sentence can be marked as a *segment* (to indicate a heading, a partial sentence, etc.) or not a segment (to indicate a normal sentence).

3.2 Sentence Level SSF

Several formalisms have been developed for such descriptions, but the two main ones in the field of NLP are Phrase Structure Grammar (PSG) (Chomsky, 1957) and Dependency Grammar (DG) (Tesniere, 1959). In PSG, a set of phrase structure rules are given for the grammar of a language. It is constituency based and order of elements are a part of the grammar, and the resulting tree. DG, on the other hand, is relational and shows relations between words or elements of a sentence. It, usually, tries to capture the syntactico-semantic relations of the elements in a sentence. The resulting dependency tree is a tree with nodes and edges being labelled.

The difference in the two approaches are shown below with the help of the following English example:

```
Ram ate the banana.
```

The phrase structure tree is drawn in Fig. 2 using a set of phrase structure rules. Fig. 3 shows the dependency tree representation for this sentence. SSF can represent both these formats.

[4]Thus SSF becomes a part of CML.

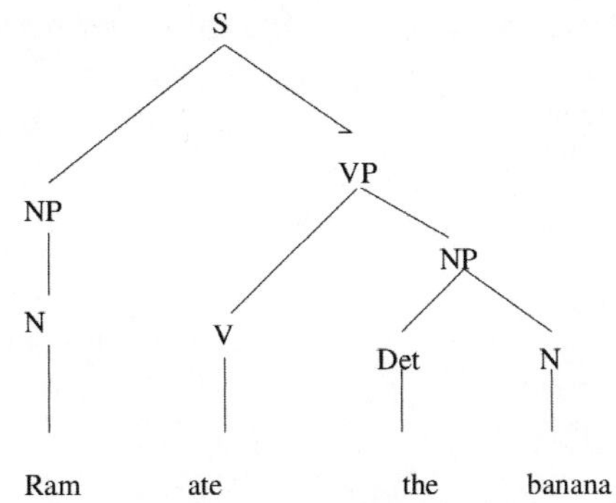

Figure 2: Phrase structure tree

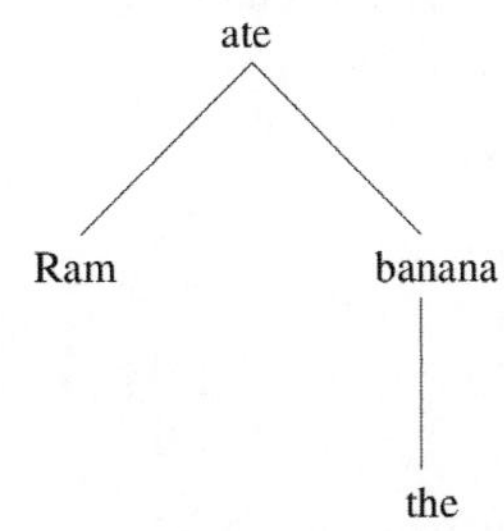

Figure 3: Dependency tree

Sentence level SSF is used to store the analysis of a sentence. It occurs as part of text level SSF. The analysis of a sentence may mark any or all of the following kinds of information as appropriate: part of speech of the words in the sentence; morphological analysis of the words including properties such as root, gender, number, person, tense, aspect, modality; phrase-structure or dependency structure of the sentence; and properties of units such as chunks, phrases, local word groups, bags, etc. Note that SSF is theory neutral and allows both phrase structure as well as dependency structure to be coded, and even mixed in well defined ways.

Though the format in SSF is fixed, it is extensible to handle new features. It also has a text representation, which makes it easy to read the output. The following example illustrates the SSF. For example, the following English sentence,

```
Children are watching some programmes on television in the house. -- (1)
```

The representation for the above sentence is shown in SSF in Fig. 4. As shown in this figure, each line represents a word/token or a group (except for lines with '))' which only indicate the end of a group). For each group, the symbol used is '(('. Each word or group has 3 parts. The first part stores the tree address of each word or group, and is for human readability only. The word or group is in the second part, with part of speech tag or group/phrase category in the third part.

```
Address   Token         Category      Attribute-value pairs
 ----------------------------------------------
 1        ((            NP
 1.1      children      NNS       <fs af=child,n,m,p,3,0,,>
          ))
 2        ((            VG
 2.1      are           VBP       <fs af=be,v,m,p,3,0,,>
 2.2      watching      VBG       <fs af='watch,v,m,s,3,0,,' aspect=PROG>
          ))
 3        ((            NP
 3.1      some          DT        <fs af=some,det,m,s,3,0,,>
 3.2      programmes    NNS       <fs af=programme,n,m,p,3,0,,>
          ))
 4        ((            PP
 4.1      on            IN        <fs af=on,p,m,s,3,0,,>
 4.1.1    ((            NP
 4.1.2    television    NN        <fs af=television,n,m,s,3,0,,>
          ))
          ))
 5        ((            PP
 5.1      in            IN        <fs af=in,p,m,s,3,0,,>
 5.2      ((            NP
 5.2.1    the           DT        <fs af=the,det,m,s,3,0,,>
 5.2.2    house         NN        <fs af=house,n,m,s,3,0,,>
          ))
          ))
 ----------------------------------------------
          Figure 4: Shakti Standard Format
```

The example below shows the SSF for the first noun phrase where feature information is also shown, as the fourth part on each line. Some frequently occurring attributes (such as root, cat, gend, etc.) may be abbreviated using a special attribute called 'af' or abbreviated attributes, as follows:

```
1         ((                  NP
1.1       children            NNS        <fs af='child,n,m,p,3,0,,' >
                                                |     | | | | |
                                                |     | | | |  \
                                              root    | | |pers |
                                                      | | |     case
                                            category  | number
                                                      |
                                                    gender
```

The field for each attribute is at a fixed position, and a comma is used as a separater. Thus, in case no value is given for a particular attribute, the field is left blank, e.g. last two fields in the above example.

Corresponding to the above SSF text stream, an in-memory data structure may be created using the APIs. (However, note that value of the property *Address* is not stored in the in-memory data structure explicitly. It is for human reference and readability only, and is computed when needed. A unique name, however can be assigned to a node and saved in the memory, as mentioned later.)

There are two types of attributes: user defined or system defined. The convention that is used is that a user defined attribute should not have an underscore at the end. System attribute may have a single underscore at its end.

Values are of two types: simple and structured. Simple values are represented by alphanumeric strings, with a possible underscore. Structured values have progressively more refined values separated by double underscores. For example, if a value is:

```
vmod__varg__k1
```

it shows the value as 'vmod' (modifier of a verb), which is further refined as 'varg' (argument of the verb) of type 'k1' (karta karaka).

3.3 Interlinking of Nodes

Nodes might be interlinked with each other through directed edges. Usually, these edges have nothing to do with phrase structure tree, and are concerned with dependency structure, thematic structure, etc. These are specified using the attribute value syntax, however, they do not specify a property for a node, rather a relation between two nodes.

For example, if a node is karta karaka of another node named 'play1' in the dependency structure (in other words, if there is a directed edge from the latter to the former) it can be represented as follows:

1	children	NN	$< fs\ drel =' k1 : play1' >$
2	played	VB	$< fs\ name = play1 >$

The above says that there is an edge labelled with 'k1' from 'played' to 'children' in the 'drel' tree (dependency relation tree). The node with token 'played' is named as 'play1' using a special attribute called 'name'.

So the syntax is as follows: if you associate an arc with a node C as follows:

```
<treename>=<edgelabel>:<nodename>
```

it means that there is an edge from $< nodename >$ to C, and the edge is labelled with $< edgelabel >$. Name of a node may be declared with the attribute 'name':

```
name=<nodename>
```

3.4 Cross Linking across Sentences

There is a need to relate elements across sentences. A common case is that of co-reference of pronouns. For example, in the following sentences:

```
Sita saw Ram in the house. He had come all by himself.   -- (2)
```

the pronoun 'he' in the second sentence refers to the same person as referred to by 'Ram'. Similarly 'himself' refers to same person as 'he' refers to. This is show by means of a co-reference link from 'he' to 'Ram', and from 'himself' to 'he'. SSF allows such cross-links to be marked.

The above text of two sentences is shown in SSF below.

```
<document docid="gandhi-324" docnumber="2">
<header> ...  </header>
<body>
<tb>
  <sentence num=1>
  ...
  2 Ram              <fs name=R>
  ...
  </sentence>
  <sentence num=2>
  1 He                <fs coref="..%R"  name=he>
  ...
  6 himself           <fs coref=he>
  7 .
  </sentence>
</tb>
```

Note that 'himself' in sentence 2 co-refers to 'he' in the same sentence. This is shown using attribute 'coref' and value 'he'. To show co-reference across sentences, a notation is used with '%'. It is explained next.

Name labels are defined at the level of a sentence: Scope of any name label is a sentence. It should be unique within a sentence, and can be referred to within the sentence by using it directly.

To refer to a name label in another sentence in the same text block (paragraph), path has to be specified:

```
..%R
```

To refer to a name label R in a sentence in another text block numbered 3, refer to it as:

```
..%..%3%1%R
```

4 Shakti Natural Language Analyzer

Shakti Analyzer has been designed for analyzing natural languages. Originally, it was available for analyzing English as part of the Shakti[5] English-Hindi machine translation system. It has now been extended for analyzing a number of Indian languages as mentioned later (Section-6.1).

The Shakti Analyzer can incorporate new modules as black boxes or as open-source software. The simplicity of the overall architecture makes it easy to do so. Different available English parsers have been extensively adapted, and the version used by Shakti system runs using Collins parser.

Shakti analyzer combines rule-based approach with statistical approach. The SSF representation is designed to keep both kinds of information. The rules are mostly linguistic in nature, and the statistical approach tries to infer or use linguistic information. For example, statistical POS tagger tries to infer linguistic (part-of-speech) tags, whereas WSD module uses grammatical relations together with statistics to disambiguate the word sense.

The system has a number of innovative design principles which are described below.

4.1 System Organization Principles

A number of system organization principles have been used which have led to the rapid development of the system. While the principles by themselves might not appear to be new, their application is perhaps new.

4.1.1 Modularity

The system consists of a large number of modules, each one of which typically performs a small logical task. This allows the overall machine translation task to be broken up into a large number of small sub-tasks, each of which can be accomplished separately. Currently the system (as used in the Shakti system)

[5] http:/shakti.iiit.ac.in

has 69 different modules. About 9 modules are used for analyzing the source language (English), 24 modules are used for performing bilingual tasks such as substituting target language roots and reordering etc., and the remaining modules are used for generating target language.

4.1.2 Simplicity of Organization

The overall system architecture is kept extremely simple. All modules operate on data in SSF . They communicate with each other via SSF.

The attribute value pairs allow features or properties to be specified with every node. Relations of different types across nodes can also be specified using an attribute-value like representation. The representation is specially designed to allow different levels and kinds of linguistic analyses to be stored. The developer uses APIs to store or access information regarding structure of trees and attribute value pairs.

4.1.3 Designed to Deal with Failure

NLP analysis modules are known to have limited coverage. They are not always able to produce an output. They fail to produce output either because of limits of the best known algorithms or incompleteness of data or rules. For example, a sentential parser might fail to parse either because it does not know how to deal with a construction or because a dictionary entry is missing. Similarly, a chunker or part of speech tagger might fail, at times, to produce an analysis. The system is designed to deal with failure at every step in the pipeline. This is facilitated by a common representation for the outputs of the POS tagger, chunker and parser (all in SSF). The downstream modules continue to operate on the data stream, albeit less effectively, when a more detailed analysis is not available. (If all modules were to fail, a default rule of no-reordering and dictionary lookup would still be applied.)

As another example, if the word sense disambiguation (WSD) module fails to identify the sense of a word in the input sentence, it does not put in the sense feature for the word. This only means that the module which substitutes the target language root from the available equivalents from dictionary, will use a default rule for selecting the sense because the detailed WSD was not successful (say, due to lack of training data).

The SSF is designed to represent partial information, routinely. Appropriate modules know what to do when their desired information is available and use defaults when it is not available. In fact, for many modules, there are not just two but several levels at which they operate, depending on availability of information corresponding to that level. Each level represents a graceful degradation of output quality.

The above flexibility is achieved by using two kinds of representation: constituent level representation and feature-structure level representation. The former is used to store phrase level analysis (and partial parse etc.) and the latter for outputs of many kinds of other tasks such as WSD, TAM computation, case computation, dependency relations, etc.

4.1.4 Transparency for Developers

An extremely important characteristic for the successful development of complex software such as a machine translation system is to expose the input and output produced by every module. This transparency becomes even more important in a research environment where new ideas are constantly being tried with a high turnover of student developers.

In the Shakti system, unprecedented transparency is achieved by using a highly readable textual notation for the SSF, and requiring every module to produce output in this format. In fact, the textual SSF output of a module is not only for the human consumption, but is used by the subsequent module in the data stream as its input. This ensures that no part of the resulting analysis is left hidden in some global variables; all analysis is represented in readable SSF (otherwise it is not processed at all by the subsequent modules).

Experience has shown that this methodology has made debugging as well as the development of the system convenient for programmers and linguists alike. In case an output is not as expected, one can quickly find out which module went wrong (that is, which module did not function as expected). In fact, linguists are using the system quite effectively to debug their linguistic data with ease.

5 Implementations

A considerable repository of implementations (in code) has evolved around SSF and the analyzer. In this section we consider two of the kinds of implementations that have accumulated so far.

5.1 SSF API

Application Programming Interfaces (APIs) have been implemented in multiple programming languages to allow programmers to transparently operate on any data stored in SSF. Of these, the better designed APIs, such as those in Perl and Java, allow all kinds of operations to be performed on the SSF data. These operation include basic operations such as reading, writing and modifying the data, as well as for advanced operations such as search and bulk transformation of the data. The Java API is a part of Sanchay [6], which is a collection of tools and APIs for language processing, specially tailored for the needs of Indian languages which were not (till very recently) well supported on computers and operating systems.

The availability of decently designed APIs for SSF allow programmers to use SSF for arbitrary purposes. And they have used it successfully to build natural language systems and tools as described below.

5.2 Sanchay Corpus Query Language

Trees have a quite constrained structure, whereas graphs have somewhat anarchic structure. Threaded trees (Ait-Mokhtar et al., 2002; Larchevelque, 2002) provided a middle ground between the two. They start with trees as the core structure, but they allow constrained links between the nodes of a tree that a pure tree would not allow. This overlaying of constrained links over the core trees allows multiple layers and/or types of annotation to be stored in the same structure. With a little more improvisation, we can even have links across sentences, i.e., at the discourse level (see section-3.3). It is possible, for example, to have a phrase structure tree (the core tree) overlaid with a dependency tree (via constrained links or 'threads'), just as it is possible to have POS tagged and chunked data to be overlaid with named entities and discourse relations.

The Sanchay Corpus Query Language (SCQL) (Singh, 2012) is a query language designed for threaded trees. It so turns out that SSF is also a representation that can be viewed as threaded trees. Thus, the SCQL can work over data in SSF. This language has a simple, intuitive and concise syntax and high expressive power. It allows not only to search for complicated patterns with short queries but also allows data manipulation and specification of arbitrary return values. Many of the commonly used tasks that otherwise require writing programs, can be performed with one or more queries.

6 Applications

6.1 Sampark Machine Translation Architecture

Overcoming the language barrier in the Indian sub-continent is a very challenging task[7]. Sampark[8] is an effort in this direction. Sampark has been developed as part of the consortium project called Indian Language to India Language Machine translation (ILMT) funded by TDIL program of Department of Information Technology, Government of India. Work on this project is contributed to by 11 major research centres across India working on Natural Language Processing.

Sampark, or the ILMT project, has developed language technology for 9 Indian languages resulting in MT for 18 language pairs. These are: 14 bi-directional systems between Hindi and Urdu / Punjabi / Telugu / Bengali / Tamil / Marathi / Kannada and 4 bi-directional systems between Tamil and Malayalam / Telugu. Out of these, 8 pairs have been exposed via a web interface. A REST API is also available to acess the machine translation system over the Internet.

[6] `http://sanchay.co.in`

[7] There are 22 constitutionally recognized languages in India, and many more which are not recognized. Hindi, Bengali, Telugu, Marathi, Tamil and Urdu are among the major languages of the world in terms of number of speakers, summing up to a total of 850 million.

[8] `http://sampark.org.in`

The Sampark system uses Computational Paninian Grammar (CPG) (Bharati et al., 1995), in combination with machine learning. Thus, it is a hybrid system using both rule-based and statistical approaches. There are 13 major modules that together form a hybrid system. The machine translation system is based on the analyze-transfer-generate paradigm. It starts with an analysis of the source language sentence. Then a transfer of structure and vocabulary to target language is carried out. Finally the target language is generated. One of the benefits of this approach is that the language analyzer for a particular language can be developed once and then be combined with generators for other languages, making it easier to build a machine translation system for new pairs of languages.

Indian languages have a lot of similarities in grammatical structures, so only shallow parsing was found to be adequate for the purposes of building a machine translation system. Transfer grammar component has also been kept simple. Domain dictionaries are used to cover domain specific aspects.

At the core of the Sampark architecture is an enhanced version of the Shakti Natural Language Analyzer. The individual modules may, of course, be different for different language pairs, but the pipelined architecture bears close resemblance to the Shakti machine translation system. And it uses the Shakti Standard Format as the blackboard (Erman et al., 1980) on which the different modules (POS taggers, chunkers, named entity recognzier, transfer grammar module etc.) operate, that is, read from and write to. SSF thus becomes the glue that ties together all the modules in all the MT systems for the various language pairs. The modules are not only written in different programming languages, some of them are rule-based, whereas others are statistical.

The use of SSF as the underlying default representation helps to control the complexity of the overall system. It also helps to achieve unprecedented transparency for input and output for every module. Readability of SSF helps in development and debugging because the input and output of any module can be easily seen and read by humans, whether linguists or programmers. Even if a module fails, SSF helps to run the modules without any effect on normal operation of system. In such a case, the output SSF would have unfilled value of an attribute and downstream modules continue to operate on the data stream.

6.2 Annotation Interfaces and Other Tools

Sanchay, mentioned above, has a syntactic annotation interface that has been used for development of treebanks for Indian languages (Begum et al., 2008). These treebanks have been one of the primary sources of information for the development the Sampark machine translation systems, among other things. This syntactic annotation interface provides facilities for everything that is required to be done to transform the selected data in the raw text format to the final annotated treebank. The usual stages of annotation include POS tagging, morphological annotation, chunking and dependency annotation. This interface has evolved over a period of several years based on the feedback received from the annotators and other users. There are plans to use the interface for similar annotation for even more languages.

The underlying default format used in the above interface is SSF. The advantages of using SSF for this purpose are similar to those mentioned earlier for purposes such as building machine translation systems. The complete process of annotation required to build a full-fledged treebank is complicated and there are numerous issues that have to be taken care of. The blackboard-like nature of SSF allows for a smooth shifts between different stages of annotation, even going back to an earlier stage, if necessary, to correct mistakes. It allows all the annotation information to be situated in one contiguous place.

The interface uses the Java API for SSF, which is perhaps the most developed among the different APIs for SSF. The API (a part of Sanchay) again allows transparency for the programmer as far as manipulating the data is concerned. It also ensures that there are fewer bugs when new programmers work on any part of the system where SSF data is being used. One recent addition to the interface was a GUI to correct mistakes in treebanks (Agarwal et al., 2012).

The syntactic annotation interface is not the only interface in Sanchay that uses SSF. Some other interfaces do that too. For example, there are sentence alignment and word alignment interfaces, which also use the same format for similar reasons. Thus, it is even possible to build parallel treebanks in SSF using the Sanchay interfaces.

Then there are other tools in Sanchay such as the integrated tool for accessing language resources (Singh and Ambati, 2010). This tool allows various kinds of language resources, including those in SSF, to be accessed, searched and manipulated through the inter-connected annotation interfaces and the SSF API. There is also a text editor in Sanchay that is specially tailored for Indian languages and it can validate SSF (Singh, 2008).

The availability of a corpus query language (section-5.2) that is implemented in Sanchay and that can be used for data in SSF is another big facilitator for anyone who wants to build new tools for language processing and wants to operate on linguistic data.

Apart from these, a number of research projects have used SSF (the representation or the analyzer) directly or indirectly, that is, either for theoretical frameworks or as part of the implementation (Bharati et al., 2009; Gadde et al., 2010; Husain et al., 2011).

7 Conclusion

We described a readable representation scheme called Shakti Standard Format (SSF). We showed how this scheme (an instance of the blackboard architectural model), which is based on certain organizational principles such as modularity, simplicity, robustness and transparency, can be used to create not only a linguistic analysis engine (Shakti Natural Language Analyzer), but can be used for arbitrary other purposes wherever linguistic analysis is one of the tasks. We briefly described the machine translation systems (Shakti and Sampark) which use this scheme at their core level. Similarly, we described how it can be used for creation of language resources (such as treebanks) and the annotation interfaces used to create these resources. It has also figured in several research projects so far. We mentioned one query language (Sanchay Corpus Query Language) that operates on this representation scheme and has been integrated with the annotation interfaces. Overall, the representation scheme has been successful at building infrastructure for language technology over the last more than a decade. The scheme is theory neutral and can be used for both phrase structure grammar and for dependency grammar.

References

Rahul Agarwal, Bharat Ram Ambati, and Anil Kumar Singh. 2012. A GUI to Detect and Correct Errors in Hindi Dependency Treebank. In *Proceedings of the Eighth International Conference on Language Resources and Evaluation (LREC)*, Instanbul, Turkey. ELRA.

S. Ait-Mokhtar, J.P. Chanod, and C. Roux. 2002. Robustness beyond shallowness: incremental deep parsing. *Natural Language Engineering*, 8(2-3):121144, January.

Alessandro Di Bari, Alessandro Faraotti, Carmela Gambardella, and Guido Vetere. 2013. A Model-driven approach to NLP programming with UIMA. In *UIMA@GSCL*, pages 2–9.

Rafiya Begum, Samar Husain, Arun Dhwaj, Dipti Misra Sharma, Lakshmi Bai, and Rajeev Sangal. 2008. Dependency Annotation Scheme for Indian Languages. In *Proceedings of The Third International Joint Conference on Natural Language Processing (IJCNLP)*, Hyderabad, India.

Ashkar Bharati, Vineet Chaitanya, and Rajeev Sangal. 1995. *Natural Language Processing: A Paninian Perspective*. Prentice-Hall of India Pvt. Ltd.

Akshar Bharati, Samar Husain, Phani Gadde, Bharat Ambati, Dipti M Sharma, and Rajeev Sangal. 2009. A Modular Cascaded Approach to Complete Parsing. In *Proceedings of the COLIPS International Conference on Asian Language Processing 2009 (IALP)*, Singapore.

Steven Bird. 2002. NLTK: The Natural Language Toolkit. In *In Proceedings of the ACL Workshop on Effective Tools and Methodologies for Teaching Natural Language Processing and Computational Linguistics. Philadelphia: Association for Computational Linguistics*.

Noam Chomsky. 1957. *Syntactic Structures*. The Hague/Paris: Mouton.

Hamish Cunningham, Diana Maynard, Kalina Bontcheva, Valentin Tablan, Niraj Aswani, Ian Roberts, Genevieve Gorrell, Adam Funk, Angus Roberts, Danica Damljanovic, Thomas Heitz, Mark A. Greenwood, Horacio Saggion, Johann Petrak, Yaoyong Li, and Wim Peters. 2011. *Text Processing with GATE (Version 6)*.

Lee D. Erman, Frederick Hayes-Roth, Victor R. Lesser, and D. Raj Reddy. 1980. The Hearsay-II Speech-Understanding System: Integrating Knowledge to Resolve Uncertainty. *ACM Comput. Surv.*, 12(2):213–253, June.

D. Ferrucci and A. Lally. 2004. UIMA: an architectural approach to unstructured information processing in the corporate research environment. *Natural Language Engineering*, 10(3-4):327–348.

Phani Gadde, Karan Jindal, Samar Husain, Dipti Misra Sharma, and Rajeev Sangal. 2010. Improving Data Driven Dependency Parsing using Clausal Information. In *Proceedings of 11th Annual Conference of the North American Chapter of the Association for Computational Linguistics (NAACL-HLT)*, Los Angeles.

Samar Husain, Phani Gadde, Joakim Nivre, and Rajeev Sangal. 2011. Clausal Parsing Helps Data-driven Dependency Parsing: Experiments with Hindi. In *Proceedings of Fifth International Joint Conference on Natural Language Processing (IJCNLP)*, Thailand.

J.M. Larchevelque. 2002. Optimal Incremental Parsing. *ACM Transactions on Programing Languages and Systems*, 17(1):115, January.

Yaoyong Li, Kalina Bontcheva, and Hamish Cunningham. 2009. Adapting SVM for Data Sparseness and Imbalance: A Case Study on Information Extraction. *Natural Language Engineering*, 15(2):241–271.

Tae-Gil Noh and Sebastian Padó. 2013. Using UIMA to Structure An Open Platform for Textual Entailment. In *UIMA@GSCL*, pages 26–33.

Anil Kumar Singh and Bharat Ambati. 2010. An Integrated Digital Tool for Accessing Language Resources. In *Proceedings of the Seventh International Conference on Language Resources and Evaluation (LREC)*, Malta. ELRA.

Anil Kumar Singh. 2008. A Mechanism to Provide Language-Encoding Support and an NLP Friendly Editor. In *Proceedings of the Third International Joint Conference on Natural Language Processing (IJCNLP)*, Hyderabad, India. AFNLP.

Anil Kumar Singh. 2012. A Concise Query Language with Search and Transform Operations for Corpora with Multiple Levels of Annotation. In *Proceedings of the Eighth International Conference on Language Resources and Evaluation (LREC)*, Instanbul, Turkey. ELRA.

L. Tesniere. 1959. *Elements de syntaxe structurale*. Paris: Klincksieck.

Quo Vadis UIMA?

Thilo Götz
IBM Germany R&D

Jörn Kottmann
Sandstone SA

Alexander Lang
IBM Germany R&D

Abstract

In this position paper, we will examine the current state of UIMA from the perspective of a text analytics practitioner, and propose an evolution of the architecture that overcomes some of the current shortcomings.

1 Introduction

UIMA (Unstructured Information Management Architecture, (UIMA, 2014)) became an Apache open source project in 2006. By that time, it had already seen about 5 years of development inside IBM. That is, it was already quite mature when it came to Apache. The core of UIMA has seen relatively little development since then, but the world around it has moved on. Thus, we should ask ourselves: how does UIMA currently fit into the software landscape, and what could be directions for future development to ensure that the fit remains good?

At its core, UIMA is a component framework that facilitates the combination of various text analytics components. Components are combined into analysis chains. Simple chains are relatively easy to build, more complex workflows are difficult.

UIMA components define and publish their own data models. The actual data is handled by the framework, and created and queried via APIs. Methods to serialize the data, e.g., for network transport, are also provided by the framework. The data access and component APIs exist for Java and C/C++, so that it is possible to combine Java and native components in a single analysis chain.

Over the years, the UIMA eco system has grown to include scale out frameworks that sit on top of the core and provide single or multinode scale out for UIMA analysis.

2 How does UIMA integrate with other frameworks?

The short answer is: it doesn't, and that is where we see the biggest chance of evolution for the future. UIMA is a framework itself, and does not integrate well with other frameworks. It has its own component architecture, its own idea of logging, its own idea of controlling file system access, etc.

This was fine at the time UIMA was built as we didn't have generic component frameworks as we have them today (actually they did exist, but they were not successful). It is still fine today if you just want to run a few files from disk, or simply don't need another framework.

However, nowadays general purpose (component) frameworks are in widespread use. On the one hand, we have enterprise frameworks such as J2EE (J2EE, 2014) and Spring (Spring, 2014) that host classic n-tier applications with some kind of http frontend. On the other, we have big data scale out frameworks such as Apache Hadoop (data at rest, (Hadoop, 2014)) or Apache Storm (data in motion, streaming, (Storm, 2014)). If you are building a non-trivial application, chances are good that you will make use of the many services such frameworks offer and base you application on one of them.

For example, imagine you want to scale out your analytics with Apache Hadoop. As long as you run your entire pipeline in a single mapper, everything is fine. There may be a few details that need to be ironed out, but in general, this kind of scale out scenario works pretty well. However, suppose you want

Proceedings of the Workshop on Open Infrastructures and Analysis Frameworks for HLT, pages 77–82, Dublin, Ireland, August 23rd 2014.

to run part of your analytics in a mapper, and another in a reducer, because you need to do aggregation of some kind. So you need to serialize the results of your first analysis step, and pass them on to the the second one. While this can be done with quite a bit of work and deep UIMA skills, it is much more complicated than it ought to be.

When we consider data-in-motion scenarios that are handled by Apache Storm or similar frameworks, this issue becomes even more pressing. There the individual units of processing are usually very small, and the framework handles the workflow. This is completely incompatible with the UIMA approach where UIMA needs to know about the entire processing pipeline to be able to instantiate the individual components. If every annotator works by itself and doesn't know where its next data package will come from, coordinating the data transfer between all those components becomes a huge effort.

It should be noted that even if you are willing to stay completely within the UIMA framework, there are things you might reasonably want to do that are difficult to impossible. For example, you can not take two analysis chains that somebody else has configured and combine them into one. Suppose you obtained a tokenizer and POS tagger from one source (so an aggregate analysis engine in UIMA speak), and some other chain that builds on that from somewhere else. You can't just combine the two, because it isn't possible to make an aggregate of aggregates. You need to take everything apart and then manually reassemble the whole thing to make one big analysis chain. Generally, this is possible, but it can be very difficult for something that should be really simple to do.

Over the years, UIMA has accumulated its own set of scale out frameworks. While this is ok if all you want to do happens in UIMA, that is rarely the case for most industrial applications. Instead, the framework is chosen for the kinds of data that are expected, or for how it fits into the rest of the software landscape. So a UIMA specific scale out framework extension is at best a niche solution.

Another area of business computing where UIMA plays no role at all today is mobile. UIMA is just too fat to run on a mobile device. That is not to say that there isn't a place for something like UIMA on mobile devices, but it would need to be much more lightweight than what we have today. We will make some suggestions in a later section how that could be achieved.

On a positive note, uimaFIT (Ogren and Bethard, 2009) is a move in the right direction. It allows you to configure your analysis engine from code, avoiding a lot of the top-level XML configuration that makes dealing with UIMA pipelines so cumbersome. However, UIMAFit is a layer on top of the base UIMA framework, and while it addresses some concerns, it does not do away with the underlying issues.

3 The data model

The UIMA data model is very strict in the sense that it is statically typed. That is, when an analysis chain is instantiated, all information about the kind of data that can be created in the chain needs to be known ahead of time. This approach has certain advantages, which is why it was chosen at the time. Specifically, it allows for a very compact encoding of the data in memory, and very fast access to the data.

On the other hand, such a strict data model is quite cumbersome to work with, particularly when you need to combine analysis components that may come from very different sources. For example, a common scenario is that you are using a tokenizer from some source, and want to add information to the tokens (e.g., POS tags or some kind of dictionary lookup information). You can't do this unless you modify the type system for the entire chain, even though it is only relevant from the time you actually add the information.

What we are facing is a classic trade-off between performance (memory and CPU) and developer convenience. While we still need efficient processing, given the size of the data sets we are looking at nowadays, we would still like to argue that developer time is a more expensive resource than machine power. Thus, it is time to move away from the static type system for data, and move towards a dynamic model that is a lot easier to handle from the perspective of the developer.

It should be noted that some of the constraints on data were realized by UIMA developers very early on, basically as soon as people started running analyses in more than one process (or on more than one node). Options were added on top of UIMA to make communication between loosely coupled components easier. Again however, these were added on top the base UIMA framework and are essentially just used by UIMA's own scale out frameworks. That is, they are quite difficult to use by end users who want to use a different framework for scale out.

Another point that is made difficult by a static type system is the caching of analysis results in (relational or other) databases. This is a point that comes up again and again on the UIMA users' mailing list. Actually, it is not so much the writing out as the reading in of previous results when your data model has changed in some minor way that doesn't even affect what you want to do with the data. Here also, a dynamic approach to data modelling would go a long way towards simplifying this process.

Finally, the need for the JCas (a system where you can offline create Java classes for your data structures) would go away entirely.

4 Analysis component reuse

The main raison d'être for UIMA is analysis engine reuse. Why then do we often find it so difficult to reuse existing components?

The main obstacle for an implementor who wants to make an analysis engine (AE) reusable is that the target type system is not known to and varies between users. The best a reusable AE can do is to allow users to map the input and output types as part of the configuration. Sadly, UIMA doesn't support this use case explicitly. There are no types for configuration values which are intended to contain type system values such as UIMA type or feature names.

Certain type systems are too complex for a type mapping and sometimes an AE is programmed against a specific type system. To integrate an existing AE in such a scenario is only possible with an adapter in front and behind the AE in order to convert the input and output types dynamically. The adapters must be implemented as an AE and they increase the complexity of the UIMA pipeline.

An implementor who updates an AE can only update the jar file used to distribute it to the users. An AE consists of two parts, the implementing classes and a XML Descriptor file. The descriptor file contains both the schema for the configuration and the user defined configuration values. Users typically copy this file and change the configuration values. An implementor can't update the users' XML descriptor to a newer version. A user will have to manually merge the changes of the customized file and the updated descriptor.

Even though it is possible to build reusable UIMA AEs, users repeatedly prefer integrating common open source NLP components themselves rather than dealing with the existing UIMA integrations (e.g., Apache OpenNLP). This is quite sad given that UIMA set out to make this sort of manual integration effort redundant.

5 Generic analysis engines

Another advantage of having a dynamic type system that can be added to at runtime would be to make generic analysis engines easier to develop and more convenient to use. By a generic annotator, we mean an annotator that is configured by the end user to perform a certain task. This could be for example a generic dictionary matcher, or a regular expression matcher as they already exists on Apache as a downloadable components.

So what is the issue then? Today in UIMA, the type system is defined ahead of time. So it is not possible to write, e.g., a regex matcher that creates a new kind of annotation, unless that annotation is also added in the type system. So you can either require users of such generic annotators to always change things in two locations at the same time: the type system specification, and the regex configuration. We all know what kind of chaos that leads to. Or you can have the generic annotator produce a generic annotation, such as a `RegexAnnotation`. The results range from the awkward (because results need to be transferred to the real target annotation) to the unusable (because the fixed generic annotations are not flexible enough to represent the intended results).

If on the other hand the type system was dynamic, generic annotators could create new data types at runtime from an end user specification, with no extra effort.

6 Design point: a layered architecture

In this section, we will propose a design that should overcome the shortcomings of UIMA that we have identified. While there are many specifics to be worked out, there are sufficient details to form the basis of an ongoing discussion. We'll begin with an overview of the design we envision, and then drill down into some details.

1. Off-line, serialized data layer (JSON and/or XML)
2. In-memory data access and creation APIs
3. Data (de)serialization
4. Component instantiation (with data source and sink)
5. Workflow
6. Application layer (logging, disk access etc.)

This is to be read from top to bottom as layers that only depend on the previous layers and are fully functional by themselves (without lower layers). We'll look at some aspects of this design proposal below.

6.1 Serialized data definition

As the basic layer of UIMA, we propose a non-programmatic, off-line format for UIMA data. Independently of what that format actually is, it is the basic level at which software components can interoperate. This is what goes over the wire/air, what is written to storage. So it is important that there is one well-defined serial format that everybody understands.

We follow the OASIS UIMA standard (Ferrucci et al., 2009) in this approach. Of course the format chosen in the standard (XMI) is very complicated. The argument given at the time was that XMI is itself a standard and that it would thereby be easy to achieve integration with other tools using this standard. If any such integration has ever materialized, we don't know about it. It seems much more important to use a format that is just powerful enough to do what needs to be done, and which is at the same time as simple as possible.

A likely candidate for such a format is JSON (ECMA, 2013). It is a simple, human readable format with very widespread use and good tooling support. There is also built-in support for many of the constructs we are used to in UIMA. Special support would have to be defined for annotations, and for references to build true graph structures (JSON just defines trees, like XML). There is no reason not to have an XML format as well, if that is desired, and tools that translate between the two.[1]

6.2 In-memory data access

By this we essentially mean what is now the UIMA Common Analysis System (CAS, (Götz and Suhre, 2004)). Apart from the changes for a dynamic type system, which might not be so large, our layering approach requires that a CAS should be independent of the rest of the framework, which is not the case today. However, if we give up on the idea of a global static type system, we are most of the way there.

If we take the approach from the last section seriously (i.e., that the serialized data format is the basis of our architecture), then the in-memory APIs need to map pretty directly to the external data definition.

6.3 Data serialization and deserialization

There is not much to say about this point. Data that was defined in terms of the in-memory API needs to be serialized to the external format, and vice versa. A more relaxed approach to the data model should make things a lot easier on this front.

[1] Two reviewers have independently remarked that if that is the case, we might as well stick with XMI, and have a translation to/from JSON. At a certain level, that is correct. However, that would require anybody who wants to deliver a compliant service to read/write the verbose and complicated XMI format. That seems counterproductive as the whole idea is to make the use of UIMA at lot easier than it is today.

6.4 Type System mapping and adapters

A type system mapping specifies which input and output types an analysis engine should use. A dynamic type system allows an analysis engine to create or extend the specified output types. Analysis engines are typically chained together in a pipeline, where the outputs of the previous analysis engines are the inputs of the following analysis engines. Just by defining the type mappings, the analysis engines will be able to dynamically create the necessary types.

We see the type system mapping as a useful tool for analysis engines when there is a common understanding in the community on how to encode the information in types. If there is a disagreement on how to model the data, the analysis engine should use an adapter to translate between the two type system worlds. With a dynamic type system the analysis engine can create input and output types in the flavor the implementor prefers and adapters can create the output types the user prefers.

6.5 The upper layers

Our proposal de-emphasizes the upper layers of the architecture, simply because we expect that many, if not most, applications will run on some sort of component framework anyway. What we have defined up to now is sufficient to run the kinds of scenarios that we described in the earlier sections.

We also believe that the configuration information that currently must be defined in the UIMA XML component descriptors is much better left to specific code of the individual components (note that one of the goals of uimaFIT is just that). If a component has a few settings you can adjust, then let there be APIs for those settings. It is so much easier to do this in your programming IDE than to fiddle with some poorly documented options in XML.

Nonetheless, for analysis workflows where the entire flow is running in a single process, it is still useful to have standard APIs that facilitate component instantiation, definition of analysis chains or simple workflows, and finally an application layer that can do some sort of simple document I/O. This is still useful for debugging, tooling and to build demo applications.

7 Conclusion

As we hope to have illustrated, UIMA is faced with a number of challenges. The UIMA framework doesn't integrate well with other framworks. Although UIMA can be used together with other frameworks, the integration is much more complicated than it should be. The statically typed data model is troublesome to work with. The type system is specified ahead of time and can't be modified during runtime. Type systems are often defined on a per-project basis and are incompatible with each other. Due to these limitations the reuse of UIMA analysis components across projects is often avoided.

For similar reasons the development of generic annotators is very limited. A generic annotator can't create new types during runtime and must either put a heavy burden on the end user, or return limited results.

To overcome these challenges, we have proposed the following changes:

- Move to a dynamic data model
- Standardize on an easy-to-use data interchange format (replace XMI by JSON, for example)
- Create a stratified architecture that supports framework integration

We have spent relatively more time talking about the perceived UIMA shortcomings than about our proposed solution. Why is that? The entire approach hinges on the decision to move to a dynamic data model. Once this step is taken, only then do certain architectural options become available. It is the crucial step, and execution of the rest of the design would not be very difficult in our opinion.

Our point of departure was the fact that UIMA analysis is difficult to integrate with other frameworks. However, we have seen that many current issues are also addressed by this evolution. We hope this paper will spawn a discussion among UIMA users and developers both, so we can make sure UIMA stays abreast of technical developments and continues to be relevant to the text analytics and computational linguistics communities at large.

References

ECMA. 2013. The JSON data interchange format. ECMA-404 (RFC 4627). Technical report, ECMA International. http://www.ecma-international.org/publications/files/ECMA-ST/ECMA-404.pdf.

David Ferrucci, Adam Lally, Karin Verspoor, and Eric Nyberg. 2009. Unstructured Information Management Architecture (UIMA) Version 1.0, OASIS Standard. Technical report, OASIS.

Thilo Götz and Oliver Suhre. 2004. Design and implementation of the UIMA Common Analysis System. *IBM Syst. J.*, 43(3):476–489, July.

Hadoop. 2014. Apache Hadoop. http://hadoop.apache.org/.

J2EE. 2014. Java Enterprise Edition. http://www.oracle.com/technetwork/java/javaee/overview/.

Philip Ogren and Steven Bethard. 2009. Building test suites for UIMA components. In *Proceedings of the Workshop on Software Engineering, Testing, and Quality Assurance for Natural Language Processing (SETQA-NLP 2009)*, pages 1–4, Boulder, Colorado, June. Association for Computational Linguistics.

Spring. 2014. Spring Framework. http://projects.spring.io/spring-framework/.

Storm. 2014. Apache Storm. http://storm.incubator.apache.org/.

UIMA. 2014. Apache UIMA. http://uima.apache.org/.

Integrated Tools for Query-driven Development of Light-weight Ontologies and Information Extraction Components

Martin Toepfer[1] **Georg Fette**[1] **Philip-Daniel Beck**[1] **Peter Kluegl**[12] **Frank Puppe**[1]

[1]Department of Computer Science VI
University of Würzburg, Am Hubland
Würzburg, Germany
first.last@uni-wuerzburg.de

[2]Comprehensive Heart Failure Center
University of Würzburg, Straubmühlweg 2a
Würzburg, Germany
pkluegl@uni-wuerzburg.de

Abstract

This paper reports on a user-friendly terminology and information extraction development environment that integrates into existing infrastructure for natural language processing and aims to close a gap in the UIMA community. The tool supports domain experts in data-driven and manual terminology refinement and refactoring. It can propose new concepts and simple relations and includes an information extraction algorithm that considers the context of terms for disambiguation. With its tight integration of easy-to-use and technical tools for component development and resource management, the system is especially designed to shorten times necessary for domain adaptation of such text processing components. Search support provided by the tool fosters this aspect and is helpful for building natural language processing modules in general. Specialized queries are included to speed up several tasks, for example, the detection of new terms and concepts, or simple quality estimation without gold standard documents. The development environment is modular and extensible by using Eclipse and the Apache UIMA framework. This paper describes the system's architecture and features with a focus on search support. Notably, this paper proposes a generic middleware component for queries in a UIMA based workbench.

1 Introduction

According to general understanding, a specification of relevant concepts, relations, and their types is required to build Information Extraction (IE) components. Named Entity Recognition (NER) systems in the newspaper domain, for example, try to detect concepts like persons, organizations, or locations. Regarding clinical text, it has been shown that lookup-based approaches (Tanenblatt et al., 2010) can achieve high precision and recall if a terminology exists that maps terms to their meanings. However, this approach is not directly applicable if such resources are not available for a certain language or subdomain, or if the domain and its terminology are changing. Unsupervised methods can help to find and to group the relevant terms of a domain, for example, into concept hierarchies (Cimiano et al., 2005). Nevertheless, automatically derived terminologies are not perfect, and there are many applications that require high precision knowledge resources and representations, for instance, to build up a clinical data warehouse. In this case, automatically generated ontologies have to be refined by domain experts like clinicians, which imposes special requirements on the usability of the tools.

There have been several efforts to support ontology extraction and refinement (Cimiano and Völker, 2005), predominantly with text processing based on the GATE (Cunningham et al., 2011) infrastructure. In the Apache UIMA (Ferrucci and Lally, 2004) community[1], several tools exist that ease system development and management. Much work has, for instance, been spent on pipeline management, rule development (Kluegl et al., 2009), or evaluation. Terminology and ontology development support, however, have not gained as much attention in the context of this framework by now. This is surprising since the integration of tools for terminology development and especially terminology generation and information extraction into existing infrastructure for text processing is promising. Actually, the approach

[1]http://uima.apache.org/

Proceedings of the Workshop on Open Infrastructures and Analysis Frameworks for HLT, pages 83–92,
Dublin, Ireland, August 23rd 2014.

taken in this paper regards terminology creation and information extraction as two related tasks. The proposed system aims to assist users in the development of components that extract information with lexical resources gathered during the specification of the concepts of the domain.

This paper introduces *Edtgar*: a user-friendly integrated terminology development environment. It provides many features that help domain experts to construct and refine light-weight ontologies driven by flexible corpus queries. In this work, "light-weight ontology" means that we focus on simple relations, as well as restricted inference. We call the knowledge representation "terminology" since the tool aims to manage lexical information for information extraction. The major components of the system are a terminology editor, a plug-in concept for terminology extraction and an information extraction API, as well as support for corpus queries. Special views show extraction statistics, provide semi-automatic annotation of gold standard documents, as well as evaluation and deployment support. The tool comprises an implementation for terminology induction and an information extraction algorithm that considers contexts. In order to keep the system modular and extensible, it integrates into Eclipse[2] and uses the Apache UIMA framework. Apache UIMA provides a well-established framework for text processing, hence, a variety of natural language processing components can easily be integrated, for example, by accessing component repositories like DKPro Core[3]. At the technical level, the default processing components of the proposed system use a combination of Apache UIMA Ruta[4] scripts and custom analysis engines implemented in Java. As a consequence, the tight integration of the terminology development tools into Apache UIMA's Eclipse Tools and Apache UIMA Ruta's rule engine and workbench allows technical engineers to use several existing features.

The structure of the paper is as follows: Section 2 gives a brief overview of ontology development systems and tools. Section 3 and 4 introduce the tool and its support for corpus queries. Results of a case study are given in Section 5. Finally, we conclude in Section 6.

2 Related Work

Most of all, our work relates to environments and frameworks for ontology learning, editing, and refinement. We first give a brief overview of such systems with a focus on open source and research related systems[5]. Afterwards, we discuss some popular query tools that come into question for integration into natural language processing environments.

OntoLT (Buitelaar et al., 2004) is a plugin for the ontology editor Protégé. It aims to derive ontological concepts and relations from plain text by defining XPath expressions over linguistic structures, e.g., subject object relations under constraints like specific lemmas. Manual annotation of ontology concept mentions can be performed with the Protégé plugin Knowtator[6].

Very similar to our work is the *NeOn toolkit*[7]. It is an Eclipse based ontology development environment. There are many plugins available that extend NeOn toolkit's functionality. For instance, the GATE Webservice plugin[8] and its TermRaider component automatically generate ontological information. One of the plugins for NeOn is the work by Cimiano and Völker, who proposed *Text2Onto*[9] (Cimiano and Völker, 2005), which is a framework that allows to apply ontology learning and change discovery algorithms. Its central data structure is called probabilistic ontology model (POM). It is not providing statistics but stores values that represent concept or relation extraction certainty. Text2Onto's natural language processing is based on GATE and the rule engine JAPE. Similar to our work, Text2Onto aims to provide an easy-to-use user interface.

Most of the tools mentioned above either use GATE or proprietary data formats for linguistic representations. We believe that there is a need for a tool based on UIMA. Our tool aims to provide an integrated

[2] `http://eclipse.org/`
[3] `https://www.ukp.tu-darmstadt.de/software/dkpro-core/?no_cache=1`
[4] `https://uima.apache.org/ruta.html`
[5] There are related commercial solutions, for instance, `http://www.poolparty.biz/`
[6] `http://knowtator.sourceforge.net/`
[7] `http://neon-toolkit.org`
[8] `http://neon-toolkit.org/wiki/Gate_Webservice`
[9] `https://code.google.com/p/text2onto/`

development environment that includes terminology development and allows to use already available features provided by Eclipse plugins related to UIMA. Thereby, we ease development, introspection, debugging, and testing of all kinds of UIMA annotation engines involved in system and terminology development. Hence, the components that extract and refine terminologies based on natural language processing can easily be adapted, for example, segmentation rules written in UIMA Ruta's workbench. The same argumentation applies to information extraction components or linguistic preprocessors like chunkers that are involved in both tasks. Contrary to most other tools, we do not consider complex relations. Instead, we focus on easy-to-understand inference and relations.

In the UIMA community, Fiorelli et al. proposed the computer-aided ontology development architecture (CODA) (Fiorelli et al., 2010) that consists of the tasks: ontology learning, population of ontologies, and linguistic enrichment. Fiorelli et al. describe how an integrated ontology development system based on UIMA could look like, however, their system *UIMAST* concentrates on ontology population aspects. By contrast, this paper also considers construction tasks and describes tooling for editing and refining light-weight ontologies either manually or based on document collections.

Table 1 compares qualitative features of different query tools which are described below. Since semantic search is an active field of research, we can only give a brief overview focused on popular tools for UIMA and GATE. We put special emphasis on tools that can be easily integrated into an Eclipse-based environment.

Tool	Framework	Index	Syntax	IDE Integration
Ruta Query View	UIMA	no[a]	expert	Eclipse
Lucas / Lucene	UIMA	yes	user-friendly	-
GATE Mímir	GATE	yes	medium	-
GATE Annic	GATE	yes	medium	GATE Developer[b]

[a] uses only UIMA's annotation index
[b] `https://gate.ac.uk/family/developer.html`

Table 1: Qualitative comparison of query tools.

The UIMA Ruta workbench contains a *query view* that enables to search in document collections with arbitrary queries formulated as rules. For instance, `Segment{-CONTAINS(CONCEPT)}` matches segment annotations that do not contain any concept annotation. With regard to usability for domain experts, this tool has a drawback: users have to be familiar with Ruta's syntax which is in general too complex for terminology engineers. They should not have to learn a programming language to pose a query on a corpus. Another drawback of the query view is that it has no option to group search results, e.g. by their covered text. The Ruta query view is not designed for fast results on very large corpora. It iteratively processes all documents of a folder that match a user-defined filename filter, thus, queries do not run as fast as with index structures for the whole corpus. A combination of rule-based query formulation and the new middleware (Section 4) would be useful for the community.

Apache Lucene [10] is a popular search engine. Existing mapping tools like the UIMA Lucene indexer *Lucas*[11] show how UIMA pipeline results can be indexed with Lucene. This solution is attractive since Lucene's query syntax allows complex query patterns but still remains easy-to-use. For example, `valve -pulmo*` searches for documents that contain the term "valve" but do not contain terms beginning with "pulmo". Inexperienced users have a higher chance to understand the syntax because it is more similar to the one of web search engines. Lucene itself does not provide a user interface but there are tools like *Apache Solr*, or *Apache Stanbol* which is a semantic search project based on Apache Solr.

Our requirements are similar in certain aspects to *Gate mímir* [12], which is an indexing and retrieval tool for Gate. It allows to find text passages that match certain annotation or text patterns. For example,

[10] `http://lucene.apache.org/core/`
[11] `http://svn.apache.org/repos/asf/uima/addons/trunk/Lucas/`
[12] `http://gate.ac.uk/mimir/`

`transistor IN {Abstract}`[13] searches for abstracts regarding transistors. In combination with GATE's rule engine Jape[14], similar functionality can be achieved for terminology development. A query tool for document processing and retrieval based on Apache Lucene and GATE is Annic[15] (ANNotations In Context) (Aswani et al., 2005). It provides a viewer for nested annotation structures and features.

3 Edtgar: Terminology Development Environment

The system has been developed as part of a medical information extraction project that populates the data warehouse of a German hospital. Documents in clinical domains differ from the kind of text that is widely used for ontology development, hence common approaches to learn ontologies, for example, with lexical patterns, have relatively low entity acceptance rates on clinical documents (Liu et al., 2011). As a consequence, ontology learning and enrichment methods and information extraction components have to be adapted to the domain. We address this adaptation step integrating new editors, views and application logic into existing tooling for working with UIMA documents. Some features of our system are especially useful for processing clinical text but they also work for similar domains, such as advertisements, product descriptions, or semi-structured product reviews.

In order to assist users during development, we qualitatively analyzed workflows in a project with clinical reports. As a result, we identified the following steps:

1. Linguistic preprocessing: A technical engineer chooses a component for preprocessing steps like tokenization, sentence detection, part-of-speech tagging, chunking, or parsing. In our projects, a rule engineer typically adapts general rules to fit to a special domain. He modifies tokenization rules and lists of abbreviations, and specifies segmentation rules that detect relevant parts of the document, annotate sections, subsections, sentences, and segments.

2. Initial terminology generation: an algorithm automatically derives a terminology based on a corpus of plain text documents.

3. Terminology refinement: a domain expert changes the terminology until it meets subjective or objective quality criteria:

   (a) Automatically extract information according to the current state of the terminology.
   (b) Inspect extraction results.
   (c) Refine terminology: edit/add new concepts, add/update variants of existing concepts.

4. Annotation of gold standard documents. Evaluation of the information extraction component and the coverage of the terminology.

Further analysis showed different aspects of improvement that conform with common expectations:

1. Search: terminology engineers frequently need to pose different kinds of search patterns on document collections. Some of them are related to quality estimation without a gold standard.

2. Redundancy: modeling concepts independently of each other causes false negatives. Some concepts have highly redundant aspects that should be managed in a central way.

In the following, we first sketch the terminology model and then briefly report on the terminology induction, validation, and information extraction components. In this work, we put special emphasis on analysing search tools that can be used in a UIMA-based workbench. Our approach to pose queries in the workbench is discussed in Section 4.

[13] from: `http://services.gate.ac.uk/mimir/query-session-examples.pdf`
[14] `http://gate.ac.uk/sale/tao/splitch8.html`
[15] `http://gate.ac.uk/sale/tao/splitch9.html`

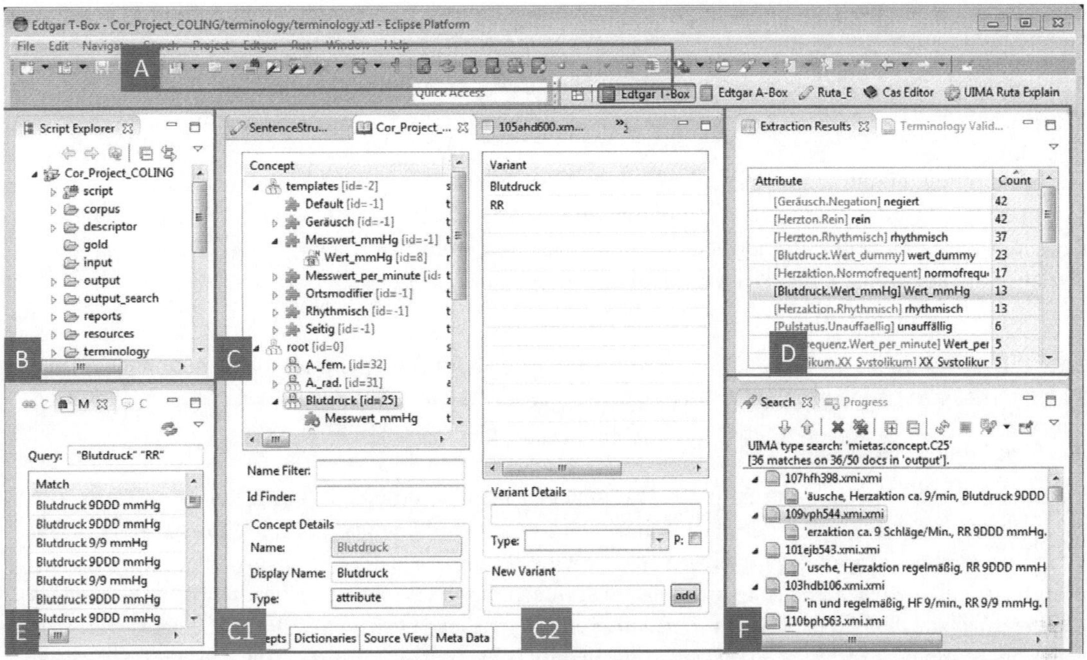

Figure 1: Edtgar T-Box Perspective: (A) Toolbar; (B) Project Structure; (C) Terminology Editor with (C1) Concept Tree, (C2) Variants; (D) Information Extraction Statistics; (E) Search View (Lucene); (F) Search Results (Filesystem: TreeViewer mode)

3.1 Terminology Model

In order to describe the information contained in documents of a domain, we follow an attribute-value model extended with concepts of type *entity* (*object*) that disambiguate different meanings of attributes.

The central aspects of our knowledge representation are given by a tuple

$$O = (T, C, D, V, R_{T\times C}, R_{T\times T}, R_{C\times V}, R_{V\times D})$$

where T, C, D, V contain templates, concepts, dictionaries, and variants, respectively. The relation $R_{T\times C}$ defines which concepts use certain templates, $R_{T\times T}$ models inter-template references. *Concepts* are the main elements of the terminology. There are several types of concepts such as objects, attributes, and values. Each concept is expressed by lexical variants (relation $R_{C\times V}$) which can be grouped by dictionaries (relation $R_{V\times D}$). *Variants* can be either simple strings or regular expressions. Attributes that belong to the same kind of semantic category typically share the same sets of values. Ontologies model this kind of relation between concepts typically by inheritance (subclass-of) or instantiation. In our terminology model, users can use *templates* to group concepts and even templates into semantic classes that share all values that are part of the template. As a consequence, the template mechanism avoids redundancy and errors in the terminology. Templates can also be used just to tag concepts. To allow users to store domain specific information, concepts can have arbitrary properties (key-value-pairs). All information of the model is de-/serializable as a single easy-to-read XML file.

3.2 Terminology Induction

Developing a terminology from scratch is costly, but some domains allow that a considerable amount of attributes and values can be automatically found. Algorithms that induce terminologies and relations can be easily plugged into the workbench through certain APIs. Per default, a simple rule-based approach based on part-of-speech tags is used. It basically finds different kinds of patterns for attributes (nouns) and values (adjectives). The algorithm uses the lemmas of lexical items to group concepts and

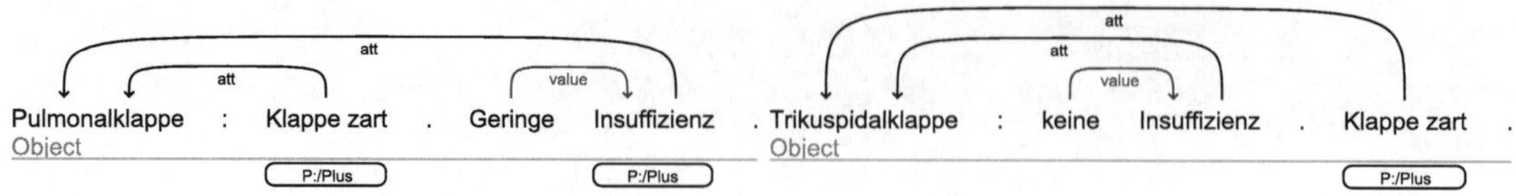

Figure 2: Ambiguous attributes: the attribute insufficiency (German: *Insuffizienz*) is both valid for the entities pulmonary valve (German: *Pulmonalklappe*) and tricuspid valve (German: *Trikuspidalklappe*). Insufficiency itself can either be negated (German: *keine*) or minor (German: *gering*). Pulmonary valve and tricuspid valve are both regular in this example (German: *Klappe zart*).

creates different variants of the concepts respectively. Probabilities that tell users how certain a concept extraction is can be optionally shown if they are provided by the algorithm.

3.3 Terminology Validation

Terminologies can become quite large, for example, in medical domains, which makes it difficult to manage them manually. For instance, it is important to avoid redundancy because keeping redundant concepts or variants in sync gets difficult. We provide different types of validators that check certain aspects of improvement and show errors and warnings. For example, missing dictionary references cause insufficient synonym lists and false negative extractions. We have a validator that creates warnings if a dictionary should be referenced instead of using only some part of this dictionary in a certain concept. There are several other validators, for instance, to detect missing template references. New validators can easily be integrated into the framework.

3.4 Information Extraction

Similar to its terminology induction module, our system has a plug-in mechanism for information extraction algorithms. By default, it contains an information extraction algorithm which allows for context-sensitive disambiguation of terms with multiple meanings. It can, for example, resolve the correct interpretation for ambiguous terms like “Klappe zart” or “Insuffizienz” as shown in Figure 2.

At first, the terminology is transformed into appropriate data structures for inference. The processing pipeline begins with finding lexemes by matching the text against regular expressions and simple strings. The next annotator segments the document into hierarchically ordered parts such as sections, subsections, sentences, segments, and tokens. This component is implemented with Ruta rules which enables rule engineers to adapt this stage to different document types and styles easily. The following stage is implemented as a Java analysis engine. At first, it finds and annotates objects, i.e., entities that are close to the root of the terminology and belong to the object type in the terminology. These concepts are typically expressed by unique variants and should not need any disambiguation. Afterwards, the algorithm tries to assign unresolved attribute entities to objects, or directly annotates special entities. Finally, the algorithm performs *light-weight inference*: first, value extractions are removed when the corresponding attribute has been negated. Second, presence annotations are added if an attribute entity requires a status value and is not negated in the sentence.

3.5 Knowledge-driven Evaluation and Status Reports

Similar to quality assurance or quality assessment in factories, users can specify assertions for text processing tasks where system behavior is expected to conform to these assertions (Wittek et al., 2013). Such expectations allow to compute quality estimates even without annotated documents. To this end, we provide special annotation types for these cases that can be categorized to distinguish different tasks or types of misclassifications. By now, knowledge-driven evaluation is realized by the contributed search commands (see Section 4). They allow to find, count, and group constraint violations which helps to estimate the quality of the text processing component and to understand the errors it makes. For example, the user can expect that all nouns should either be assigned to a concept annotation or listed in a blacklist. Elaboration of this aspect of the tool is planned for future releases.

3.6 Edtgar Workbench Overview

Edtgar's graphical user interface (see Figure 1) provides two perspectives and several views to assist the user. The heart of the tool is the *terminology editor* that allows to create or modify concepts (attributes and values, etc.), manage variants and dictionaries. If the main terminology of a project is opened, users can set the active corpus for the project, or trigger several actions. They can start terminology induction/enrichment, information extraction, or run different types of specialized or general searches on the active corpus, for example, by pressing the corresponding buttons in the toolbar. The tool also provides several other features that we do not discuss here, e.g., support for semi-automatic gold standard annotation, evaluation, documentation, and much more.

3.7 Typesystem Handling

Inspecting the results of processed documents is a visual process. Representing each concept type by a distinct annotation type has a technical advantage because occurrences of a certain type of concept can be highlighted in the UIMA CAS editor with a different color. During terminology induction, however, the terminology and the corresponding annotation types do not exist in the typesystem of the processed document. As a result, the presented framework uses a hybrid concept representation. Engines can use generic annotation types with an integer id feature to create proposal annotations for terminology generation and enrichment. These annotations are subsequently mapped to type based representations when the terminology and its typesystem have been completely defined. As a natural side-effect of terminology development, identifiers of concepts may change, for instance, if concepts are rejected or merged. The terminology editor keeps identifiers stable as long as possible since both representation schemes have problems with invalid IDs. An advantage of the ID feature based approach is that it is able to retain invalid references whereas a type-based approach looses information when documents are loaded leniently.

Besides concept annotations, the system provides framework types for different purposes. For instance, *IgnoredRegion*, *UnhandledSegment*, or *Sealed*. They allow to configure irrelevant text detection for each subdomain, enable users to find new terms, or that have been manually inspected and contain gold standard annotations, respectively.

4 Search Tools for the Workbench

An important aspect of terminology development is *search support*. It should assist users with predefined queries, e.g., to find new concepts, synonyms of concepts, or different meanings of concepts. Technical users, however, must be able to perform searches with arbitrary complex patterns. Several tasks can be regarded as corpus queries, for instance, finding measurement units or abbreviations.

In order to support domain experts, we identified three main types of queries that fit to their workflows. First of all, *Unhandled Segments Search* is a kind of false negative predictor (cf. Section 3.5). It lists all segments in the corpus that have not yet been covered either by terminological concepts or exclude patterns. This is in particular useful in clinical domains where nearly every noun phrase contains relevant information. It can, however, easily be adapted to other domains. Second, *querying specific types of extracted information* is necessary, for instance, to inspect extraction results and to judge their quality. It allows to create partial gold standards and it helps to decide if attributes have ambiguous meanings dependent on their context. Third, *constrained search* supports the terminology engineer when editing concepts or creating new entries: users often search for attributes to find their value candidates and need to see documents containing synonyms of the attribute but leaving known value terms out. Finally, if domain experts are not familiar with regular expressions, they benefit from *fast lexical search* to test their patterns.

Query Tools in Edtgar

Most of the queries mentioned above can be implemented as searches for certain annotation types (*UIMA Type Search*). For instance, segments that do not contain any extracted information (*Unhandled Segments Search*) can be annotated with a special type, and concept mentions can be annotated with types based on

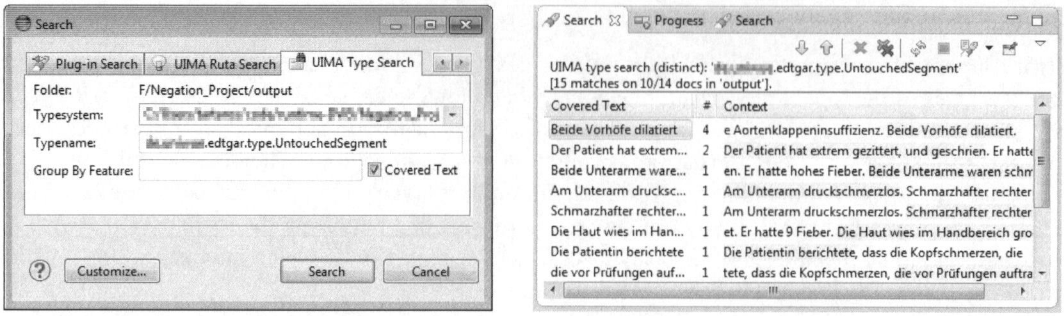

(a) Search Page for UIMA annotation types: results can be grouped by a certain feature or their covered text.

(b) Search Results Page (TableViewer mode): it shows distinct unhandled segments ordered by frequency

Figure 3: Generic Search Components

concept identifiers, e.g., `mietas.concept.C24` for the concept with the ID 24. The system provides two types of query commands that support annotation type searches.

The first query command uses a separate index over a whole corpus and provides very fast retrieval. It is based on Apache Lucene, thus Lucene's user-friendly query syntax can be used. For instance, querying "insufficiency AND aortic -moderate" retrieves sentences that contain "insufficiency" and "aortic" but not "moderate". The interface to Lucene-based queries can be seen in Figure 1 (E). The index is based on sentences and contains special fields for extracted concept annotations. For instance, "concept:24" shows sentences where the concept with the ID 24 has been extracted. Indexing can be triggered manually.

The second query command iterates over files in the filesystem and uses UIMA's index structures to find annotations of requested types. It integrates into the search framework of Eclipse. As a consequence, users can easily expand or collapse search results, browse search results, or iteratively open respective documents in a shared editor instance. The component implements a tree view (confer Figure 1 (F)) and a table view (confer Figure 3b) to show results. The programmatic search command needs a type name, a type system, and a folder. As a special feature, search results can be grouped based on their covered text or the string value of a feature of the annotations. Grouping allows to show absolute counts for each group. It helps users to find and rank relevant candidate terms and phrases. It can, however, also be used in other use cases, for example, to list all distinct person mentions in a text collection. Results can be exported as an HTML report. Figure 3a shows the generic search page for posing UIMA based queries. The folder can be selected in the script explorer (see Fig. 1 (B)). The dialog provides a combo box to choose the type system and auto-completion for the type name and group-by text widgets.

Technical users can already use the middleware in combination with rule-based queries when they create rule scripts just for this purpose. These scripts define queries and types for results. Subsequently, users apply one of the type-based search commands.

Only one of the task specific query types in the terminology development environment is not implemented as a Lucene search or an annotation type based search command: to support quick testing of regular expressions, the tool accesses the text search command of Eclipse which allows very fast search and rapid feedback.

5 Case Study

The main application of the tool is terminology generation and subsequent information extraction for a wide range of medical reports. We evaluated it in a small subdomain of the physical examination concerning the heart (cor). We gathered 200 anonymized documents from a hospital information system and divided the corpus into a training and a test set (150:50). For terminology generation, we first extracted all nouns from the training set as attributes. Then we merged similar entries and deleted irrelevant candidates. For each attribute we generated and manually adapted relevant value candidates assigning templates wherever possible. For both tasks, we applied multiple searches and used tool support for fast inspection of the relevant segments in the documents. The final terminology was used for information extraction on the test set. We measured the time necessary for terminology adaption and the precision and recall of the information extraction on the test set and additionally estimated the recall with a query as described in Section 4. The gold standard for information extraction in this feasibility study was defined by ourselves. From the training set, we extracted 20 attributes and 44 boolean and 6 numerical values. Manual correction took about 4 hours. Microaveraged precision and recall of the information extraction were 99% and 90% on the test set. The estimated recall on the test set was 84%. Roughly one half of the errors was due to unknown terminology in the test documents. The other half was mainly induced by missing variants of already known concepts. With a larger training set, these kinds of errors can be considerably reduced.

6 Summary

Ontology development and query-driven workflows have not gained as much attention in the UIMA community as, for example, pipeline management, rule development, or evaluation. Especially if ontologies are developed in order to build information extraction systems, it is desirable to have a workbench environment that integrates both tools for ontology development and information extraction. The tool suggested in this paper aims to fill this gap. It supports the creation of light-weight ontologies for information extraction, that is, it helps to find attributes and their values, and to encode simple relations between concepts. It integrates into Eclipse and lowers the bridge between different frameworks and tools. Notably, we assist users in query-driven workflows, which includes a simple way to assess quality without manually annotated documents. We plan to release the tool under an open source license.

Acknowledgments

This work was supported by the Competence Network Heart Failure, funded by the German Federal Ministry of Education and Research (BMBF01 EO1004).

References

N. Aswani, V. Tablan, K. Bontcheva, and H. Cunningham. 2005. Indexing and Querying Linguistic Metadata and Document Content. In *Proceedings of Fifth International Conference on Recent Advances in Natural Language Processing (RANLP2005)*, Borovets, Bulgaria.

Paul Buitelaar, Daniel Olejnik, and Michael Sintek. 2004. A Protégé Plug-In for Ontology Extraction from Text Based on Linguistic Analysis. In ChristophJ. Bussler, John Davies, Dieter Fensel, and Rudi Studer, editors, *The Semantic Web: Research and Applications*, volume 3053 of *Lecture Notes in Computer Science*, pages 31–44. Springer Berlin Heidelberg.

Philipp Cimiano and Johanna Völker. 2005. Text2Onto: A Framework for Ontology Learning and Data-driven Change Discovery. In *Proceedings of the 10th International Conference on Natural Language Processing and Information Systems*, NLDB'05, pages 227–238, Berlin, Heidelberg. Springer-Verlag.

Philipp Cimiano, Andreas Hotho, and Steffen Staab. 2005. Learning Concept Hierarchies from Text Corpora Using Formal Concept Analysis. *J. Artif. Int. Res.*, 24(1):305–339, August.

Hamish Cunningham, Diana Maynard, Kalina Bontcheva, Valentin Tablan, Niraj Aswani, Ian Roberts, Genevieve Gorrell, Adam Funk, Angus Roberts, Danica Damljanovic, Thomas Heitz, Mark A. Greenwood, Horacio Saggion, Johann Petrak, Yaoyong Li, and Wim Peters. 2011. *Text Processing with GATE (Version 6).*

David Ferrucci and Adam Lally. 2004. UIMA: An Architectural Approach to Unstructured Information Processing in the Corporate Research Environment. *Natural Language Engineering*, 10(3/4):327–348.

Manuel Fiorelli, Maria Teresa Pazienza, Steve Petruzza, Armando Stellato, and Andrea Turbati. 2010. Computer-aided Ontology Development: an integrated environment. In René Witte, Hamish Cunningham, Jon Patrick, Elena Beisswanger, Ekaterina Buyko, Udo Hahn, Karin Verspoor, and Anni R. Coden, editors, *New Challenges for NLP Frameworks (NLPFrameworks 2010)*, pages 28–35, Valletta, Malta, May 22. ELRA.

Peter Kluegl, Martin Atzmueller, and Frank Puppe. 2009. TextMarker: A Tool for Rule-Based Information Extraction. In Christian Chiarcos, Richard Eckart de Castilho, and Manfred Stede, editors, *Proceedings of the Biennial GSCL Conference 2009, 2nd UIMA@GSCL Workshop*, pages 233–240. Gunter Narr Verlag.

K. Liu, W. W. Chapman, G. Savova, C. G. Chute, N. Sioutos, and R. S. Crowley. 2011. Effectiveness of Lexico-syntactic Pattern Matching for Ontology Enrichment with Clinical Documents. *Methods of Information in Medicine*, 50(5):397–407.

Michael Tanenblatt, Anni Coden, and Igor Sominsky. 2010. The ConceptMapper Approach to Named Entity Recognition. In Nicoletta Calzolari (Conference Chair), Khalid Choukri, Bente Maegaard, Joseph Mariani, Jan Odijk, Stelios Piperidis, Mike Rosner, and Daniel Tapias, editors, *Proceedings of the Seventh International Conference on Language Resources and Evaluation (LREC'10)*, Valletta, Malta, may. European Language Resources Association (ELRA).

Andreas Wittek, Martin Toepfer, Georg Fette, Peter Kluegl, and Frank Puppe. 2013. Constraint-driven Evaluation in UIMA Ruta. In Peter Kluegl, Richard Eckart de Castilho, and Katrin Tomanek, editors, *UIMA@GSCL*, volume 1038 of *CEUR Workshop Proceedings*, pages 58–65. CEUR-WS.org.

Intellectual Property Rights Management with Web Service Grids

Christopher Cieri
email: ccieri

Denise DiPersio
email: dipersio

Linguistic Data Consortium
3600 Market Street
Philadelphia, PA. 10104
email: @ldc.upenn.edu

Abstract

This paper enumerates the ways in which configurations of web services may complicate issues of licensing language resources, whether data or tools. It details specific licensing challenges within the context of the US Language Application (LAPPS) Grid, sketches a solution under development and highlights ways in which that approach may be extended for other web service configurations.

1 Introduction

Growing interest in web service architectures raises questions about how such uses of language technologies and other resources interact with licensing constraints, including those that were imagined at an earlier time when resources and tools were more likely controlled by individual user organizations. Research communities that depend upon language resources (LRs) have become accustomed to, if not delighted with, the need to agree to certain limitations on the use of such resources. However, historically, negotiations concerning the use of LRs occur relatively infrequently. Even the largest data centers produce only a few new resources each month, generally under one of a small number of familiar license types. Once the resource has been acquired, integrating it in a local workflow requires time, creating a natural brake on the need to acquire new resources. Grid infrastructure, on the other hand, promises the ability to very rapidly build pipelines from existing services and resources. The common vision of web service architectures is that they reduce the burden of tool integration by presenting the tools as services and coordinating their input and output requirements. However, absent a similar mechanism for coordinating the licenses that constrain LR use, Grid operators risk creating infrastructure that simultaneously ameliorates the tool integration problem while exacerbating the licensing problem. In the sections that follow, we describe an approach that addresses the general problem of documenting, communicating and partially enforcing licensing constraints within a service grid.

2 Web Section Complexities

Human Language Technology related web services, singly and in various configurations and clusters, constitute a new ecosystem in which LRs, specifically data sets and tools, may be implemented and combined in ways not necessarily contemplated by existing intellectual property law and contracts that apply to the web services' constituent components. For example, traditional licenses may permit distribution from a data center to a licensed user organization and processing by either, but may prohibit distribution from the user to any additional parties. Even if it were clear that this constraint were intended only to block redistribution to unlicensed users, it is not clear whether all copyright holders would agree that moving the same data over the web to be processed by web services should be allowed. Another example involves the attribution and license requirements of shared software. In the past, licenses were typically described in a document included with the software source code. Attribution requirements were satisfied by listing software authors' names in similar documents or by displaying them in a header presented when the software was invoked at the commend line. However, users of web services may never see a source code repository or a command line.

Proceedings of the Workshop on Open Infrastructures and Analysis Frameworks for HLT, pages 93–100,
Dublin, Ireland, August 23rd 2014.

Service grids, as just one of multiple possible configurations of web services, have different stakeholder types: grid operators who maintain the software and servers that allow service registration and discovery; two types of service providers, those who provide access to data and those who provide access to software; and of course users. In addition to multiple stakeholder types, such Grids also have multiple instances of users, data providers and software providers. Where grids have been federated, there are also multiple grid operators. Each of these stakeholders may have different desires relative to the behavior of web services, most importantly where intellectual property protection is concerned. Beyond the obvious conflict that users typically want fewer restrictions on resources than providers, grid operators or service providers may require compensation, grid operators may wish to track and record user behavior, service providers may demand attribution, limit use of their services to the non-commercial sectors and may wish to exploit data that passes through their service nodes for purposes of further system development or evaluation.

In addition to multiple stakeholder types and multiple instances of each, grids also combine these data and software services in various combinations that affect licensing in a variety of ways. Figure 1 summarizes three simple cases. In the first, users direct data they own or control through an external service controlled by a second party. In the second case, both the data and the processing are controlled by a single entity who is not the user. In the third case, one external party controls the data while another controls the software. In each of these cases, the interaction of multiple parties may complicate licensing by introducing new and idiosyncratic constraints.

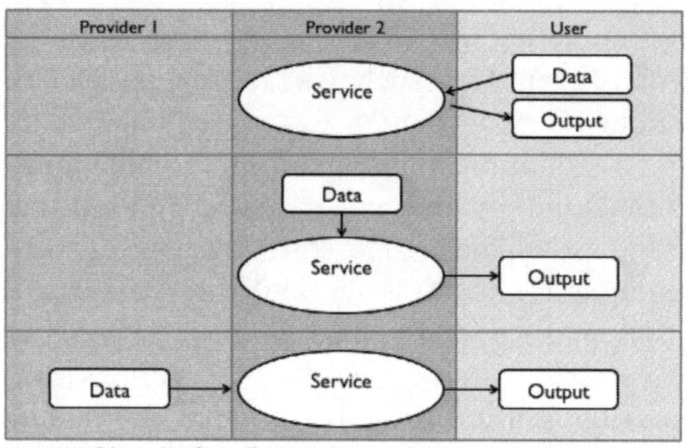

Figure 1: Simple Configurations of Web Services

Figure 2 sketches more complex cases in which data, controlled by the user or not, passes through multiple services controlled by independent parties. Examples of the first two use cases might include speech translation, configured as speech transcription followed by translation of the transcript text, in which the input speech is controlled by the users (e.g. in voicemail transcription) or is controlled by an independent party (e.g. translation of broadcast news). In the third case, not only are there multiple services operating on the same data, but these services are configured as generic engines that require models provided by other parties to operate on specific languages. One example might be language identification engines that accept new models in order to recognize new languages.

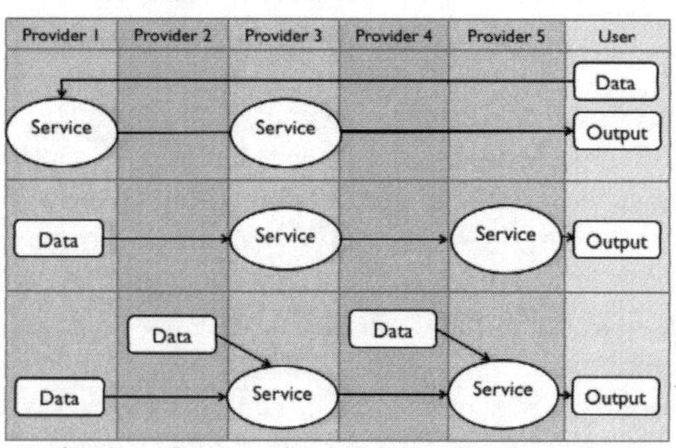

Figure 2: More Complex Web Service Configurations

Web service grids further complicate licensing because no provider or user controls the entire ecosystem. Grid operators, software service providers, data providers and users may all be distinct from one another. Indeed in the future imagined by grid proponents, there are many software and data providers and even more users on any one grid, and many grids federated to permit users of one to access services on another. In such an environment, it is clear that each user, provider and grid operator may act independently and sometimes at cross-purposes to others.

3 Approaches to Grid Licensing

One can imagine multiple approaches to harmonizing this ecosystem. First, one might choose to try to constrain service and data providers insisting that as a condition of participation in the grid, they must agree to make their services available to specific classes of users under pre-defined terms. The NICT Language Grid did this by establishing a Service Grid Agreement. However, it is equally possible to construct a grid in which service providers are not the owners or developers of all the software they use to provide services. For example, within the US NSF-funded Language Application Grid, two of the principle service providers, Brandeis University and Vassar College, have created services based on third party software such as NLTK (Bird, Klein, Loper 2009) and the Stanford Toolkit (Manning et al., 2014). In this case, the service providers do not own the tools and thus cannot enter into agreements about the terms under which the software underlying their service may be used. As a solution, one might imagine providing software services under whatever licenses the underlying software has imposed and then constrain the users to comply with these terms. A third alternative would be to assume that all parties take responsibility for their own actions during grid operations and to impose no controls over either providers or users. The fourth option is of course to constrain both providers and users. In this paper we will argue for this last hybrid.

Descriptions of the licensing approaches used by existing grids are scant, only rarely presented in published works, occasionally described on project web pages and sometimes left to be understood from the licenses used. Piperidis (2012) describes META-SHARE as a membership based infrastructure in which resources are available under one of four license types. While META-SHARE encourages within-network sharing with the fewest constraints possible, the four license types permit a range of constraints including those expressed by the Creative Commons[1] licenses and also allow for fees. META-SHARE servers harvest licensing elements from contributed services and present them to users as a table, in fact the model for our Table 2 below. The Language Grid[2] developed by NICT, includes license text, where available, in the description of each resource it provides. The Language Grid also provides a tool for composing workflows. Upon execution of a given workflow, the Grid displays the sequence of licenses that affect the use of the workflow component tools and data. Bosca et al. (2012) describe LinguaGrid[3] as "open to different operators (Universities, Research institutes, Companies) with configurable services access policies: free, restricted to registered users, research or commercial licensing". LinguaGrid is built upon the grid infrastructure developed by NICT and presumably uses the same approach to license management. CLARIN[4] documentation describes a rich set of licensing options for service providers. Many have equivalents in the Creative Common licenses though CLARIN enriches this set by allowing providers to require that published papers based on CLARIN resources are reported to the providers and that derived resources are deposited to CLARIN, a specific variant of the share-alike constraint. CLARIN also provides a legal help desk to answer questions about licensing among other issues. The LAPPS Grid has developed an explicit model for license management that is membership based, allows for a wide range of license types and fees, presents a summary of license constraints and actual licenses prior to workflow execution and even prevents the subset of license violations that can be detected at execution time.

Grid architecture constitutes a new approach to combining LRs. Providing clear documentation of the terms under which providers and users operate offers peace-of-mind to resource providers and clarity to service users either of which group may otherwise opt out of an initiative whose risks are incompletely understood. Furthermore, it is probable that for service providers who do not own the underlying data or software, imposing constraints on users may be not only a wise idea, but also a legal or contractual obligation. It is important to note that many license terms constrain behavior that

---

[1] http://creativecommons.org/
[2] http://langrid.org/en/index.html
[3] http://www.linguagrid.org/
[4] http://www.clarin.eu/

may occur long after web services have run, for example commercial use of output. Therefore, grid operators are not in a position to strictly enforce license terms. They may however, block obvious and immediate violations of licenses, make users aware of constraints that affect behavior and secure their agreement to relevant terms.

4 Dimensions of Constraints on Language Resource Use

The licenses that constrain the behavior of language resource users, and thus grid users, vary along a number of dimensions, the first of which pertains to the object being licensed. Software licenses typically constrain the use of software and derivative works. Data licenses similarly constrain the use of the data and derivative works. However, derivative work, to the extent that the term is defined at all, seems to refer to other data in the case of data licenses, and to other software in the case of software licenses. Importantly, none of the software licenses reviewed for this paper made a clear attempt to constrain the use of their output, which is often data, while many data licenses do constrain the use of processed data.

The LRs used in web services may be owned by the user, may be in the public domain or may be copyrighted by someone other than the user. Copyrighted LRs may be constrained as to use or as to user. The commonest use constraints typically prevent commercial use and the creation or commercial use of derivative works. They may prevent distribution of the LR or derivative works or they may require that products whose creation relied upon the licensed resource be shared under the same terms (also known as the Share Alike or Viral Copyleft constraint). They may require that users provide attribution of LR creators and/or cite the resource or a specific reference paper. Finally, any license may include other terms that have not been described here because they constitute the long tail of uncommon constraints. To give just one example, we are aware of at least one corpus that requires that recipients receive certification from their local Institutional Review Board that they have been trained in the treatment of human subjects.

An additional complexity in licensing constraints defined by use is that neither copyright law nor the software or data licenses reviewed for this paper provide a bright line to distinguish derivative works (which are typically constrained by such licenses) from transformative uses (which are typically not). Within HLT, we can imagine simple and stereotyped cases. Given one hour of audio recorded from a copyrighted news broadcast, the transcript of the audio and its translation into any language are derivative works subject, at least in the US, to copyright and any licensing constraints imposed on the audio. On the other hand, a unigram frequency list based on the transcript or translation is a highly transformed work generally considered immune to those same limitations.

License constraints related to the user, rather than the use, typically prevent commercial organizations from accessing the resource. In at least some cases, the intent of this constraint is to encourage potential commercial users to negotiate directly with the LR provider for access under terms that include a fee structure. More generally, the user types distinguished by LR licenses include academic and not-for-profit organizations, governments and commercial organizations. In some instances, companies engaged in pre-commercial technology development may be treated differently. In addition, a model of licensing constraints must distinguish organizations that have executed a specific license required by a LR from those that have not. Organizations may be licensed by enumeration or by features. As an example of licensing by enumeration, the Linguistic Data Consortium maintains databases of all users, all licenses required by their LRs and a table of which user organizations have executed each license. However, users may also be considered licensed if they possess certain features, for example, if they are non-profit organizations.

One use that seems to have been overlooked by existing grid licenses is the ability of service providers to derive benefit from the processing they offer. For example, one could imagine a translation service that not only outputs translations for submitted input text but also computes n-grams from that text and uses them to improve its source language models. Were this practice allowed, it would further complicate licensing within web service architectures where it is not always clear that the user who submits data for processing has the authority to permit the service providers to exploit that data.

5 Combining Licensing Constraints

Having enumerated the dimensions along which LR use may be constrained, we can easily imagine some use cases in which specific workflows should be prohibited or at least flagged. The obvious case would be one in which some input data required a specific license that the potential user had not executed. Another example would be the case in which some processing service required a fee that the potential user had not yet paid. Similarly a commercial organization seeking to process data that is only available under a no-commercial-use license should be prevented or at least warned by the service grid. At least within the United States – and this probably holds for many other jurisdictions – the law that governs copyright and the individual licenses commonly associated with LRs are relatively underspecified on a number of questions relevant to web services. For example, within US copyright law the only functional definition of "fair use" is a description of the four dimensions along which fair use claims are to be evaluated. Given this situation, we should not be surprised that current bodies of law offer no calculus for combining constraints imposed on the multiple LRs that may support any given workflow.

For example if a specific pipeline makes use of two data resources, one of which permits commercial use while the other prohibits it, what constraints apply to the final output? To make this concrete, consider a pipeline in which a language identification service detects the language of an input text and routes it to an appropriate machine translation service. If the language identification service relies on a data set available under a no-commercial-use license but neither the input text nor the translation engine are similarly constrained, may the user sell access to the translation? Our tendency may be to think this use is acceptable. Would we feel the same if the translation engine relied on data that imposed the no-commercial-use constraint? What if the input text was available under a no-commercial-use license but no other component in the pipeline constrained use? While we may have intuitions about acceptable use in these cases, there is no body of law, nor much precedent, to support one or another interpretation.

6 The Language Application Grid

In order to work through a possible solution, we now consider the specific tool and data resources implemented in the US NSF funded Language Applications Grid. To date, the LAPPS Grid has used 27 unique software packages (programs, toolkits, APIs, libraries) that are available under the 9 unique licenses summarized in Table 1.

Table 1: LAPPS Grid Software by License

License	Software
Apache 2.0	Language Grid software, NLTK, ANC2GO, UIMA, OAQA, Uimafit, guava-libraries, ActiveMQ, AnyObject, Jaxws-maven-plug-in, Jetty, OpenNLP
BSD	Hamcrest, NERsuite, CRFsuite (in NERsuite)
CDDL 1.1	Jaxws-rt
CPL 1.0	MALLET, AGTK, JUnit
Eclipse 1.0	logback (v1.0), Jetty
HTK-Cambridge	HTK
MIT	Mockito, libLBFGS (in NERsuite), GIZA (v3)
Python	NLTK
WordNet	Genia tagger library (in NERsuite)

Many of the constraints imposed by these licenses fall into recognizable categories summarized in Table 2

Table 2: LAPPS Grid Licenses and Common Constraints

License	Redistribution	Use	Derivative Use	Attribution	Share Alike	Fee
Apache 2.0	Yes	Commercial	Commercial	Yes	No	No
BSD	Yes	Commercial	Commercial	No	No	No
CDDL 1.1	Yes	Commercial	Commercial	Yes	Yes	No
CPL 1.0	Yes	Commercial	Commercial	No	No	No
Eclipse 1.0	Yes	Commercial	Commercial	Yes	Yes	No
HTK-Cambridge	No	Commercial	Commercial	No	No	No
MIT	Yes	Commercial	Commercial	No	No	Yes
Python	Yes	Commercial	Commercial	Yes	No	No
WordNet	Yes	Commercial	Commercial	Yes	No	No
LDC FP Member	No	Commercial	Commercial	No	No	No
LDC NFP Member	No	Research	Research	No	No	No
LDC Non-member	No	Research	Research	No	No	Yes
CC-Zero	Yes	Commercial	Commercial	No	No	No
CC-BY	Yes	Commercial	Commercial	Yes	No	No
CC-BY-SA	Yes	Commercial	Commercial	Yes	Yes	No
CC-BY-ND	Yes	Commercial	None	Yes	No	No
CC-BY-NC	Yes	Research	Research	Yes	No	No
CC-BY-NC-SA	Yes	Research	None	Yes	Yes	No
CC-BY-NC-ND	Yes	Research	None	Yes	No	No
GPL (v2,3)	Yes	Commercial	Commercial	Yes	Yes	No

These many license have in common a relatively small number of constraint types and values as summarized in Table 3.

Table 3: LAPPS Grid Common Constraints and Values

Constraint	Values
Redistribution	Yes/No
Use	Commercial/Research Only
Derivative Use	Commercial/Research Only/None
Transformative Use	Commercial/Research Only /None
Attribution	Yes/No
Share Alike	Yes/No
Fee	Yes/No
Other Specific License, Constraint	--

However, as one considers the complexity of licensing with the grid, it is important to also consider the limitations on the role of grid operators relative to prior practice. Traditional language resource distribution, before the era of web services, treated licensing constraints variably. For example, where users are required to pay a fee in order to access a LR, that fee is normally required in advance. If a resource requires a specific license to be executed, some data providers may withhold the resource until the agreement is signed either on paper or via a click-through agreement. Others may provide the license with the LR and a statement that by accessing the data, the user is agreeing to the terms of the license. However, beyond these cases, there is little attempt to block access to a resource until licensing terms have been satisfied. Indeed many licensing terms constrain future action and thus cannot be required as a condition of access. For example, the constraints on redistribution, use of derivative works, attribution and share alike all affect action that necessarily takes place after the LR has been accessed. Given these limitations, we expect that the ability of any web service policy or procedure to enforce such constraints is similarly limited. Thus, within the LAPPS Grid, we distinguish two types of enforcement of licensing constraints, requirement and notification as summarized in Table 4. In a small number of cases, we block the execution of a service pipeline if required conditions are not met but otherwise accumulate notifications that we present to users before allowing them to execute the pipeline. We must also note here that no summary of licensing terms can legally stand-in for the actual license executed so that any approach we use must also make reference to the actual licenses.

Table 4: Constraint Enforcement

Constraint	Action
Redistribution	Notify
Use	Notify
Derivatives Use	Notify
Attribution	Notify
Share Alike	Notify
Fee	Require
Other Specific License	Require
Other Specific Constraint	?

7 A Grid Licensing Model

Putting together the discussion to date, we propose the model in Figure 3 for managing licenses within a service grid framework. Specifically, this model benefits from features already implemented for the LAPPS Grid while imposing some limitations of its own. First, within the LAPPS Grid, users build pipelines using one of two workflow management tools developed by the project. The *Composer*, described in greater detail in Ide et al. 2014, displays for the user the set of available tool and data services allowing the user to select one or more, determine their order of application and even create branches to allow two or more tools of the same types to operate on the data in parallel so that their performance may be evaluated and compared. The Composer takes note of the input and output requirements of each tool in the chain and, in complex workflows, correctly routes data to appropriate processing services. The workflow *Planner*, still under development, allows the user to specify input data and desired output and then uses its knowledge of each tool's inputs and outputs to construct a pipeline that produces the desired result. The licensing model makes use of these workflow managers. First we require that any service registered in the grid only respond to requests from one of the workflow managers. This keeps the grid ecosystem closed and prevents a user from directing output of one of the services outside the grid where one cannot monitor use. We also require that service providers register the licenses that govern use of their services. The user initiates a session with the workflow managers by authenticating themselves. As the user builds a workflow, the manager requests from each service the list of constraints imposed. As in Table 2 and Table 4, these may be requirements for a fee or the execution of a specific license or they may be notifications of the future behavior expected of users. The workflow manager also queries a local database or API connected to a service provider or data center to determine whether the user has satisfied the payment and specific license requirements. If not, the pipeline is blocked. Otherwise the user continues to build the pipeline while the manager accumulates a summary of the click-through licenses required and general licensing constraints imposed. Before the user can execute the pipeline, the workflow manager presents a summary of the licenses required, with links to the original text, as well as a summary of the general constraints imposed. The user must click to agree to the terms before processing will begin. For each service that provides processing, the workflow manager also displays any attribution requirements or license statements normally displayed at the command line or in a README file since these are generally invisible to a grid user.

Of course, this model only works if the grid or other collection of web services constitutes a closed system where a small number of management programs can control the inputs and outputs to each process. Naturally, the grid licensing model is unable to resolve issues that remain unresolved in general such as the lack of a bright line distinguishing derivative and transformative use of linguistic data and tools. In such cases it takes a legally conservative approach, acting for example as though as uses may be considered derivative and issuing appropriate warnings.

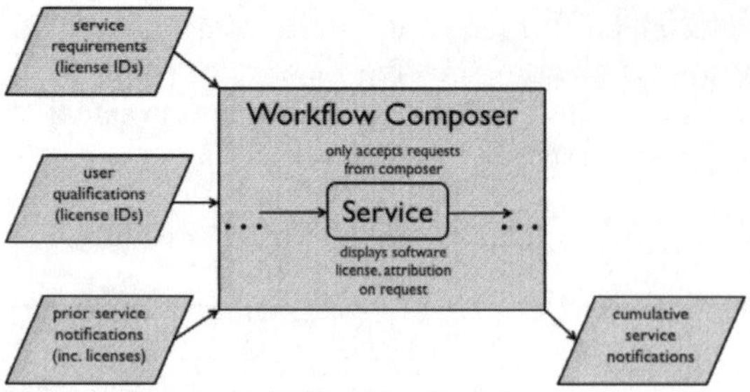

Figure 3: Service Grid Licensing Model

8 Conclusion

We discussed the features of web service architectures that complicate the licensing of LRs, including data and tools, both by introducing ecosystems not contemplated during the drafting of relevant intellectual property law and the development of the LR and by creating complex workflows not entirely under the control of any single user. We sketched the dimension along which licenses constrain LR use. Making the discussion more concrete, we then enumerated the license and constraint types that affect the resources used to build the US LAPPS Grid. Finally, we sketched a model for protecting intellectual property via the use of workflow managers while allowing users with appropriate credentials to construct complex pipelines. This approach relies on the closed nature of the service grid and would need to be extended in cases where the pipeline could combine web services without bounds.

9 Acknowledgments

This work was supported by National Science Foundation grants NSF-ACI 1147944 and NSF-ACI 1147912.

References

Bird, S., Klein, E., Loper, E. (2009) Natural Language Processing with Python. O'Reilly Media.

Bosca, A., Dini, L., Kouylekov, M., Trevisan, M. (2012) Linguagrid: A network of Linguistic and Semantic Services for the Italian Language. In Proceedings of the Eighth International Language Resources and Evaluation (LREC12), Istanbul, Turkey. European Language Resources Association (ELRA).

Ide, N., Pustejovsky, J., Cieri, C., Nyberg, E., DiPersio, D., Shi, C., Suderman, K., Verhagen, M., Wang, D., Wright, J. (2014) The Language Application Grid. In Proceedings of the Ninth International Language Resources and Evaluation (LREC14), Reykjavik, Iceland. European Language Resources Association (ELRA).

Ide, N. and Suderman, K. (2014). The Linguistic Annotation Framework: A Standard for Annotation Interchange and Merging. Language Resources and Evaluation.

Manning, C., Surdeanu, M., Bauer, J., Finkel, J., Bethard, S., McClosky, D. (2014) The Stanford CoreNLP Natural Language Processing Toolkit. In Proceedings of 52nd Annual Meeting of the Association for Computational Linguistics: System Demonstrations, pp. 55-60.

Piperdis, S. (2012). The META-SHARE Language Resources Sharing Infrastructure: Principles, Challenges, Solutions. In Proceedings of the Eighth International Language Resources and Evaluation (LREC12), Istanbul, Turkey. European Language Resources Association (ELRA).

EUMSSI: a Platform for Multimodal Analysis and Recommendation using UIMA

Jens Grivolla
Universitat Pompeu Fabra
Barcelona, Spain
jens.grivolla@upf.edu

Maite Melero
Universitat Pompeu Fabra
Barcelona, Spain
maite.melero@upf.edu

Toni Badia
Universitat Pompeu Fabra
Barcelona, Spain
toni.badia@upf.edu

Cosmin Cabulea
Deutsche Welle
Bonn, Germany
cosmin.cabulea@dw.de

Yannick Estève
Université du Maine
Le Mans, France
yannick.esteve@lium.univ-lemans.fr

Eelco Herder
L3S Research Center
Hannover, Germany
herder@l3s.de

Jean-Marc Odobez
IDIAP Research Institute
Martigny, Switzerland
odobez@idiap.ch

Susanne Preuß
Gesellschaft zur Förderung der Angewandten Informationsforschung
Saarbrücken, Germany
susannep@iai.uni-sb.de

Raúl Marín
VSN Innovation and Media Solutions
Alicante, Spain
rmarin@vsn.es

Abstract

The EUMSSI project (Event Understanding through Multimodal Social Stream Interpretation) aims at developing technologies for aggregating data presented as unstructured information in sources of very different nature. The multimodal analytics will help organize, classify and cluster cross-media streams, by enriching its associated metadata in an interactive manner, so that the data resulting from analysing one media helps reinforce the aggregation of information from other media, in a cross-modal semantic representation framework. Once all the available descriptive information has been collected, an interpretation component will dynamically reason over the semantic representation in order to derive implicit knowledge. Finally the enriched information will be fed to a hybrid recommendation system, which will be at the basis of two well-motivated use-cases. In this paper we give a brief overview of EUMSSI's main goals and how we are approaching its implementation using UIMA to integrate and combine various layers of annotations coming from different sources.

1 Introduction

Nowadays, a multimedia journalist has access to a vast amount of data from a plurality of types of sources to document a story. In order to put information into context and tell his story from all significant angles, he needs to go through an enormous amount of records with information of very diverse degrees of granularity. At the same time, he needs to reduce the noise of irrelevant content. This is extremely time-consuming, especially when a topic or event is interconnected with multiple entities from different domains. At a different level, many TV viewers are getting used to navigating with their tablets or iPads while watching the TV, the tablet effectively functioning as a second screen, often providing background information on the program or interaction in social networks about what is being watched. Both the

Proceedings of the Workshop on Open Infrastructures and Analysis Frameworks for HLT, pages 101–109, Dublin, Ireland, August 23rd 2014.

journalist and the TV viewer would greatly benefit from a system capable of automatically analysing and interpreting unstructured multimedia data stream and its social background, and, with this understanding, be able of contextualising the data, and contributing with new, related information.

The FP7-ICT-2013-10 STREP project EUMSSI, which started in December 2013, is developing methodologies and techniques for identifying and aggregating data presented as unstructured information in sources of very different nature (video, image, audio, speech, text and social context), including both online (e.g., YouTube) and traditional media (e.g. audiovisual repositories), and for dealing with information of very different degrees of granularity.

This will be accomplished thanks to the integration in a UIMA-based[1] multimodal platform of state-of-the-art information extraction and analysis techniques from the different fields involved (image, audio, text and social media analysis). The multimodal interpretation platform, in an optimized process chain, will analyze a vast amount of multimedia content, aggregate all the resulting information and semantically enrich it with additional metadata layers. The resulting system will be potentially useful for any application in need of cross-media data analysis and interpretation, such as intelligent content management, recommendation, real time event tracking, content filtering, etc. In particular, the EUMSSI project will use the semantically enriched information to make personalized content-based recommendation.

2 Multimodal analytics and Semantic Enrichment

For reasoning with and about the multimedia data, the EUMSSI platform needs to recognize entities, such as actors, places, topics, dates and genres. A core idea is that the process of integrating information coming from different media sources is carried out in an interactive manner, so that the metadata resulting from analyzing one media helps reinforce the aggregation of information from other media. For example, the quality of speech recognition heavily depends on the audio quality and background noise. Existing text, tags and other metadata will be exploited for disambiguation. Further, OCR on video data, speech analysis and speaker recognition mutually reinforce one another. The combined and integrated results of the audio, video and text analysis will significantly enhance the existing metadata, which can be used for retrieval and recommendation. In addition, the extracted entities and other annotations will be exploited for identifying specific video fragments in which a particular person speaks, a new topic begins, or an entity is mentioned. Figure 1 illustrates some of the different layers of analysis that may exist for a video content item.

Once the entities and concepts have been identified in the different modalities, all the information is aggregated and semantically enriched, using general ontologies or structured knowledge bases. Wikipedia categories have been successfully exploited with this purpose in different works: e.g. to describe chemical documents (Köhncke and Balke, 2010), to identify topics of interest for Twitter users (Michelson and Macskassy, 2010), and also to improve Web video categorization (Chen et al., 2010). Moreover, (Hahn et al., 2010) have shown that the structured information gathered from Wikipedia infoboxes can be used to answer complex questions, like "Which Rivers flow into the Rhine and are longer than 50 kilometers?" For this purpose, text documents need to be previously annotated using DBpedia Spotlight (Mendes et al., 2011), which automatically annotates text with links to articles in Wikipedia. The process of semantic enrichment is still largely domain-dependent; therefore, apart from the available general-purpose knowledge bases and ontologies (DBpedia, FOAF, DublinCore...), the EUMSSI platform needs specialized resources for categorizing videos on different dimensions. Linked Data technologies (Heath and Bizer, 2011) and the Linked Open Data cloud[2] provide access to several of these resources, including geodata, movie databases and program information.

3 Content-based Recommendation and the Demonstrators

The semantically enriched information is then used by the EUMSSI system to make personalized content-based recommendation. We propose a novel recommender system that leverages matrix factorization (Koren, 2008) with implicit feedback in order to integrate content-based similarity, usage history

[1]Unstructured Information Management Architecture: http://uima.apache.org/

[2]http://lod-cloud.net/

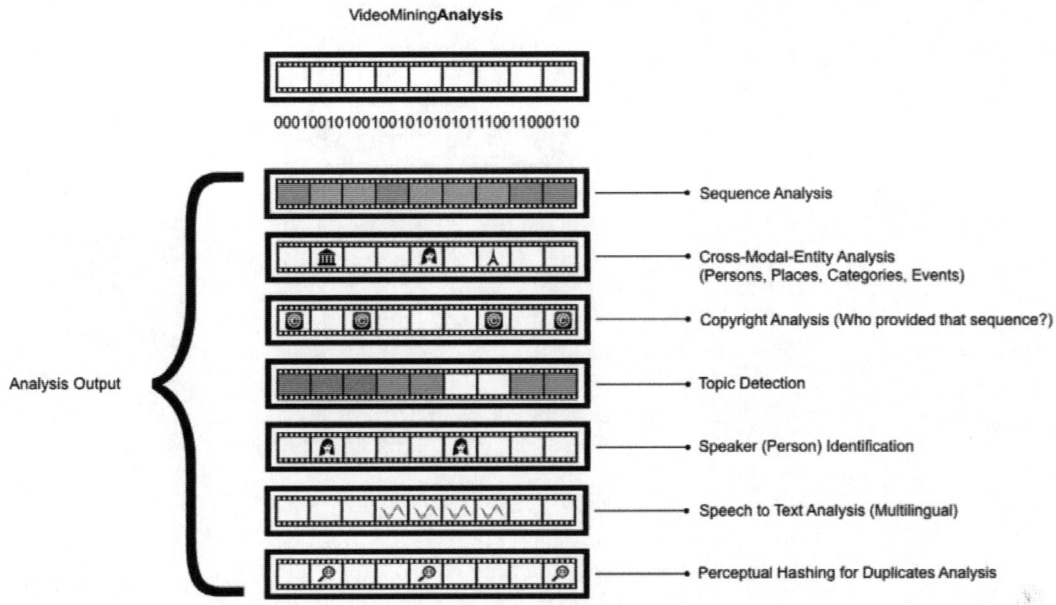

Figure 1: Video Mining Analysis

(i.e. collaborative filtering), as well as user demographics. This integrated approach reduces the cold-start problems typical of collaborative filtering, both for new users and for new content. Recommendation and aggregation of related content in EUMSSI is expected to use varying degrees of personalization, giving more weight in some cases to the individual user's interests, based on his viewing history, but being based primarily on the similarity to the currently shown content in other cases.

On top of the recommender, two demonstrators will be implemented within the EUMSSI project, each catering to a different use-case: (i) a computer-assisted *storytelling* tool integrated in the workflow of a multimedia news editor, empowering the journalist to monitor and gather up-to-date documents related with his investigation, without the need of reviewing an enormous amount of insufficiently annotated records; and (ii) a *second-screen* application for an end-user, able to make relevant suggestions of multimedia content based on what the user is watching, what other people have watched, and what people are saying about these contents in the social networks. Figure 2 shows how both applications build on a common base of multimedia analysis and content aggregation/recommendation algorithms.

4 Architecture overview

All new content coming into the system is first normalized to a common metadata schema (based on schema.org) and stored in a database (MAM/media asset manager, or MongoDB[3]) to make it available for further processing. Analysis results, as well as the original metadata, are stored in CAS format to allow integration of different aligned layers of analysis.

The process flow, pictured in Figure 3, can be summarized as follows:

1. new data arrives (or gets imported)
2. preprocessing stage
   (a) make content available through unique URI (from central MAM)
   (b) create initial CAS with aligned metadata / text content and content URI

[3]it will be developed in parallel as an open source MongoDB based solution, as well as integrated into VSN's proprietary platform

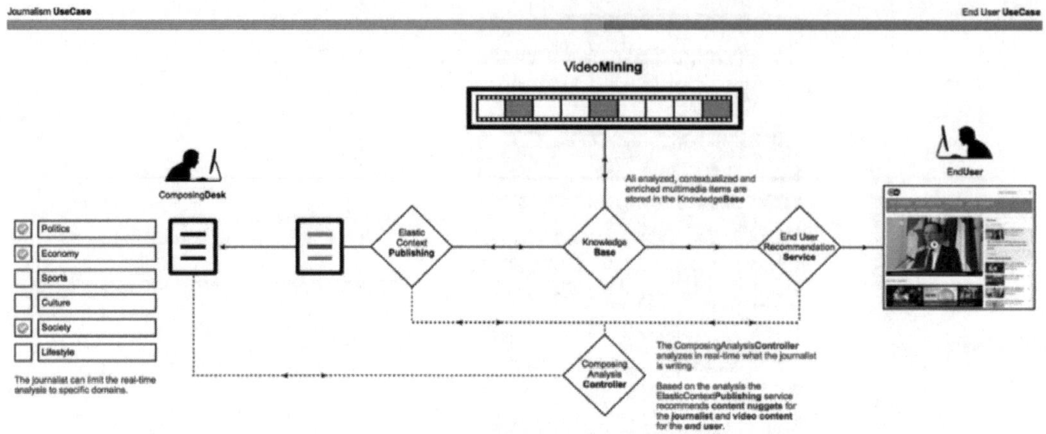

Figure 2: Multimodal platform catering both for the journalist and the end-user's use-cases

   (c) add content to processing queues

3. processing / content analysis
   (a) distributed analysis systems query queue when they have processing capacity
   (b) retrieve CAS with existing data (or get relevant metadata from wrapper API)
   (c) retrieve raw content based on content URI
   (d) process
   (e) update CAS (possibly through wrapper API)
   (f) update queues
      i. mark as processed
      ii. add to queues for other processes that depend on previous analysis results
4. indexing when processing is complete for a content item (e.g. with Solr)

Note that this architecture design mainly depicts the data analysis part of the EUMSSI system – the deployment by Web applications is not visible in the figure. These will be built upon the Solr indexes created from the CAS.

5 Aligned data representation

Much of the reasoning and cross-modal integration depends on an aligned view of the different annotation layers, e.g., in order to connect person names detected from OCR with corresponding speakers from the speaker recognition component, or faces detected by the face recognition.

The Apache UIMA[4] CAS (common analysis structure) representation is a good fit for the needs of the EUMSSI project as it has a number of interesting characteristics:

- Annotations are stored "stand-off", meaning that the original content is not modified in any way by adding annotations. Rather, the annotations are entirely separate and reference the original content by offsets

[4]http://uima.apache.org/

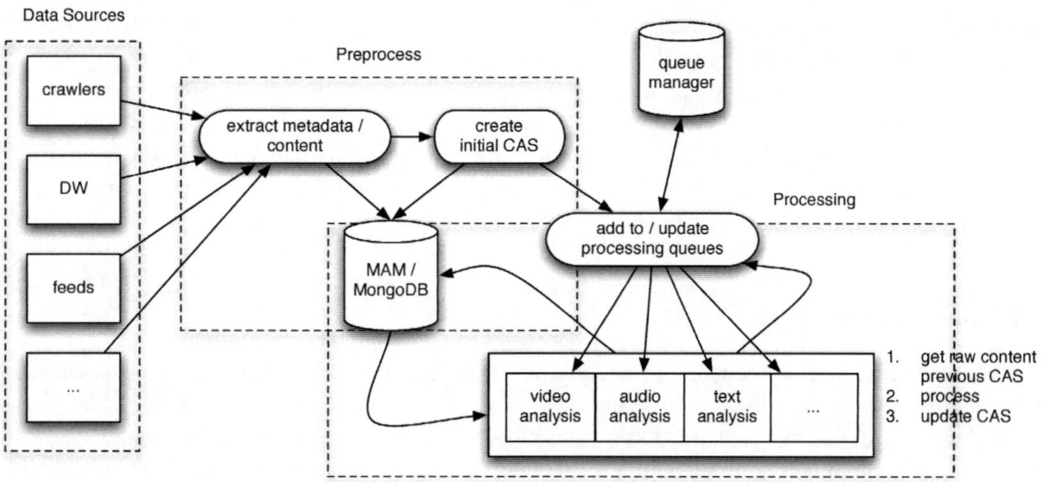

Figure 3: Architecture design

- Annotations can be defined freely by defining a "type system" that specifies the types of annotations (such as *Person, Keyword, Face,* etc.) and the corresponding attributes (e.g. *dbpediaUrl, canonicalRepresentation, ...*)
- Source content can be included in the CAS (particularly for text content) or referenced as external content via URIs (e.g. for multimedia content)
- While each CAS represents one "document" or "content item", it can have several *Views* that represent different aspects of that item, e.g. the video layer, audio layer, metadata layer, transcribed text layer, etc., with separate source content (SofA or "subject of annotation") and separate sets of annotations
- CASes can be passed efficiently in-memory between UIMA analysis engines
- CASes can be serialized in a standardised OASIS format[5] for storage and interchange

In the case of the EUMSSI project, the common base for alignment for different annotation layers referring to multimedia content is timestamps relative to the original content.

Annotations based directly on multimedia content (video and audio) will naturally refer to that content via timestamps, whereas text analysis modules normally work with character offsets relative to the text content. It is therefore fundamental that any textual views created from multimedia content (e.g. via ASR or OCR) refer back to the timestamps in the original content. This will be done by creating annotations, e.g. tokens, that include the original timestamps as attributes in addition to the character offsets.

As an example, we may have a CAS with an audio view on which we apply automatic speech recognition (ASR), providing the transcription as a series of tokens/words with a timestamp for each word. The system then creates a new view in the CAS that has the full plain-text transcription as SofA and a series of *Token* annotations with both character offsets relative to the plain-text SofA, and timestamp offsets relative to the multimedia content.

In this way it is possible to apply standard text analysis modules (that rely on character offsets) on the textual representation, while maintaining the possibility to later map the resulting annotations back onto the temporal scale.

Timestamps will be represented in milliseconds in order to avoid floating point values. In this way, all annotations can be subtypes of the standard UIMA Annotation type[6], which provides access to a number

[5] http://docs.oasis-open.org/uima/v1.0/uima-v1.0.html

[6] otherwise annotations would need to derive from the more generic TOP type

of utility functions that help find sets of overlapping annotations, retrieve annotations in offset order, etc.

SofA-aware UIMA components are able to work on multiple views, whereas "normal" analysis engines only see one specific view that is presented to them. This means that e.g. standard text analysis engines don't need to be aware that they are being applied to an ASR view or an OCR view; they just see a regular text document. SofA-aware components, however, can explicitly work on annotations from different views and can therefore be used to integrate and combine the information coming from different sources or layers, and create new, integrated views with the output from that integration and reasoning process.

6 Flow management

UIMA provides a platform for execution of analysis components (*Analysis Engines* or *AEs*), as well as for managing the flow between those components.

CPE or uimaFIT[7] (Ogren and Bethard, 2009) can be used to design and execute pipelines made up of a sequence of AEs (and potentially some more complex flows), and UIMA-AS[8] (*Asynchronous Scaleout*) permits the distribution of the process among various machines or even a cluster (with the help of UIMA DUCC[9]).

Analysis Engines can either be "natively" written for UIMA or can be wrappers that translate inputs and outputs for existing analysis components so they can be integrated in UIMA. All text analysis components, as well as the integration and reasoning components, will be available as UIMA AEs and can therefore be configured and executed directly within the UIMA environment.

There are some components of the EUMSSI platform, however, that do not integrate easily in this fashion. This is the case of computationally expensive processes that are optimized for batch execution. A UIMA AE needs to expose a *process()* method that operates on a single CAS (= document), and is therefore not compatible with batch processing. This is particularly true for processes that need to be run on a cluster, with significant startup overhead, such as many video and audio analysis tasks.

It is therefore necessary to have an alternative flow mechanism for offline or batch processes, which needs to integrate with the processing performed within the UIMA environment.

The main architectural and integration issues revolve around the data flow, rather than the computation. In fact, the computationally complex and expensive aspects are specific to the individual analysis components, and should not have an important impact on the design of the overall platform.

As such, the design of the flow management is presented in terms of transformations between data states, rather than from the procedural point of view. The resulting system should only rely on the robustness of those data states to ensure the reliability and robustness of the overall system, protecting against potential problems from server failures or other causes. At any point, the system should be able to resume its function purely from the state of the persisted data.

To ensure reliability and performance of the data persistence, we expect to use a well-established and widely used database system such as MongoDB.

Figure 4 shows the general flow of the EUMSSI system, focusing on the data states needed for the system to function.

In order to avoid synchronization issues, the state of the data processing is stored together with the data, and the list of pending tasks can be extracted at any point through simple database queries.

For example in order to retrieve the list of content items that have been crawled or received from feeds, but still need to be converted to the unified EUMSSI schema, it is sufficient to query for items that have a "source_meta:original" but no "source_meta:eumssi".

Similarly, the queues for analysis processes can be constructed directly from the "processing_state" of an item by selecting (for a given queue) all items that have not yet been processed by that queue and that fulfil all prerequisites (dependencies).

[7] https://uima.apache.org/uimafit.html
[8] http://uima.apache.org/doc-uimaas-what.html
[9] http://uima.apache.org/doc-uimaducc-whatitam.html

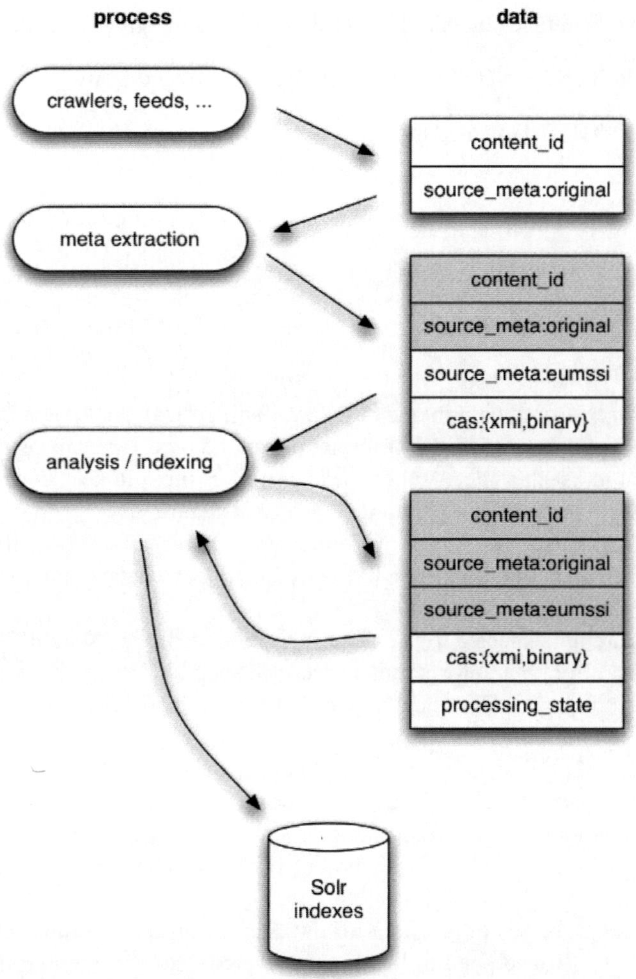

Figure 4: data flow and transformations

As an illustration, each content item has approximately the following structure:

```
{
  "content_id" : UUID,
  "source_meta" : {
    "original" : ORIGINAL_SOURCE_METADATA,
    "eumssi" : EUMSSI_SOURCE_METADATA
  },
  "cas" : {
    "xmi" : XMI_CAS,
    "binary" : BINARY_CAS
  },
  "processing_state" : {
    "queue1" : "done",
    "queue2" : "in_process",
    ...
    "queueN" : "pending"
  },
  "extracted_meta" : METADATA_FROM_CAS
}
```

where:

- **UUID** is a system-wide unique content id, created when first inserting the content into the system
- **ORIGINAL_SOURCE_METADATA** is the metadata as provided from the original content fields
- **EUMSSI_SOURCE_METADATA** is the original metadata mapped to the EUMSSI vocabulary / schema
- **XMI_CAS** is the CAS serialized in XMI format (and possibly compressed)
- **BINARY_CAS** is the CAS serialized in binary format (alternative to XMI_CAS)
- **METADATA_FROM_CAS** is metadata that is generated by EUMSSI analysis processes, using the EUMSSI schema

Normally, the CAS will be stored only in one of the available formats, but potentially different serializations could be used. The "extracted_meta" information can be used for analysis results that are used as inputs to other annotators (such as detected Named Entities as input to speech recognition), to avoid the overhead of extracting that information from the CAS on demand.

MongoDB allows to stored structured information (corresponding to a JSON structure), so that the content of fields like ORIGINAL_SOURCE_METADATA can reflect whatever internal structure the original data had.

The final applications are not expected to use the information stored in MongoDB directly, but rather access Solr indexes created from that information to respond specifically to the types of queries needed by the applications. Those indexes will typically be created from the CAS when all analysis steps have been performed.

It is, however, possible to have indexing processes that only depend on a subset of analyses, and thus make content items (at least partially) accessible to the applications before they have been fully processed (which may take a relatively long time). The indexing processes can be managed in the same way as any analysis process, with their own queues that specify the necessary dependencies, and taking the current state of the CAS as input.

In its simplest form, the processes responsible for the data transitions are fully independent and poll the database periodically to retrieve pending work. Those processes can then be implemented in any language that can communicate comfortably with MongoDB. As an efficiency improvement, in order to reduce the polling load, message queues (such as managed by ActiveMQ[10]) can be used to notify processes of pending work after performing the preceding steps.

7 Conclusions and future work

In this paper, we have presented the main goals and approaches of the EUMSSI project, which aims to innovatively integrate state-of-the-art text and A/V analysis technologies, semantic enrichment and reasoning, social intelligence and collaborative content-based recommendation, in order to build a multimodal, interoperable platform potentially useful for any application in need of automatic cross-media data analysis and interpretation, such as intelligent content management, personalized recommendation, real time event tracking, content filtering, etc.

The project is still in an early stage, and many aspects will need to be defined later on. The different analysis modalities are handled by separate research groups that will each improve the individual types of analysis in their are of expertise. This paper only reports on the platform that will integrate and combine the analysis results.

Additionally, possible interactions between modalities will need to be defined as it becomes clearer what information each analysis can provide or benefit from. We have at this point identified some of the more obvious interactions, such as doing text analysis on speech recognition output, or adding Named Entities from surrounding text to the vocabulary known to the ASR system, but many more may become apparent as the different research groups learn from each other.

[10]http://activemq.apache.org/

One of the main innovative aspects of the project also lies in the combination of the outputs of different analysis layers, and the capacity to perform reasoning or inference over this combined view to create a richer model of the content than can be obtained individually. This is an important research task that has not started yet, and we hope to report on it in the near future. As such, this article is limited to the technological foundation that will enable this work by providing a flexible platform with easy access to all available information layers.

Development of the platform has recently begun and all developments will become publicly available at https://github.com/EUMSSI/.

Acknowledgements

The work presented in this article is being carried out within the FP7-ICT-2013-10 STREP project EUMSSI under grant agreement n° 611057, receiving funding from the European Union's Seventh Framework Programme managed by the REA-Research Executive Agency http://ec.europa.eu/research/rea.

References

Zhineng Chen, Juan Cao, Yicheng Song, Yongdong Zhang, and Jintao Li. 2010. Web video categorization based on Wikipedia categories and content-duplicated open resources. In *Proceedings of the international conference on Multimedia - MM '10*, page 1107, New York, New York, USA, October. ACM Press.

Rasmus Hahn, Christian Bizer, Christopher Sahnwaldt, Christian Herta, Scott Robinson, Michaela Bürgle, Holger Düwiger, and Ulrich Scheel. 2010. Faceted wikipedia search. In *Business Information Systems*, pages 1–11. Springer.

Tom Heath and Christian Bizer. 2011. Linked data: Evolving the web into a global data space. *Synthesis Lectures on the Semantic Web: Theory and Technology*.

Benjamin Köhncke and Wolf-Tilo Balke. 2010. Using Wikipedia categories for compact representations of chemical documents. In *Proceedings of the 19th ACM international conference on Information and knowledge management - CIKM '10*, page 1809, New York, New York, USA, October. ACM Press.

Yehuda Koren. 2008. Factorization meets the neighborhood. In *Proceeding of the 14th ACM SIGKDD international conference on Knowledge discovery and data mining - KDD 08*, page 426, New York, New York, USA, August. ACM Press.

Pablo N. Mendes, Max Jakob, Andrés García-Silva, and Christian Bizer. 2011. DBpedia spotlight. In *Proceedings of the 7th International Conference on Semantic Systems - I-Semantics '11*, pages 1–8, New York, New York, USA, September. ACM Press.

Matthew Michelson and Sofus A. Macskassy. 2010. Discovering users' topics of interest on twitter. In *Proceedings of the fourth workshop on Analytics for noisy unstructured text data - AND '10*, page 73, New York, New York, USA, October. ACM Press.

Philip V. Ogren and Steven J. Bethard. 2009. Building test suites for UIMA components. *SETQA-NLP '09 Proceedings of the Workshop on Software Engineering, Testing, and Quality Assurance for Natural Language Processing*, pages 1–4, June.

Author Index

Association for Computational Linguistics
209 N. Eighth Street
Stroudsburg, Pennsylvania 18360

International Conference on e-Learning 2019

Held at the Multi-Conference on Computer Science and Information Systems (MCCSIS 2019)

Porto, Portugal
16-19 July 2019

iadis